D1130362

"Facts, historical background, wonderful photos, and personal experiences are woven together in this first-rate story of the King James Bible. Guaranteed to deepen your appreciation of the English Bible."

Charles C. Ryrie, editor, *Ryrie Study Bible*

"Never before in history have so many people been curious about the Bible. Some hunger for its truth; others seek to disparage its message. Donald Brake brilliantly clarifies for our generation, with simplicity and pictorial reality, what to many is a dusty, out-of-date tome. Here is a creative masterpiece from a reputable scholar, verifying God's Word to every human being. Pleasantly readable, it is an outstanding, authentic book to enrich every Christian's library."

Howard G. Hendricks, Distinguished Professor Emeritus, Christian education and leadership, Dallas Theological Seminary

"No one is more knowledgeable about English Bible translation than Donald Brake. In this book he has brought together an impressive array of information about the King James Bible. What makes the book distinctive is the abundance of photographs."

Leland Ryken, professor of English, Wheaton College

"Every English-speaking Christian—and indeed, every native English speaker—should own a King James Bible. It is the single greatest monument to the English language—and it was done by a committee! It has impacted our history, heritage, culture, art, and language in ways that cannot be described in a single volume. The King James Version's history is bound up with the Reformation and the struggle to get the Word of God to laypeople. It is the single most important Bible translation produced in the last millennium.

"This is not to say that the King James Bible is the only translation that one should read, nor that it's the best. But Donald Brake has shown, through meticulous research, engaging style, irenic tone, and exquisite illustrations, that this translation deserves a place on our shelves and in our hearts. Dr. Brake is the right man to write this book, as the many illustrations and anecdotes will show. This is his passion and his life. I recommend *A Visual History of the King James Bible* to every English-speaking Christian because here you will discover a part of the rich tapestry of the Christian faith in which you find yourself today."

Daniel B. Wallace, executive director, The Center for the Study of New Testament Manuscripts

"On the 400th anniversary of the most famous of English Bible translations, Donald Brake has written an engaging account of the history of the King James Bible. Brake's accounts of the translation process, the textual basis of the translation, and seventeenth-century printing and design techniques are all interwoven with his personal stories as a collector of rare Bibles. Photos of many of the rare volumes from Brake's collection, now in the Dunham Bible Museum, fill the pages of this beautifully illustrated book."

Diana Severance, director, Dunham Bible Museum

"Whether deeply loved or deemed archaic, the King James Version of the Bible has had a profound effect not only on the English-speaking world but on the very language we speak. With the passion of a collector and the skilled insights of a scholar, Donald Brake relates the fascinating story of how English politics of the sixteenth and seventeenth centuries molded the translation, which was accepted by both the Anglican and Puritan wings of the English church. Regardless of one's preferred English translation, this is a book well worth reading."

Michael A. Harbin, chair, biblical studies, Christian education, and philosophy department, Taylor University

"Donald L. Brake possesses the talents and experiences of a scholar, professor, collector of early English editions of the Bible, historian, and missionary to produce such an instructive work. As a scholar, Dr. Brake understands the biblical languages behind the King James Version and the challenges all translators must grapple with. As a professor, he taught generations of students on the King James Version and other early English versions. Moreover, he taught the Bible to these students through early and modern English versions. As a collector, he mastered the various revisions, corrections, and editions of the King James Version, becoming expert in the physical characteristics of the editions, including their printing and binding. As a historian, he is thoroughly familiar with the various controversies, both ancient and modern, concerning the translation. As a missionary, he witnessed the influence of the King James Version on translations in other languages and cultures. Clearly Dr. Brake is thoroughly qualified to write this authoritative work."

Russell Fuller, professor of Old Testament, The Southern Baptist Theological Seminary; author of *Invitation to Biblical Hebrew*

"Dr. Brake's *A Visual History of the King James Bible* is truly a masterful work! Scholarly yet highly readable, this book presents King James Bible history clearly, concisely, and with many interesting, full-color illustrations. His accuracy of Bible history is also spiced frequently with lively descriptions of events surrounding the birth and production of this capstone of English Bible history. Some of Don's personal experiences as a lifelong Bible collector keep the reader's interest high. Truly this book is the fruitful product of Don's lifetime of study and teaching the Bible, as well as his passion for persons to know those committed scholars who have given us our English Bible."

John Hellstern, cofounder, The Living Word National Bible Museum

A VISUAL HISTORY

of the

KING JAMES BIBLE

The Dramatic Story
of the World's Best-Known Translation

DONALD L. BRAKE

WITH SHELLY BEACH

BakerBooks

a division of Baker Publishing Group
Grand Rapids, Michigan

Published by Baker Books
a division of Baker Publishing Group
P.O. Box 6287, Grand Rapids, MI 49516-6287
www.bakerbooks.com

Printed in Singapore.

Library of Congress Cataloging-in-Publication Data
Brake, Donald L., 1939–
        A visual history of the King James Bible : the dramatic story of the world's best-known translation / Donald L. Brake with Shelly Beach.
            p.   cm.
        Includes bibliographical references (p.   ) and indexes.
        ISBN 978-0-8010-1347-8 (cloth)
        1. Bible. English—Versions—Authorized—History. 2. Bible. English—Versions—Authorized—History—Pictorial works. I. Beach, Shelly. II. Title.
    BS186.B695   2011
    220.5′2038—dc22   2010021092

Interior design by Brian Brunsting and Robin Black

11   12   13   14   15   16   17   7   6   5   4   3   2   1

To my family for their years of input into my life
and their sacrifice for my work as Bible collector, missionary,
pastor, teacher, educator, and author

Francis and Anna Mae Brake, father and mother (deceased)
Donnie and Beth Taylor Brake, son and daughter-in-law
DL, Josh, and Caleb, grandsons
Debbie and Robert Stoppa, daughter and son-in-law
Brianna and Isaiah, granddaughter and grandson
Michael Brake, son (deceased)

Contents

Illustrations

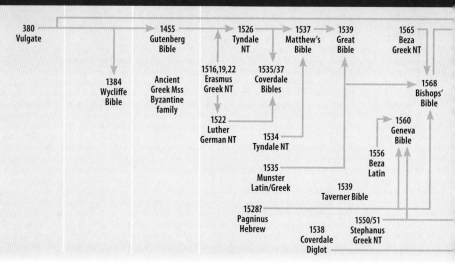

Versions and editions produced during

Richard II 1377–99	Henry VII 1455–1509	Henry VIII 1509–47	Edward VI 1547–1553	Mary I 1553–58
Wycliffe *(1384–88)*	Gutenberg *(1455)* Golden Legend *(1483)*	Tyndale NT *(1526)* Coverdale *(1535)* Matthew *(1537)* Taverner *(1539)* Great Bible *(1539)*	No new transl. Tyndale *(17 eds)* Coverdale *(3 eds)* Matthew *(3 eds)* Great Bible *(8 eds)* Taverner *(4 eds)*	No Prot. Bible Geneva NT *(1557)*

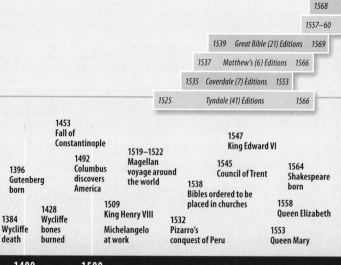

1568

1557–60

1539 Great Bible (21) Editions 1569

1537 Matthew's (6) Editions 1566

1535 Coverdale (7) Editions 1553

1525 Tyndale (41) Editions 1566

1453
Fall of
Constantinople

1547
King Edward VI

1492
Columbus
discovers
America

1519–1522
Magellan
voyage around
the world

1545
Council of Trent

1396
Gutenberg
born

1538
Bibles ordered to be
placed in churches

1564
Shakespeare
born

1428
Wycliffe
bones
burned

1509
King Henry VIII

1558
Queen Elizabeth

1384
Wycliffe
death

1532
Pizarro's
conquest of Peru

1553
Queen Mary

1384
Wycliffe
death

1396
Gutenberg
born

1509
Michelangelo
at work

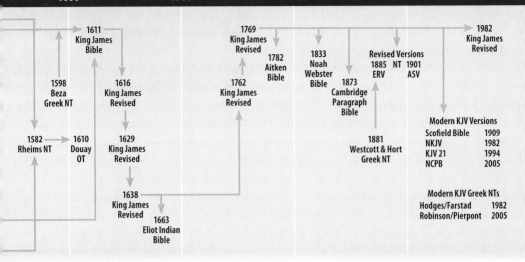

THE KING JAMES VERSION

the reigns of the monarchs of England

Elizabeth I *1558–1603*	James I *1603–25*	Charles I *1625–49*	Charles II *1660–85*	George III *1760–1820*
Geneva *(1560)* Bishops' *(1568)* Rheims NT *(1582)*	Douay OT *(1610)* KJV *(1611)* KJ revision *(1616)* Geneva banned *(1616)*	KJ revision *(1629)* KJ revision *(1638)*	Eliot Indian *(1663)* American printing	Aitken *(1782)* Americans began printing English Bibles

| 1611 | King James Version | Present |

| 1582 | Rheims / Douay | 1750 |

| Bishops' (19) Editions | 1617 |

| Geneva Bible (140) Editions | 1644 |

1620
Pilgrims land at Plymouth

1609
Milton born

1607
Jamestown founded

1776
Declaration of
Independence

2003
Iraq War

1605
Gunpowder Plot

1685
George F. Handel
born

1754–63
French and
Indian War

1861
American
Civil War

1965
Vietnam War

1588
Defeat of
Spanish
Armada

1604
Hampton Court Conference

1603
King James I

1732
George Washington
born

1812
War

1941
World War II

1917
World War I

Hear Ye, Hear Ye . . .

The hall of Hampton Court Palace exploded with shouts and cheering as His Majesty King James I entered the room and ascended the royal box. The clamor only subsided as the gavel banged, announcing the second day of the Hampton Court Conference on January 16, 1604. The three-day conference had been called in response to a document formulated by the Puritans and submitted to James I requesting reforms within the church. As the hours wore on and views clashed over the lengthy list of controversial issues, the Puritans' frustrations grew as the king consistently ruled in favor of the majority Anglicans. Beneath the growing tension lay the Puritans' knowledge that the Anglicans favored the use of the Bishops' Bible, which had been produced in 1568 and which the Puritans rejected in favor of the Geneva Bible, with its extensive cross-references, introductions, and study tools.

His Majesty King James I, attired in a high-crowned Spanish hat and sitting a royal distance from the bareheaded clergy, could scarcely be heard as he stood to address the court: "We have assembled here again on Monday, this our second day of a conference that shall change the Church of England."

The crowd pressed in to hear the royal words, but His Majesty's voice did not match his commanding presence. He had been born with a tongue too large for his mouth, preventing him the dignity of projecting his words with the force of royalty.

The actions of one man in this critical moment of time would reshape the language of the Christian faith and initiate a new Bible translation that would come to be known as England's greatest literary achievement. John Rainolds,

Hampton Court. 29 -11-53 LSLupton

The suggestion for the translation of the famous King James Version was made at Hampton Court in 1604. Photo: Original art, L. Lupton.

a stubborn, opinionated, and uninhibited Puritan, rose to his feet to be recognized. He knew full well the king's reprimand could fall like a stroke of a sword for such a bold act.

"May Your Majesty be pleased." The room went deadly silent as John spoke.

"May Your Majesty be pleased. May a new translation be made that will answer to the intent of the original rather than allowing for the corrupt interpretations of Henry VIII and Edward VI."

All eyes turned toward His Majesty and scanned his face for his response. With one word, the hope that Rainolds voiced for the Puritans could be extinguished.

The voice of Lord Bishop of London Richard Bancroft, the king's advocate and supporter of the Anglican Bible, rose from the crowd. "If every man's humor be followed, there would be no end of translating." His words dripped with sarcasm.

The audience withdrew even further into silence in the cold shadow of the challenge and waited for His Majesty to respond. Whether courtier or servant, every person in the room knew that the Puritans supported the Geneva Bible and the Anglicans supported the Bishops' Bible. But what would Rainolds's challenge mean to King James and the Church of England?

The glare of the king's steely blue eyes deeply penetrated Rainolds as he rose. "I would that England had one uniform translation, but I have never yet seen a Bible well translated in English, and I think the Geneva is the worst of all."[1]

Had a pin dropped to the floor, all those present in Hampton Court Palace hall that day would have heard it. The king raised his arm and extended a finger of warning at the group. "This new translation must not be burdened with marginal notes that are partial, untrue, seditious, and treacherous toward kingship but rather must spread the idea of divine rule by monarchs."

The king had thrown down the gauntlet. He had commissioned a new translation with a new mission. The King James Bible would be *His Majesty*'s version of Scripture.

Out of the foment of controversy arose the greatest literary achievement the English language has ever produced and the defining achievement of the reign of James I. Like most men and women who step out in courage, Puritan Rainolds did not know his simple act would become a pivotal point in history and that he would father one of the most influential books of all time.

Echoes of the Call

Four hundred years ago, a book was born that left a legacy not only within the scope of literature but also within the timelines of history and the Christian church—the King James Version of the Bible. As the world's bestseller during the past four centuries, the King James Version has stood unsurpassed by all other English books in its popularity and influence. From its mysterious beginnings to its resilience amid winds of criticism, the King James Version remains unmatched in its melodic prose and majestic poetry. A survivor, it stands as a legacy to our thirst for spiritual truth.

Acquiring my first King James Version collector's copy fueled my dream to write a book that celebrates this enduring literary masterpiece. My story begins decades ago, when my interest in collecting rare manuscripts and Bibles was sparked as a second-year seminary student. Sitting on the floor in Professor Charles Ryrie's den with a small group of fellow students, I was mesmerized as he delicately turned the pages of rare Bibles and manuscripts I'd never dreamed of seeing or holding. My seminary years were financially challenging with my income barely supporting my family. So, in spite of my newfound passion, I slipped the thought of Bible collecting onto a back shelf for more than a decade while I finished seminary and administered a Bible school in Ethiopia.

Then in the late 1970s, Richard Estes, a collector, awakened my passion. He gave me a book written by Robert Dearden Jr. in 1929. *The Guiding Light of the Great Highway*, a book that provides a history and review of old Bibles, sparked my first venture into the collecting world, shaped my lifelong philosophy of collecting, and served as my guide as I built my collection of rare and significant Bibles. I have read and handled this book so much that the dust jacket is dog-eared and the spine is split in several places. Each page bears the residue of my hands, and the corners are worn in especially favored areas of research.

From the earliest days of collecting, I sought one treasured Bible: a first edition of the King James Version. Considered the cornerstone of any Bible collection, first-edition KJV Bibles are rare and expensive. My salary at Mult-nomah School of the Bible (today Multnomah University), where I began teaching in 1977 after returning from Ethiopia, supported my family, but little money remained for collecting rare Bibles. So I decided to designate the use of an assistant basketball coaching stipend to fund my growing addiction to Bible collecting.

Late one afternoon I received a call from Richard Estes, with whom I talked regularly about Bibles available on the market, the prices they brought, and the collectors who purchased them. Richard offered to sell me a 1611–13 King James Version "She" edition. Often considered a second edition or first edition, second issue, this edition is called the "She Bible" because of the reading in Ruth 3:15, "She went into the city," instead of the reading in a first edition 1611 version, "He went into the city."

Richard's opening offer sent my heart racing. While the Bible lacked the general title page, it was in its original state; even the spine was original—a rare find. The price was beyond my means, but I thought it was the op-portunity of a lifetime. To ease my conscience, I called Dr. Ryrie, my former professor, to seek his advice. His words would either give me the affirmation I needed to move forward with a crucial purchase or to refuse the offer. I can still remember the excitement that rushed over me with Dr. Ryrie's observa-tion. Although the Bible lacked the important title page, the original binding and spine maintained its value.

My next call was to Richard to complete the transaction.

A sense of accomplishment swept over me in that moment. I had ac-quired my heart's desire, the cornerstone of my collection: a first edition of the King James Version.

I invite you to enter into these pages chronicling the wonderful and fasci-nating story of the creation of the King James Version. Don't rush; absorb the significance of the story slowly. Be prepared to lose a little sleep, and travel at your own peril, for you too may be destined to lose your heart along the way and become a lover of the world's bestselling Bible.

1

A Nation Finds Her Tongue

English Develops as a National Language

T
he story of language is the story of the historical movements and cultural influences that channel the words and thoughts, not to mention the hearts and lives, of people throughout the ages. Language shapes and defines us. To glimpse the history of the language of the King James Bible is to glimpse our own story.

The English language, like all languages, has been evolving for centuries and will continue to do so throughout the twenty-first century. It changes even at this moment. In the past five hundred years the evolution of words and language has been dramatic, and those language changes are often well traced through texts of Scripture that have been preserved over the centuries. The 1388 Wycliffe translation, the 1611 King James Version, and the 2002 *Message* translation evidence the variety of changes in the English language.

Compared with language development of many civilizations, however, English developed relatively rapidly. For instance, while the development of Greek and other ancient languages spanned several thousand years, the time it took for the Anglo-Saxon language (forerunner of modern English) to develop into words similar to those we speak today can be measured in a few hundred years.

Three distinct periods mark the development of English: (1) Old English, the period from the sixth century to the Norman Conquest of 1066; (2) Middle English, 1100 to 1500; and (3) Modern English, 1500 to the present. The Norman Conquest (when the troops of William, Duke of Normandy, invaded England) significantly altered the old Anglo-Saxon language with the influence of French. Subsequently, the Anglo-Norman language gave way in the fourteenth century to a genuine, recognizably English language.

Old English Period (Sixth Century to 1066)

Difficult as it might be to imagine, when the Romans landed on the island of England a few years before the birth of Christ, English did not exist. The language of this time and place included both Germanic and Celtic elements. It was not until the sixth century that a small percentage of people in Britain spoke a prototype of English.

During this period, from the sixth century until the Norman Conquest, the British were tossed about by an influx of invasions and missionary endeavors that added to the flavor and texture of the English language. The development of English was shaped, in part, by the Germanic tribes, Angles, Saxons, and Jutes, who battled for supremacy among themselves and with the tribal Picts, Scots, and Gaels who inhabited the island. Then in the sixth century, Pope Gregory, who viewed the island dwellers as pagans, sent a monk named Augustine[1] to convert King Ethelbert to Christianity. The third king of the kingdom of Kent, Ethelbert, ruled over an alliance of the Angles, Saxons, and Jutes. Augustine's mission was successful, and over time Latin and Greek words found their way into the English vocabulary. Over the course of one thousand years, these combined cultural forces created a hybrid language that assimilated elements of Roman, Saxon, Danish, and Norman into a new strain of English.

The politics of invasion and conquest take language captive, along with its people. The early invaders' language, today known as Old English or Anglo-Saxon English, formed a rudimentary base for the English we speak today.

They Are Like the Angels in Heaven

Stately and commanding, Gregory strolled through Rome's famous market-place, bustling with merchants selling their wares. He often walked this path, which ultimately led to the slave-trading pit at the end of the street. Peering at the slaves on this bright, sunny day, he saw a number of beautiful, white-bodied, fine-haired young men and boys up for auction.

He was not interested in purchasing any of the boys for himself, but he was inquisitive. Something that particular day drove him to ask the seller, "Where are these young men from? Are they Christians or pagans?"

The reply came quickly. "They are pagans from the Isle of Britain."

"Alas! What a pity that the devil himself possesses men with such fair countenances." He was oblivious to the condescending tone that so often marked men of his position.

He inquired a second time as if he did not fully understand. "Where did you say they come from?"

"They are *Angles* from Britain," replied the slave trader.

"And where in Britain?" Gregory seemed intent on finding out more about these curious creatures.

"They are from the province of Deira." The slave owner turned away, irritated and anxious to conclude the conversation.

"And what is the name of the king of Deira? I find it interesting that the Latin term for his province means *wrath*—'de ira.' I don't suppose you knew that." Gregory ignored the impatient man's lack of interest.

"Please, sir, business calls me," the man continued. "But the man is called Aella."

Gregory paused. "Aella—Alleluia—praise the God of creation whose name shall be sung in the Isle of Britain, and these Angles, these angels, shall be plucked from the wrath of God."

With those words the future Pope Gregory found his mission. His story, as related by the Venerable Bede, a church historian, goes on to report that when Gregory became pope, he sent missionaries led by Augustine to evangelize the Angles.[2]

The Anglo-Saxon conquest was so successful that very few words have survived from the original British language (Celtic). The Anglo-Saxons' love for ambiguity, innuendo, and wordplay characterized their writings and filtered into English literature in every age.[3]

It is not surprising to learn that the earliest written portions of the English language came to life and survived over the ages in the form of Scripture. Caedmon (ca. 657–84), a Yorkshire layman attached to a monastery now known as Whitby Abbey, set songs to verse in Anglo-Saxon English. A legend describes his habit of singing portions of Scripture in a highly complicated vernacular meter. His poem known as *Caedmon's Hymn*—a praise poem in honor of God—is known due to its survival in more than twenty manuscript copies. One manuscript (ca. 737), believed to be the earliest surviving copy of *Caedmon's Hymn*, is held in a collection at the Cambridge University Library.

The Old English period is characterized by Latin manuscripts that used interlinear glosses, a type of word-for-word translation that was placed directly into the text. Glossing was an Anglo-Saxon pedagogical tool for introducing Latin to the reader by using visual juxtaposition. The most famous example is the Lindisfarne manuscript—a tenth-century, literal rendering of the text into an Anglo-Saxon dialect by a scribe named Aldred (d. 968).[4] Latin influences sometimes paved the way for the acceptance of new words in Old English. The Latin terms *spiritus sanctus* (Holy Spirit), *evangelium* (Good News), and *feond* (judgment day) became *Halig Gast* (Holy Ghost), *god-spell* (gospel), and *Doomsday*.[5]

Between 750 and 1050, the massive Viking (or Danish) invasions from the north influenced the development of English. The king of Wessex, Alfred the Great (849–99), defeated the Vikings at Ethandune in a critical victory. Alfred's victory meant the Britons retained the English language—Old English would not die or be absorbed under the rule of conquering Norsemen. But the Norsemen did have some influence on English, though it is difficult to evaluate because English and Norse are similar. It is clear, however, that *sky*, *skin*, *root*, and other monosyllabic words have been assimilated into English from the Old Norse language.

Alfred the Great rebuilt schools and insisted that education be conducted in the vernacular English. He demonstrated his dedication to the development of English when he committed to learn Latin at the age of forty in order to carry out the critical work of translation.[6] This resulted in his translations of the Ten Commandments, excerpts from Exodus and Acts, and a negative form of the Golden Rule.[7]

One writer stands out among the others during the era of the Old English period: Aelfric of Eynsham (955–ca. 1010). While Aelfric was not a true translator, he developed the use of the vernacular language and set the stage for the translation of the Wessex Gospels, a circa 990 translation of the Gospels from the Latin Vulgate Bible into the West Saxon dialect of Old English. Aelfric's translations of lessons from the Pentateuch, Joshua, Judges, Kings, Job, Esther, and the Maccabees set him apart as an important figure in language development and laid a foundation for translation of the Bible into English.[8] Even though Aelfric did not translate the Scriptures, he proclaimed biblical and religious truth in simple, everyday English for those who knew no Latin.

It was not until the tenth century that a translation of the four Gospels into Old English emerged. The Wessex Gospels, anonymously written, do not bear a date, but several extant manuscripts, none of which is the original, bear witness to an early date. In fact, the Wessex Gospels continued to be read even after the Norman invasion of 1066.[9] This successful invasion by the French significantly altered the English language and influenced efforts to translate the Bible. Old English was fading, and the seeds of Middle English had been planted. With their growth, new translation efforts would be born.

A significant Old English document, but written in the Gothic language, is called *Codex Argentens* or *Silver Book* because it was copied in letters of a silvery hue. This translation of the Gospels, completed around AD 360 by the famous missionary scholar Ulfilas (ca. 310–83) for the heathen Goths, represents a pre–Old English version of Scripture. One can see the progression of the language by juxtaposing key phrases from *Codex Argentens* next to the Old English, Middle English, and Modern English versions of the same phrases.

Gothic (360)[10]	Old English, Anglo-Saxon (995)	Middle English, Wycliffe (1388)	Modern English, King James (1611)
in bokom Psalmo	on tharn Sealme	in the book of salms	in the book of Psalms
Ik in thata dour	Ic eom geat	Y am the dore	I am the door
kaurno whaiteis	hwaetene corn	a corn of whete	a kernel of wheat
wheitos swe snaiws	swa hwite swa snaw	as whijt as snowe	as white as snow

Middle English Period (1066–1500)

Spoken English came to an end among British royalty for two hundred years following the Norman victory at Hastings in 1066. The invaders declared Norman French the official language of England, formally bringing to a close the Anglo-Saxon English period and introducing Middle English. The ruling French aristocracy repressed the Anglo-Saxon language, and the dominance of the French language delayed the long-awaited translation of an English Bible.

During that period of two hundred years, the Anglo-Saxon language assimilated French influences and eventually evolved into the Anglo-Norman or Middle English language. French speakers in Paris looked down on the sub-French spoken in England. But the story of the English language would not be brought to an end by the whim of French rule or cultural assimilation. Over the course of decades, the primitive Old English written language withstood the Norman-French invasion.[11]

The first English Bible was yet to appear, but the English people received religious instruction in Anglo-Saxon liturgy, lyric songs, theatrical plays, and poems.[12] Many of these theatrical plays were absorbed into the national culture over the course of the development of the English language.[13] Nevertheless, the common people were deprived of the use of an English Bible as their rule of faith. Their religious life depended on popular medieval dramas, oral transmissions of biblical stories, Latin and French language Bibles (used mostly by the aristocracy), and instruction by the priesthood.

It was not until the close of the twelfth century that genuine, distinguishable Middle English surfaced in written form as homilies and translations of short passages of the Gospels. Men and women pressed forward in their

Middle English is represented in this facsimile of the late fourteenth-century Wycliffe New Testament. Facsimile.

quest for spiritual growth in their faith with a desire to interact with Scripture and, more importantly, claim it as their own.

The thirst for spiritual guidance centered on the importance of the book of Psalms during this era, further promoting the development of English as a written language. Two influential Anglo-Norman translations of the Psalter appeared in the thirteenth and fourteenth centuries. William of Shoreham and Richard Rolle, both translating from the Latin Vulgate, produced Psalters. Rolle's elaborate commentary stood as a standard reference for more than a century. Not only did his work influence John Wycliffe in the fourteenth century, but his commentary continued to be printed in the infancy period of the fifteenth-century printing press.

A genuine English language gradually replaced the Anglo-Norman language. Accompanying the development of a unique English language came a groundswell of English nationalism in the fifteenth century. Alister

McGrath observes: "Where once an English Bible was derided as crude and potentially heretical, it would now be seen as a symbol of national pride and international status."[14]

Growing Church Unrest

Amid this period of literary growth, the church faced internal conflict. The laity, discontent with the claims of the Roman Church, refused to accept the church as supreme. France and England's attempts to unite over their support of popes Urban and Clement had brought the respect for the church to an all-time low. England, in an age immortalized by Chaucer, grew eager for the Scriptures in her own tongue.

In response, the church tried to enforce the rule that clergy alone could own and read the Scriptures—but reading should not be done in English. If simple laypeople wanted to know what Scripture said, they could gaze upon the pictures in stained glass windows. The clergy not only prevented the laity from reading the Scriptures, they also prohibited copies of the sacred text from becoming available in the vernacular or for an affordable price.

John Wycliffe (1320–84): The Morning Star of the Reformation

For Bible lovers around the world, it may be surprising to learn that no complete English Bible existed before the fourteenth century. The modestly educated clergy studied only large, awkward copies of the church's authorized Latin Bible. The exorbitant price and the scarcity of copies made reading and study nearly impossible. The clergy could only hope to put their hands on portions of Scripture and, for the most part, relied heavily on their prayer books for spiritual development. The use of these fragmented portions of biblical texts made it impossible to understand the flow, context, and meaning of the Scriptures as originally intended. This state of affairs undoubtedly contributed to the poor standard of Bible interpretation and the faulty worship of words and phrases used out of context. As a result, the medieval church easily succumbed to strange and grotesque doctrines.

The first complete Bible in English, however, was a strict, literal translation from the Latin Vulgate that was probably produced by John Wycliffe, known as "the Morning Star of the Reformation."[15] Wycliffe was born in 1320 in the small village of Wycliffe-on-Tees in the north of England. He attended Balliol College in Oxford and received his Doctor of Theology in 1372–73. He later became warden of Canterbury Hall. Some of Wycliffe's translation work is so literal that it is difficult to understand without the use of a Latin dictionary. Although a few scholars in medieval Europe studied Greek, they used common Latin as the primary medium of study and instruction, so it was only natural to translate Scripture from their Latin Bible.[16] The widespread teaching of Greek and Hebrew had not yet reached England, and Wycliffe did not know either language, but he believed a Bible in the people's language would help balance the abusive authority of the established church. Not long after his cumbersome and awkward English translation in 1382, one of Wycliffe's associates began a revision in 1388.

Faith often leads to political action, whether one lives in the fourteenth or twenty-first century. John Wycliffe was fully aware of the religious climate and political unrest in his

A portrait of John Wycliffe from an engraving by H. Cook. Wycliffe is credited with the translation of the first complete Bible in the English language. Photo: Emily Sarah Holt, John de Wycliffe (c. 1900), 38.

world, but his life was compelled by a passion for Scripture to be the principal rule of life. The church wielded great power over the people in the pews and governed their behavior through fear of excommunication and the dread of purgatory, but it was Wycliffe's faith that stood in contrast to the popular thought among the religious authorities who stood over him. He believed that reading Scripture with understanding and obedience to its precepts precluded worshipping the words as oracles from God.

John Wycliffe dared to take a stand against the established church and began preaching the doctrine of the authority of Scripture against the many abuses of the church's power.[17] He stood firm upon the conviction that the Scriptures are the sole authority for faith and practice. Therefore, he reasoned, the Bible should be in the hands of the people who are individually responsible to God. He declared that the Bible must be in the language of the common people so they could grasp the clear teaching of Scripture.

Wycliffe insisted that translations in languages other than Latin could not negatively affect the meaning of Scripture. His conviction was expressed in a Latin sermon found in an Oxford manuscript, which translated reads:

> Although the common expressions may change over time, the truthful principles that are articulated from the Gospel are the same in number. Likewise, even though the languages are different, the evangelical truths do not change. Therefore the Scriptures should be written and spoken in Latin and Greek, in Gaelic, in English, and should also be articulated in all other languages. But especially, the Scriptures should be written in English because a translation does not have to be true to the idioms but rather the translation should rely on the perfection of truth confirming the truths of God.[18]

The Wycliffe Bible

Only 250 copies of the Wycliffe Bible exist today, and each one differs from the other. This is not surprising since each was hand-copied from different manuscripts by various monks using a handmade stylus and lamp-black ink. Nineteenth-century scholars identified at least two distinct families of manuscripts, known as the Early Version (EV) and the Later Version (LV). Recent scholarship has found variances even within these two families.

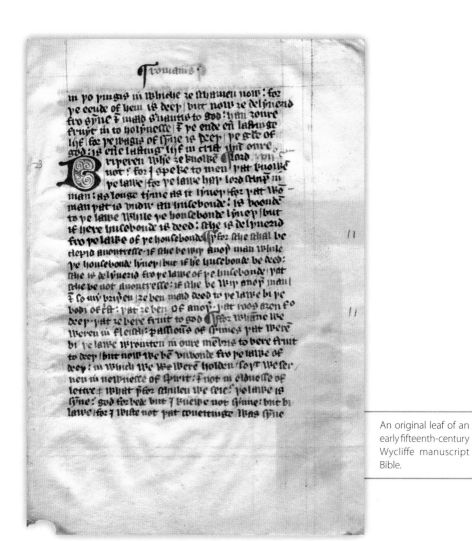

An original leaf of an early fifteenth-century Wycliffe manuscript Bible.

The early version of the Wycliffe Bible was probably completed about 1382, and the later version is from 1388 or later, perhaps as late as 1395. The early version follows the Latin word order, while the later version makes use of idiomatic expressions.

Many of the differences in the manuscripts were the result of copying in an atmosphere of persecution shrouded by a need for secrecy. Scribes often hurried to complete manuscripts with little attention to accuracy, frequently relying on whatever manuscript could be acquired quickly. In spite of the pressure of perilous times, many of the copies were beautifully adorned, most likely by professional illuminators. Even after the 1408 Constitutions of Oxford,[19]

"We Do Not Teach Latin Here"

I paused to take a long look at the impressive doors of the Bodleian Library before I entered. In those few moments I absorbed the magnificent architecture and imagined John Wycliffe, in a long, flowing academic gown and "Tudor bonnet" and with a bundle of books tucked under his arm, entering these great halls of learning. I had spent nearly a year getting permission from the Bodleian Library to publish an exact facsimile of a Wycliffe manuscript. I was ready for an investigation of multiple copies of Wycliffe manuscripts. I felt somehow unworthy to enter the sanctuary where these manuscripts were housed, but the librarian's helpfulness eased my nerves and set me to the task at hand.

Since no exact facsimile or accurate reproduction of a Wycliffe manuscript had ever been done, I felt it was a worthy project for me to give back to Bible collecting—the hobby I so enjoy. After viewing nearly every manuscript in their library, I chose a New Testament manuscript, Rawlinson C259, for its small size and potential use by fourteenth-century laity. I contracted with a London printer who was familiar with the Bodleian Library to photograph the manuscript. The printer agreed to keep the two thousand copies at its facility in England, and I could pay for the storage and shipping as I sold them.

A few months after the project was completed, I received a letter informing me the printer had gone bankrupt and I had one month to collect the copies or the total inventory would be sold at auction. I scraped together the funds and sent the money to the printer. A month later the inventory appeared at the Portland docks with customs due. Now at the mercy of market demand and without a public auction house like eBay, I quickly expanded my prospect list and sent out brochures to smaller libraries to find a quick sale for my Wycliffes.

An immediate response came from an English teacher in Alabama who enthusiastically ordered a copy for her school. I mailed her a copy, expecting a check by return mail. To my surprise, when I opened the return mail I found the Wycliffe facsimile, along with a startling explanation.

"I am returning your Bible because we do not teach Latin here."

Latin? Apparently the archaic spellings and ancient letters had confused this twentieth-century teacher into believing that instead of receiving a copy of a Bible produced in Middle English, she had purchased a Latin text.

which forbade the reading or production of English translations of Scripture unless approved by diocesan authorities, many copies of the Wycliffe Bible appeared. Today the extraordinary number of existing Wycliffe copies can be attributed to durable, fire-retardant, water-resistant parchment and the vast number of copies that were hand-produced.

The Early Wycliffe Bible (1382)

A mystery surrounds the translators of the earlier version. Their identities are somewhat uncertain, but it is believed that Nicholas of Hereford collaborated with Wycliffe, possibly with the assistance of John Purvey and John Trevisa. At least three manuscripts of the early version provide a variety of translation information. MS Bodley 959, housed at the Bodleian Library in Oxford, is a large manuscript with many corrections and alterations formerly believed to be the original autograph of the Wycliffe Old Testament. The manuscript includes the Old Testament book of Baruch among the prophetical books.[20] Baruch 3:20 ends abruptly at the bottom of the page: "*ye place hem / risen / ye (the) yunge.*" A cryptic postscript follows verse 20: "Here ends the translation of Nicholas."

The Bodleian Library's MS Douce 369, another early version, also ends abruptly at the same place in the text but a quarter of the way down the second column of the page. This passage ends with a similar abrupt ending, "*Explicist translacom Nicholay de herford*" ("Here ends the translation of Nicholas of Hereford"). Nicholas of Hereford most likely translated this portion of the Old Testament, and Lollards were undoubtedly involved in the translation of the rest of the Bible.

A third early manuscript, MS Ee.10, housed in the Cambridge University Library, ends at exactly the same place in Baruch and records, "*Here endith the translacioun of N and now bigynneth the translacioun of J & of othere men.*" Perhaps "N" refers to Nicholas of Hereford, but the "J" poses a problem. The letter could refer to John Wycliffe, John Trevisa, or John Purvey, Wycliffe's secretary at Lutterworth, where Wycliffe had pastored. Purvey was

Oxford educated, ordained to the priesthood, and most likely a doctor of theology. His contemporaries acknowledged him as a scholar.

The earliest mention of Wycliffe's association with the Bible translation is Henry Knighton's reference in his *Chronicon*. Writing in the 1390s, Knighton refers to 1382 as the period when John Wycliffe translated the Gospels. John Wycliffe's name became forever linked with his work in translating what is known as the Wycliffe Bible.

The Later Wycliffe Bible (1388–95)

John Purvey, one of Wycliffe's most devoted associates, worked from the earlier version to translate the revised Wycliffe Bible. Many scholars refer to him as "Lollard's librarian," testifying to his scholarship and access to the resources necessary for translation and writing. For many years it has been accepted that Purvey wrote the general prologue that introduces this later version of the Wycliffe Bible, but modern scholars debate this authorship. The prologue contains fifteen chapters encouraging princes, lords, justices, and commoners to read the Law of God; in addition, it includes principles for interpretation and methods for translating.

Wycliffe awakened the latent desire of the faithful to read and study the Bible. His 1382 translation and the revised version created a thirst that led to the insatiable desire for Bible translations that culminated in the Golden Age of the sixteenth century. Wycliffe died of natural causes in 1384, but contention did not stop when he was buried. In 1428, almost fifty years later, the Council of Constance under the rule of Pope Martin V declared him a "stiff-necked heretic." Church officials ordered that his bones be exhumed and burned and the ashes be cast into the River Swift.

So effective was the Wycliffe English Bible that the church made a specific statement to prevent further translations of the Bible in English. The Oxford Council summoned in 1407–8 by Thomas Arundel, archbishop of Canterbury, made a direct restriction of English translations. Church historian John Foxe quoted the seventh enactment:

We therefore decree and ordain, that no man, hereafter, by his own authority translate any text of the Scripture into English or any other tongue, by way of a book, libel, or treatise, now lately set forth in the time of John Wickliff, or since, or hereafter to be set forth, in part or in whole, privily or apertly, upon pain of greater excommunication, until the said translation be allowed by the ordinary of the place, or, if the case so require, by the council provincial. He that shall do contrary to this, shall likewise be punished as a favourer of error and heresy.[21]

But neither enactments nor political threats could quell the hunger that stirred in the hearts of men like John Wycliffe to produce a Bible that would be accessible to all men and women. Even after his death, Wycliffe's passion for a Scripture delivered into the hands of all people burned in the hearts of a new generation.

Modern English Period (1500 to Present Day)

During the Modern English period, economic and social factors exerted influence over the progression of English. Social unrest in Western Europe brought a shift in wealth and economic power from the traditional feudalistic system and the social structure of a few governing families to a burgeoning middle class. The newfound interest in literacy among the common plowmen and their increased wealth and power led to the rise of entrepreneurs who initiated local and foreign trade.

The languages of the aristocracy and the church—Parisian French and Latin—fell out of favor when the Hundred Years' War (1337–1453) between the English and the French positioned French as the language of England's enemies and English as the language of the commoners and the educated. The Renaissance fueled a rapid learning curve, increasing the popularity of words, reading, and the communication of ideas. And the go-to source for reading and study became the most popular book in society: the English Bible.

Due to the design efforts of goldsmith Johann Gutenberg in Germany (Gutenberg Bible printed 1454–56), by the sixteenth century the printing press was making a widespread impact throughout England. Gutenberg, the so-called man of the millennium, popularized the mass production of books through the printing press and his development of movable type. The Western world was ready for words to be printed in the English language. The Gutenberg press paved the way for William Caxton (1422–91) to print the first book in English: an edition of *Canterbury Tales* (1476). Caxton soon found that England was anxious to become literate and had an appetite for books in the English language.

The story of bringing the Bible into the language of common people— an epic drama captured in my book *A Visual History of the English Bible:*

This 1611 King James Version is one of England's greatest literary treasures.

Photo: R. Maisel.

The Forbidden Book in the Twentieth Century

Breathless with excitement, the young father and Bible school student ordered five Amharic Bibles, which were written in the official and most widely spoken Semitic language of Ethiopia.

"Why do you want five Bibles?" I asked. It was an odd number, and the man did not seem to possess the means to own many books. I tried to hide my curiosity, but something in his face intrigued me. (I managed the bookstore and taught Bible and theology at the Grace Bible Institute in Jimma, Ethiopia, as a missionary with the Sudan Interior Mission.) "You can read only one at a time, and they last for many years."

"We know once the government takes control of the area, they will seize all the Bibles and destroy them. I am going to bury a copy for each of my children in plastic bags in a secret place over the hill behind my house. When it is safe to dig them up, our children will each have their own copy to read."

I fought the swell of tears as he spoke.

Only days before this, the Communists had taken over the country, and the future for Christians was fearfully uncertain. As we prepared to exit the country for Addis Ababa before the new regime took over, news of our bookstore's fire sale had reached even the outskirts of the province. The local Communist group had already searched our homes for weapons, rifled through our belongings, and confiscated various items from the mission compound. Evidence of the persecutions of Christians in several down-country provinces had already surfaced.

I was touched by this father's determination and foresight, and I bid him Godspeed. With his treasured Bibles safely in hand, he set off to leave a legacy for his children. One Bible at a time, one hole at a time, dug by a father's hands.

The story of the *forbidden book* is not a phenomenon of the Middle Ages only. It is a real and living testimony of a worldwide thirst for the Word of God that spans cultures and generations—a thirst that was a driving force in the souls of men and women centuries ago, and a thirst that will drive modern-day souls to seek, sacrifice, and dig until the end of ages.

The Tumultuous Tale of the World's Bestselling Book (Baker, 2008)—is littered with the deaths of martyrs. Those who harbored sinister interests within the church opposed the Bible in the English language. At the provincial council meeting at St. Paul's Church in London in 1407, Archbishop of Canterbury Thomas Arundel adopted the prohibition of not only the translation of any portion of Scripture into English but also the public or private reading of Scripture, under penalty of excommunication or punishment for heresy. The sentiments of the church to block the common people's access to Scripture could not have been clearer.

It wasn't until Henry VIII championed a national English language and the Great Bible in English that the effects of the Constitutions were finally nullified.[22] The English-speaking world stood poised to receive a Bible that would shape the English language for all time.

The endorsement of an authorized English language in the sixteenth century, during the monarchies of Henry VIII through Elizabeth I, set the stage for extensive Bible translation work during this era, culminating in such works as the Bishops' Bible (1568), the Coverdale Bible (1535), the Douay-Rheims (alternate spelling, Rhemes) Bible (1582–1610), the Geneva Bible (1560), the Great Bible (1539), the Matthew's Bible (1537), and the Tyndale New Testament and portions of the Old Testament (1526–34). The monarchs during this period fostered the development of a language that gave birth to the greatest English literary period of all time, which produced not only a heritage of great English Bible translations but also the works of William Shakespeare and John Donne.

2

Fanning the Flames

Early English Printed Bibles, King Henry VIII to Queen Mary

The fifteenth century saw the birth of a movement that would influence the world for centuries: the Reformation. The instigation for this massive sociological, cultural, and theological phenomenon was men and women—the masses were disgruntled with the church's decadence and abuses. This was also the period of the Renaissance, when people hungered for education and the arts. This hunger led to the development of Gutenberg's printing press, which led to the inexpensive proliferation and distribution of Scripture to commoners in the pew and paved the way for the Reformation. Once the Bible reached the hands of those who so long had thirsted for the Scriptures, their passion for truth fanned the flames of the Reformation to white-hot intensity that was felt around the world.

A Commoner Influences History

It fell to the destiny of a commoner, Johann Gutenberg (ca. 1396–1468), to alter the course of world history. Prior to Gutenberg's invention, printers had carved outlines of simple pictures and texts from solid blocks of wood. The blocks were inked with wool-stuffed leather pads and then placed in handpresses similar to winepresses that forced the ink from the block to the paper or vellum.

Gutenberg's invention of practical movable type allowed printers to reuse lead composite letters, creating a far more efficient and accelerated printing process, resulting in exponentially increased book production.

William Caxton brought the art of printing to England in 1475, and he translated and printed Jacobus de Voragine's *Golden Legend* (1483). This

The *Golden Legend* was the first portion of the Bible printed in English. It described the lives of the saints from the Old Testament to the time it was published.

work is a hagiography, or collection of biographies and lore about venerated saints from the Old and New Testaments, such as Abraham, Joshua, David, Matthew, Luke, and Paul; it also includes passages summarizing the life of Christ. The summaries of saints' lives in the *Golden Legend* are drawn from Scripture but are mixed with apocryphal stories and church lore.

While Caxton could have chosen to print the Wycliffe Bible, he disassociated himself from Wycliffe's work for fear of the negative consequences imposed by the Constitutions of 1408. No one was allowed to produce or use an English Bible that was not endorsed by the church. Consequently, he chose to print Jacobus de Voragine's book that included only elements of biblical text. The *Golden Legend* became a popular work that served as the primary print source for religious teaching for the English-speaking world for more than forty years. It wasn't until 1526 that the Tyndale New Testament finally replaced the *Golden Legend* as a reliable version of the New Testament.

William Tyndale (ca. 1494–1536): "God's Outlaw"

Sometime between 1493 and 1495, an ordinary Welsh family living in Stinchcombe, Gloucestershire, welcomed a newborn son, William Tyndale. Few men have influenced history and affected Christianity as powerfully as Tyndale. For centuries he remained relatively unknown among the laity until he was recognized in the twentieth century as a significant contributor to the English Bible, a recognition long overdue.

When Tyndale entered Oxford University in 1510, the influences

An anonymous portrait of William Tyndale. Tyndale translated the first Bible into English from the Greek New Testament, and it was the first Bible published by printing press. Some have suggested this is actually a portrait of John Knox in 1580 and forty years later was presumed to be Tyndale.[1] Photo: George Offor, The New Testament (Editor's Extra Illustrated copy, 1836), 98.

of John Colet and Desiderius Erasmus were making inroads among the English academic society. Colet, dean of St. Paul's Cathedral in London, studied abroad and then returned to London, where he preached from the Epistles of the apostle Paul and implemented the *new learning* of humanism. Erasmus, influenced by Colet, was a Dutch humanist who worked on Greek and Latin translations of the New Testament. Erasmus's humanism placed increased emphasis on man's rationality while shifting emphasis away from clericalism and the supernatural. His philosophies, as well as his Greek New Testament, shaped the academic atmosphere in English universities. Many scholars believe Tyndale spent time studying Erasmus's Greek New Testament at Cambridge University.[2]

While Tyndale was studying for his Bachelor of Arts degree, both Oxford and Cambridge introduced the study of ancient languages. He became a diligent student of the original biblical languages; so intensely, in fact, that he rejected the teaching presented in many of his biblical and theological studies, going so far as to call some of the university teachers "apostles of ignorance." Soon after he was ordained in 1515, Tyndale was granted a Master of Arts degree, which included the study of theology.

Erasmus was a humanist and editor of the first published Greek New Testament.   Photo: Original art, L. Lupton.

Erasmus by Holbein

John Colet, humanist and theologian, influenced the Christian atmosphere in the late fifteenth century.

With England facing religious turmoil with enemies in abundance, Tyndale quickly recognized the impossibilities of translating the Bible in his homeland. But a second and even more important factor forced his hand. The Oxford Constitutions of 1408 required the approval of the bishops before he could translate the Bible, and neither Cuthbert Tunstall, bishop of London, nor Cardinal Wolsey would grant Tyndale such authority. Sensing the growing climate of hostility in England, Tyndale considered alternate plans.

"God's Outlaw" Flees England

Realizing he could not wait for a more positive political climate in London, Tyndale set sail for Hamburg, Germany, in May of 1524. Luther's Germany was a hotbed of the Reformation, and Tyndale optimistically believed he could proceed with his translation work with less opposition.

He found a shifting theological atmosphere in Hamburg and all of Germany, which was in the throes of the Protestant Reformation. Disgruntled clergy were abandoning cloisters; priests and nuns were marrying; vows were being relinquished; indulgences and certificates of forgiveness were no longer being sold in public. The Lord's Supper had replaced masses and rites, and commoners were reading Luther's German Bible and openly discussing current theological issues.

Because Tyndale was unable to find the printing presses and scholarly research tools he needed to conduct his work in Hamburg, he spent most of the year in Wittenberg translating the New Testament. While scholars disagree as to whether he met Luther while there, most researchers agree that Luther was in Wittenberg at the time and he may have influenced Tyndale's translation work. In fact, some scholars debate whether Tyndale may have relied on Luther's German translation. He did, of course, support Luther theologically. But because Tyndale's knowledge of Greek and Hebrew was superior to his German, it is more likely that he consulted Luther's work only for comparison purposes.

> Tyndale found a shifting theological atmosphere in Hamburg and all of Germany, which was in the throes of the Protestant Reformation.

During August of 1524, with the ink barely dry on his work, Tyndale made his way to Cologne, Germany, where he engaged Peter Quentel, a local printer, to begin production of the New Testament. After Quentel produced approximately ten sheets (eighty quarto pages, with a quarto representing one-fourth the size of the original sheet of paper), the city senate, hearing of progress on the New Testament and influenced by anti-Lutheran forces within the city, forbade the printing to continue. Tyndale, who had been warned of impending danger, fled to Worms with the sheets, which contained most of the Gospel of Matthew and, some believe, portions of Mark. He took the documents to Peter Schoeffer, a German printer who had apprenticed with Johann Gutenberg, and Schoeffer resumed the project.

The first printed New Testament in English was completed as a small octavo (each leaf of an octavo represents one-eighth of the original sheet) at Worms, Germany, in 1526. (The earlier eighty-page quarto edition was abandoned for the new smaller edition.) Today only one fragment of Tyndale's New Testament survives from the Cologne (1525) printing. While some spelling changes separate the editions, the two translations are much the same. The Worms printing omitted numerous marginal notes from the Cologne edition, perhaps because of added cost or Tyndale's fear that controversy over the politically charged notes might detract from the Testament's distribution.

The Cologne printing established the format for future editions of the New Testament, even though later translators challenged the inclusion of the marginal notes. In addition to the marginal notes and an extensive prologue, the Cologne printing included a list of the books of the New Testament with Hebrews, James, Jude, and Revelation separated from the other books. This format follows the collation of Luther's New Testament of 1522. Luther believed these four books did not share the same canonical authority as the rest of the New Testament. Tyndale did not necessarily hold to this canonical view, but he was influenced by Luther's formatting changes. The Cologne printing also provides evidence that Tyndale most certainly possessed a copy of Luther's German translation and had referred to it.

Bishop Cuthbert Tunstall of London, a key player in the English church hierarchy, feared Tyndale's translation would cause people to abandon the principles, practices, and traditions of the church. In October of 1526 he began confiscating Tyndale's New Testaments as they were smuggled into England. Copies were publicly burned, and men and women who dared to defy the ban were punished with fines and imprisonment as well as other means. As the church's restraints tightened, people's spirits plummeted.

Tunstall also used merchants to purchase copies on the continent in order to cut off the supply of Bibles to England. One man, however, raised a voice in objection. Augustine Packington, a London businessman, felt the bishop had overstepped his authority and met with Tyndale to inform him of the plot. To Packington's surprise, Tyndale embraced the news with enthusiasm and encouraged Packington to carry out Tunstall's orders.

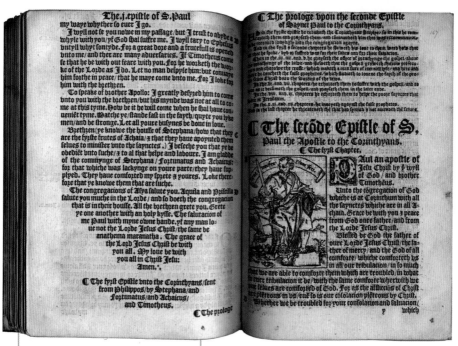

The Tyndale New Testament was the first New Testament printed in the English language. Pictured here is the 1536 edition.

Tyndale felt the church's response to the confiscation and burning of God's Word would heighten condemnation of the English church in the world's eyes, and profits from Bible sales would reduce Tyndale's debt and fund another revision.[3]

Tyndale was right; Tunstall's book-burning program proved an abysmal failure. New Testaments poured into England, and the demand for more grew daily. Pirated copies circulated and sold in England in spite of threats of punishment. William Tyndale had produced a bestseller!

Success breeds success. With the obvious triumph of the 1526 edition, Tyndale launched into the 1534 revision—a small octavo edition of approximately four hundred pages. His 1534 revision shows improvement in his understanding of Greek terms and grammatical constructions, reflecting his continual study to improve his translation abilities. With the publication of this revised edition of the New Testament, William Tyndale experienced for the first time the distinction of having his name attached to the Bible that would be considered his finest work.

The Outlaw's Hideout Discovered

While Tyndale lived in Germany, his concealment was secure and his English enemies could not gain access to him. But in 1534 Tyndale concluded that the progress of the Reformation had made it possible for him to move in with the Poyntz family. Thomas Poyntz, an English merchant who had moved to Belgium, and his wife Anna, offered Tyndale a hideout in their home. Antwerp was under the jurisdiction of Charles V, a staunch Roman Catholic who believed that an accusation of heresy against Tyndale would promote the best interests of the church. On May 21, 1535, Henry Phillips, Tyndale's supposed friend, betrayed him. He was kidnapped and imprisoned in the castle of Vilvorde near Brussels. By this time, Thomas Cromwell and even Henry VIII had become sympathetic toward an English translation and made token attempts to intervene on Tyndale's behalf. But Charles V, the nephew of Henry's recently divorced wife, the staunchly Catholic Catherine of Aragon, refused to respond to their requests.

Tyndale spent his final days in prison at Vilvorde castle.

Beware the "Ides" of May

"William, you must find out more about this Henry Phillips," Thomas Poyntz insisted. "There is something about him I do not trust."

William Tyndale shook his head. "He is an honest man, a learned man, and a man of means who has much to lose in associating with me. Don't worry. He has protected my identity on several occasions and has been supportive of my translation work." William valued Thomas's opinion; he had risked his own safety and reputation by hosting an "outlaw" from the Roman Church in his home in Antwerp.

"But William, you know your enemies in England are searching all of Europe for you. Sooner or later they will find you, and you know what that means. For a price, someone will be willing to turn you over to the authorities."

William could read the worry on his friend's face. Thomas knew William had fought against a false sense of security over the years of his stay with the Poyntz family in Antwerp. By 1535 life tucked away in their home had taken on its own measured pace.

By the time Henry Phillips had arrived on the scene in Antwerp in 1535, three years had passed in relative safety. From all appearances, Phillips seemed no threat. He came from a wealthy English family, and his only vice seemed to be gambling away the family inheritance. He had expressed interest in William's translation work and had even made bold statements that he was no friend of Henry VIII. William, a man of easy confidences, had readily opened his heart to Phillips.

William knew the hunt for him had escalated. No one knew the source of the search order: Henry VIII himself, Sir Thomas More, or, more likely, the bishop of London. But no matter the source, William chafed under the mounting pressure.

Poyntz had scarcely finished his pleading when Henry Phillips appeared in the doorway. More and more of late he seemed to appear at odd moments, William noted. Henry greeted them, "This is an especially beautiful spring day—a perfect morning for you to shake off winter and enjoy the reawakening of the city."

The idea appealed to William. The thought of walking even a short distance in the open sunshine after hiding from authorities all winter seemed a small privilege after months of work on his beloved translation. "I believe sunlight is just what I need," he agreed. Tyndale nodded reassuringly in Poyntz's direction as he joined Henry and stepped through the door. Thomas called out an objection behind them, but it was too late.

"Please, Sir William," the younger Henry feigned a polite attitude. "You make your way ahead of me down the path." With a gesture, he motioned to William to precede him. William paused to move forward before his eye caught a movement in his peripheral vision. His heart dropped. Before the men broke through the protection of the hedge, William felt the truth fall hard across his soul. For a price, Henry Phillips had betrayed him. He had pre-arranged a meeting with the king's officers beyond the protected property of the English house. Peace settled on William with the warmth of the sunshine as the authorities seized his arms and took him into custody. Without a struggle, William Tyndale gave up his freedom.

From May 1535 to October 1536 he was housed in the Vilvorde prison near Brussels. On Friday, October 6, in the midst of the town square before the local officials and in front of a crowd of onlookers, William Tyndale, bound in irons, was led to the stake. With the piles of brush nestled around the platform, the executioner tightened the noose, strangled him, and then set the brush ablaze.

But before the noose of the executioner forever silenced his earthly voice, Tyndale spoke: "Lord, open the eyes of the king of England!" Moments later, this man of God received his eternal reward as he met the Savior whom he had served faithfully in life.

Within four years of William Tyndale's death, four English translations of the Bible were circulating in England. All were based upon his work. One was the official English Bible.

Pictured is the only known handwriting of William Tyndale, a letter written while he was in prison at Vilvorde near modern Brussels. The letter requests that the procurer send him warmer clothes, a Hebrew Bible, a grammar, and a dictionary. It is unknown if his captors fulfilled his request. Some historians suggest that while Tyndale was in prison, he translated portions of the Old Testament. Photo: Francis Fry, *A Bibliographical Description of the Editions of the New Testament* (1878), xiv.

Tyndale's legacy is of inestimable value, surpassing his work on the Tyndale English New Testament and Old Testament books and extending to the influence of his work on succeeding Bible translations. Even the most popular English Bible, the King James Version (also known as the Authorized Version), owes a debt to William Tyndale. The highly qualified translators of the 1611 King James Version relied heavily upon Tyndale's work, basing an estimated 80 to 90 percent of their Bible on Tyndale's translation. Recognizable readings from Tyndale survive nearly word for word in the King James Version:

> Matthew 11:28 "Come unto me all ye that labor and are laden and I will ease you."
>
> Matthew 7:7 "Ask, and it shall be given you; seek, and ye shall find; knock, and it shall be opened unto you."
>
> Acts 17:11 "The noblest . . . searched the scriptures daily whether those things were even so."
>
> Hebrews 12:2 "Looking unto Jesus, the author and finisher of our faith."
>
> Revelation 3:20 "Behold I stand at the door and knock. If any man hear my voice and open the door, I will come in unto him and will sup with him, and he with me."
>
> Revelation 7:17 "And God shall wipe away all tears from their eyes."

Although the King James Version of 1611 dwarfed the work of previous translations in popularity, William Tyndale's work stands to date as a very influential English translation.

In spite of his humble birth, William Tyndale's voice echoed from the halls of sixteenth-century courts and manors to the huts of the lower classes. He stepped out in leadership on behalf of those seeking church reformation. He stood as a resolute rogue among a religious hierarchy steeped in dogma. He sacrificed his life on behalf of those seeking a voice for their faith, and his death shook the foundation of English religious society. William Tyndale stands as a hero of the faith who made the ultimate sacrifice as a martyr. His legacy to "the man behind the plow" surpasses his own work in

John Foxe (1517–87), a significant church historian, wrote about the period of history from John Huss (priest and martyr, ca. 1372–1415), John Wycliffe (ca. 1320–82), and William Tyndale (ca. 1494–1536) to the beginning of Queen Elizabeth's reign in 1559. Catholic Queen "Bloody" Mary's brutal reign of terror (1553–58) greatly affected Foxe's life. At the request of Lady Jane Grey, a committed Protestant who ruled as queen for just more than a week before her overthrow and execution at the hands of Queen Mary, Foxe published his *Acts and Monuments* in 1563.[4]

The Roman Catholic Church immediately attacked the book for its use of inflammatory language against the church as well as its inaccuracy. In response, Foxe issued a second edition in 1570 that was more conservative in language choice.

While he had access to documents of the period about which he wrote, Foxe's views may have been influenced by the stories he heard about the evil deeds of the Roman Catholic Church. Although he has been accused of deliberately falsifying records, Foxe often appeals to living witnesses who reported the stories, so the contemporary reader can verify his information. While Foxe's *Acts and Monuments* stands as a tremendously important chronicle of history, readers must apply caution in assuming that all reports are unbiased, since many of the accounts cannot be verified by supporting sources.

Bible translation. Because of William Tyndale's unwavering courage, Scripture passed into the hands of all men and women. No longer would the Bible be read by priests and clergy alone.

Miles Coverdale (ca. 1488–1569): The Dean of Translators

William Tyndale paved the way for the approval of an English Bible; however, his untimely death in 1536 prevented his translation of the entire Bible. But Miles Coverdale, a translator and scholar in his own right, completed Tyndale's task and brought the Bible in its entirety to every church in England.

The Byble in Englyshe, that is to saye the content of all the holy scrypture, bothe of ý olde and newe testament, truly translated after the veryte of the Hebrue and Greke textes, by ý dylygent studye of dyuerse excellent learned men, expert in the forsayde tonges.

Prynted by Rychard Grafton & Edward Whitchurch.

Cum priuilegio ad imprimendum solum.

1539.

Henry VIII ordered that the Great Bible be placed in every English church.

An Augustinian monk with a sense of political savvy, Coverdale played a pivotal role in the history of Bible translation. He was born around 1488 and was admitted into the priesthood in 1514. But by 1528 Coverdale had been influenced by the Reformed movement and abandoned his priestly habit and Augustinian order to fully embrace the Lutheran cause.

Miles Coverdale's carefully veiled shrewdness gave him the ability to move among political enemies without alienating them and helped him curry court favor while other Bible translators were dying for the cause. Coverdale attracted powerful protectors whose support enabled his translation to become the first authorized Bible in the British Empire. Where Tyndale had failed to gain ecclesiastical endorsement and was openly opposed by King Henry VIII, Coverdale cultivated support from the royal family, and his Bible includes an elaborate dedication to the king. Some scholars believe Henry, under the influence of Cromwell and More, encouraged Coverdale to translate the Bible—hence the dedication. The support from both More and Cromwell helps explain Coverdale's successful, long life as a translator.

> An Augustinian monk with a sense of political savvy, Coverdale played a pivotal role in the history of Bible translation.

Coverdale's introductory Bible dedication cites Henry's second wife, Anne. She had long supported Coverdale's work on the Bible, and she no doubt used her court influence on his behalf. But after Henry's divorce from Anne and her eventual execution, surviving copies show a correction of "Anne" (Boleyn) with "Jane" (Seymour), Henry's third wife, who died after giving birth. While the support of a sovereign typically guarantees an endeavor's success, Queen Anne Boleyn's evangelical leanings and patronage of the 1535 Coverdale Bible hastened its downfall. In May of 1536, her arrest and execution prevented the king from officially authorizing the Bible she had supported. History's long-awaited *authorized* Bible would not be the 1535 Coverdale Bible.

Modern Christians might be disappointed that a new Bible was translated by a scholar who did not have an academic's skill in the original languages, but such was the case with the first complete printed English Bible. Coverdale's limited knowledge of the original languages forced him to consult

German, Swiss, and Latin texts. His choice among English expressions reflected aesthetic judgment, linguistic taste, and an attempt to produce a more stylistic rendering. While Coverdale's work was admirable, he seldom exceeded Tyndale's readability, which sought linguistic faithfulness to the intended meaning of the original languages.

In 1535 Jacobus van Meteren, a financier and printer of early English Bibles, published Coverdale's first complete English language Bible in Antwerp. By this time the Bible was in great demand in England. In 1533 a new act had been passed, forcing foreign printers to sell their loose pages to London binderies.[5] In this bold act of protectionism, the English bindery industry placed a stranglehold on the market. Van Meteren was forced to sell the sheets from the Coverdale Bible to James Nicholson of Southwark. As a result, although printed in Antwerp, all extant copies of the Coverdale Bible have English bindings.

Although study notes are helpful in understanding the Bible, notes became a suspicious element from the moment of their conception because of the controversial nature of theological content. Coverdale wisely omitted potentially offensive notes and introductions. His margins contained only alternate readings, general interpretations, and references to parallel passages. To decorate the Bible after the fashion of earlier hand-illuminated Bibles, about 150 small woodcuts adorned the text of his 1535 first edition.

Coverdale's Bible set a precedent in one history-making matter related to the relationship between formatting and doctrine. Some may wonder why the apocryphal books are included in the English Bible. What they might not realize is that in versions predating the Coverdale, the apocryphal books are scattered throughout the Bible. In the Coverdale Bible the Apocrypha is located between the Old and New Testaments. Why the change? Since church traditions differ on what books should be contained in the canon of inspired Scripture, the word *Apocrypha* means different things to different religious groups. In its general sense, the word refers to books that are considered useful but not inspired. For instance, the Roman Catholic Church believes the Apocrypha is inspired, while the Protestant Church does not. Coverdale separated the apocryphal books from the text of the Old and New Testaments and placed them between the Testaments. He emphasized their secondary importance when he wrote, "The books and treatises, which among the father's [*sic*] of old are not reckoned to be of like authority with the other books of the Bible, neither are they found in the Canon of the Hebrews."[6] Coverdale was the first translator to set apart the apocryphal books as having a distinct place and a lesser value than the canonical books. His precedent established the standard format for Protestant English Bibles and continues today.[7]

Coverdale's work in Bible translation dovetails with the books left untranslated by Tyndale. The Psalms and prophetic books reveal the scope of Coverdale's influence:

> Psalm 1:1 "O Blessed is the man, that goeth not in the councell of the ungodly: that abydeth not in the waye off synners, or sytteth not in the seate of the scornefull."
>
> Psalm 22:1–3 (chapter 23 in KJV) "The Lorde is my shepherd, I can want nothing. He feedeth me in a green pasture, and leadeth me to a fresh water. He quickeneth my soul, and bringeth me forth in the way of rightness for his name sake."
>
> Isaiah 53:6 "As for us, we go all astraye (like shepe), every one turneth his owne waye."
>
> Jeremiah 17:1 "Graven upon the edge of your altars with a pen of iron and with an adamant claw."

Miles Coverdale lived a long life (ca. 1488–1569) marked by court intrigue. He survived the bloody persecutions of the counter-Reformation and the persistent banishments of Queen Mary, and his contributions to translation guarantee him a place in Bible history. From the first complete printed Bible in the English language (1535) to the last edition of his famous Great Bible (1569), Coverdale had a significant impact on several translations.

Thomas Matthew (ca. 1505–55): The Birth of Authorized Bibles

While Henry VIII did not translate a single word of the English Bible, his romances influenced the success of the English Bible more than any story of intrigue of the sixteenth century. Because the Roman Catholic Church refused to accept Henry's divorce from Catherine of Aragon and his marriage to Anne Boleyn, Henry broke with Rome. His position undermined church authority and set in motion the establishment of the Protestant Church of England and the Bible's translation into English.

In England, licensed Bibles meant government support and a guaranteed market share. By the end of 1537 King Henry had licensed two Bibles: the Matthew's Bible and the Coverdale Bible. To no one's surprise, the battle over an official, standard Bible soon began. The notes of the Matthew's Bible and Thomas Matthew's association with Tyndale offended the English clergy.[8] Coverdale's Bible relied on the Latin, German, and Swiss, rather than Greek and Hebrew. Amid the growing controversy, voices on each side called for a new translation. A Bible, some insisted, should be chained to every church pulpit and pronounced the "Licensed-Authorized Bible."

Thomas Cromwell, first lord protector of the Commonwealth of England, Scotland, and Ireland, boldly stepped forward to support a standardized text that could garner the support of all English people. The clergy, however, were still concerned about translations with notes that could be confusing

Pictured from the bottom up, the Matthew's Bible (1537), the first authorized Bible; the *Golden Legend* (1521); and second edition Coverdale (1537), the first with royal license on the title page.
Photo: R. Maisel.

The title to the 1540 Great Bible (also known as Cranmer's Bible) bore the coat of arms of Cromwell and Cranmer (below). After Cromwell fell out of favor with Henry VIII, Cromwell's coat of arms was expunged (top). Although most copies bear the name Edward Whitchurch as printer, this 1540 copy was printed by Richard Grafton. This was the first English Bible officially appointed to be used in the churches and to state so on the title. Photo: M. Brake.

or misleading to untrained laypeople. As a judicious choice, Cromwell chose Miles Coverdale, a proven friend of the court, to undertake the new translation. In 1539 the famous Great Bible (so called because of its size) was published. In a history-making edict, Henry VIII ordered a Great Bible placed in each church so every literate man and woman could have access to Scripture.

Coverdale's commission for the new translation was based on his friendship with Thomas Cromwell, as well as his proven ability to produce a good translation. Grafton and Whitchurch, who had published the Matthew's Bible, received the contract for publication of the Great Bible. France was chosen as the production site, in part because of advanced printing techniques and superior paper quality available there.

But France was struggling through the conflicts of a counter-Reformation. Even Henry's approval could not prevent the enemies of the Reformation from attempting to destroy English Bibles. Cromwell, aware of the potential dangers to the publication of an official translation, sent letters to the French king asking him to permit the printing of a licensed English translation. In the spring of 1538 the king granted permission, with the proviso that no "private or unlawful opinions" be included. His caveat targeted what had been perceived as antipapal marginal notes in the earlier Matthew's Bible.

Translation work pressed forward under constant threat. Translator Coverdale and printer Grafton continued to send sheets of biblical text to Cromwell in England while clouds of doom loomed over the project. Some authorities in England feared Cromwell's sponsored translation and led an effort in France to discover Coverdale, Whitchurch, and Regnault's secret work on the Bible. Word of Regnault's involvement may have leaked to autocrats in France who organized an attack on the work. In December 1538 the French inquisitor, under the authority of the Roman Catholic Church, issued an order expounding the dangers of a vernacular Scripture. The magistrates ordered Francis Regnault, the printer of the Coverdale Bible, to appear before the court to answer charges. Coverdale and Grafton escaped to England carrying sheets from the Great Bible. Regnault's printing offices were raided, and the remaining copies of Coverdale's 1538 Diglot (dual-language) were destroyed. Evidence shows that in the mayhem a large number of Great Bibles were most likely destroyed as well.

The 1538 Coverdale Diglot was the third edition of the diglot but the only authorized edition. It was a translation of English paralleled with Latin and exerted some influence on the Rheims New Testament. Pictured in front is the Coverdale Bible (1537).

For his translation, Coverdale referred to Tyndale's English translation as well as Munster's and Erasmus's Latin texts. Surprisingly, the Great Bible is a revision of the Matthew's Bible of 1537 rather than Coverdale's own translation of 1535. The 1539 Great Bible, hurriedly produced under political pressure from Cromwell, certainly needed revision. In April 1540 it was carefully revised and emended to include Thomas Cranmer's famous prologue to the work, which resulted in the work becoming known as the Cranmer Bible, even though it more accurately reflects the efforts of Thomas Cromwell.

His fall from Henry's favor in July 1540 meant Cromwell's public disgrace. An edition dated 1541 eradicated Cromwell's coat of arms on the title page. This same edition claimed Bishop Cuthbert of Duresme as a faithful supporter of the Cranmer Bible. Interestingly, Bishop Cuthbert is Bishop Tunstall, formerly bishop of London, who relentlessly fought the introduction of Tyndale's New Testament into England. Yet the Great Bible is nothing more than a slight revision of Tyndale's New Testament.

As an officially licensed and standardized translation, the Great Bible drew the support of religious authorities who once stood divided. Henry VIII's 1538 decree concerning the completed Great Bible allowed a Bible to be placed in every church.

A Clerk Becomes a Translator: The Taverner Bible

Richard Taverner (1505–75) received his education at Cambridge University and was a scholar in Greek, but he lacked a scholar's knowledge of Hebrew. After revising the Matthew's Bible, Taverner sought official license as a lay preacher. It is speculated that as a clerk in Cromwell's administration, he may have learned that the king wanted to authorize a Bible translation for use in the English church.

The Taverner Bible appeared in 1539, shortly before the Great Bible. While Taverner's work had only minimal influence on later English translations, some of his expressions have survived. Hebrews 1:3 states that the Son of God is the "express image" of his person—a Taverner rendering. Taverner also introduced a few memorable words, such as *parable* for Tyndale's

Portrait of Thomas Cranmer by Hans Holbein.

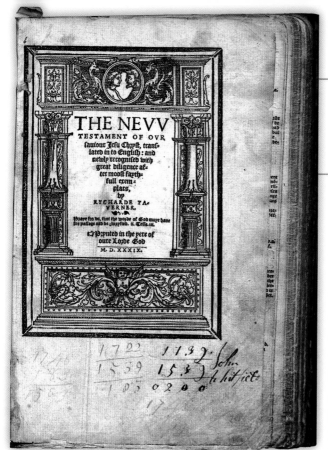

term *similitude*. In comparison to the Matthew's version, however, Taverner's primary contributions to the work of translation can be identified as stylistic and idiomatic renderings. In the Matthew's Bible, 1 John 2:1 reads, "We have an advocate with the Father." The Taverner edition reads, "We have a spokesman with the Father." While both are acceptable translations, the word *spokesman* reflects Taverner's attempt at a more idiomatic rendering.

From William Tyndale to Richard Taverner, the translators of early English Bibles made significant contributions in formatting, study notes, stylistic and idiomatic renderings, comparative language study, structural analysis, and beauty of language. The Western world's seemingly unlimited access to Scripture today rests upon the foundation of the sacrifice of committed men and their many colleagues for the cause of Bible translation.

3

The Theological Tug-of-War

Protestant, Catholic, and Anglican Factions under Elizabeth I

By the middle of the sixteenth century, commoners and courtiers alike viewed the Bible of the English Reformation with indifference. King Henry VIII himself sowed seeds of apathy when in his later years he abandoned his earlier approval of an English Bible. But with Henry's death on January 28, 1547, his successor, Edward VI, decreed that the Bible be read and services conducted in English. Once again English men and women enjoyed free access to the Bible. No less than fifty editions of the Scriptures were produced during King Edward's reign.

Eager to take advantage of the expanding market, printers raced to publish any edition they could find. During Edward's reign, three editions of the complete Coverdale Bible, seven of the Great Bible, five of the Matthew's Bible, and two of the Taverner Bible were reprinted.

Complaints about conflicting biblical teachings resulting from access to differing Bible translations marked Edward's reign, and this environment caused concern for both Protestants and Catholics. Before long the Roman Catholic Church channeled its *authorized teachings* into the notes of the Bible. This debate regarding versions also gave the established church the renewed opportunity to persecute those not holding to traditional doctrines.

The newe Testament
ofour Sauiour Iesu Christe. Faythfully translated out of the Greke.

Wyth the Notes and expositions of the darke places therein.

Viuat   *Rex.*

Mathew.xiij f.
V nio,quem præcepit emi seruator Iesus,
Hic situs est,debet non aliunde peti.

The pearle, which Christ cõmaunded to be bought
Is here to be founde, not elles to be sought.

No less than fifty editions of the English Bible were printed during Edward VI's reign.

The Protestants' relative freedom to read the Bible in English was short-lived. Mary, a zealous Catholic, ascended the throne in 1553 and ushered in a period of persecutions against freethinking Bible readers. Bishop Bonner, who became known as Bloody Bonner for his persecution of non-Catholics during the reign of Mary, attempted to extinguish zeal for reading the Scriptures. As a result, new editions of the English Bible did not appear during Mary's reign, and freedom to personally interact with Scripture was forbidden. Both John Rogers, translator of the Matthew's Bible, and Archbishop Cranmer lost their lives under Bloody Mary's reign of terror. Only the exiled Coverdale escaped martyrdom.

The Protestant Geneva Bible: The First Study Bible

Mary's opposition to the Bible prompted a migration of Protestants from England to Geneva. Situated at the center of Calvinism, Geneva became a safe haven where persecuted English men and women could peacefully study God's Word with little fear of reprisal. Exiles John Calvin, Theodore Beza, John Knox, and William Whittingham, who are named among the greatest theologians of Protestant history, as well as linguists and scholars Anthony Gilby and Thomas Sampson, engaged in the translation of the Geneva New Testament of 1557 and the complete Bible of 1560 with its many theological and exegetical notes. The newly completed 1550 Stephanus Greek New Testament and Beza's 1556 Latin translation and notes provided useful new translation tools

The 1560 Geneva Bible contributed substantially to the creation of the King James Version (front). From left to right, Stephanus (1551) was the basis of the Greek text underlying the King James Version; the Latin Bible (1495) was a small, pocket-size Bible that attempted to make Scriptures available to the common people; the Geneva New Testament (1557) was the first portion of an English text to include verse divisions and roman type; and the modern *Textus Receptus* is the basis for modern textual studies of the Greek text used in the King James Version. Photo: M. Brake.

for their work. And for the first time, Old Testament portions left untranslated by Tyndale were translated directly from the Hebrew in the Geneva Bible.

While many translations circulated prior to the Geneva Bible, no Bible existed in an easy-to-read format and a size affordable to both pastors and laypeople. William Whittingham, brother-in-law of John Calvin and the primary translator of the Geneva New Testament of 1557, responded to this problem. Using the Matthew's edition of the New Testament, Whittingham produced a very small duodecimo volume (twelve pages printed from one sheet of paper) in roman print. Some of these small volumes found their way into England even before Queen Mary died in 1558.

The 1560 edition of the Geneva Bible also addressed those needs. It was the first edition published in quarto size and printed in roman script with verse

Courage When It Counted

Exhausted after enduring months behind bars in an Oxford prison, harsh interrogations, and endless trials, Thomas Cranmer, archbishop of Canterbury, stared death in the face. In previous recantations he had agreed to submit to the authority of Queen Mary and had willingly acknowledged the pope as head of the church. But Bishop Edmund Bonner was still not satisfied with these concessions. Broken, Cranmer added to his recantations, rejected Lutheranism, and accepted the Catholic doctrine of transubstantiation and exclusive salvation in the Roman Catholic Church.

Queen Mary was unconvinced and ordered the day for his execution with the admonition that if Cranmer would make one final public recantation, she would spare his life. He was instructed to submit his speech in writing—a speech that was later published.

Staring at his written words, which acknowledged a sweeping denial of all he truly believed, Cranmer began to sob. Scenes of the gruesome, fiery deaths of Hugh Latimer and Nicholas Ridley just months before coursed through his memory. Exhausted, his brain pounded with the beating of his heart as his mind raced between conviction, then doubt, then the fires of his own impending death.

He knew that his life, though marked by conflict, had fueled the fires of the English Reformation. More than once he had compromised his convictions

divisions, which made it easier to read. Printed by Roland Hall, also a refugee from England, it was adorned with popular woodcut images and maps. The Geneva Bible remained the most popular edition for nearly seventy years until the mid-seventeenth century when the last edition came off the press in 1644.

Even before the Geneva Bible[1] was completed in 1560, Queen Elizabeth ascended the throne, bringing in a new era of freedom for the Geneva exiles. Recognizing that royal support was crucial in order for a translation to survive, the men astutely wrote a tasteful dedication to Queen Elizabeth. She supported the public reading of the Bible printed in Geneva even before Christopher Barker printed it in England in 1575.

to please the king and then the queen. Now in the final moments of life, one parting compromise was being demanded of him. But could his final words in this life be a denial of his battered faith?

In the early morning hours, weary and exhausted from his solitary debate, Thomas Cranmer found the answer he sought. Peace swept over him, and he slept.

On the day marked for Cranmer's execution, March 21, 1556, an audience gathered at a service at University Church of St. Mary the Virgin in Oxford. They expected to hear him deny a faith that had faltered over the years—one certain to crumble beneath the weight of martyrdom. Shock waves rippled through the crowd as Cranmer deviated from his prepared speech, boldly renounced all previous written recantations, and confessed his sin in compromising his faith. As he pressed into his final words, his voice gathered strength. "I will punish the hand that signed the recantations by putting it in the fire first, and as for the pope, I refuse him as Christ's enemy and Anti-christ with all his false doctrine."

As Cranmer's fiery words died away, officials dragged him to the post to be burned at the same site outside Balliol College where his colleagues Hugh Latimer and Nicholas Ridley had burned at the stake as Protestant martyrs six months before him. After a life of compromise, Thomas Cranmer found peace at the end of his life in a demonstration of courage that would withstand not only the flames, but the winds of time.[2]

The Geneva Bible was an excellent translation, but its most distinguishable feature became its marginal study notes, which became a teaching tool for Puritans in America and Britain. But the notes represented a more radical Reformed theology; they met opposition in England and ultimately sealed the doom of the Geneva Bible when the King James Version abandoned use of marginal notes some fifty years later. In Scotland, however, Reformer John Knox accepted the translation immediately. Scotland designated the Geneva Bible as its first Bible "appointed to be read in the churches."

Several unique words and phrases distinguish the Geneva Bible:

Genesis 3:7 "Breeches" for "aprons" (KJV) or "coverings" (NIV)

Luke 2:7 "Cratch" for "manger" (KJV)

Luke 4:8 "Hence from me, Satan" for "Get thee behind me, Satan" (KJV)

John 16:2 "They shall excommunicate you" for "They will put you out of the synagogue" (KJV)

The Rheims New Testament: The Catholic Counterattack

While the battle for a vernacular Bible had ended, the war for theology intertwined with Bible versions had begun. Rome responded to the popularity of sixteenth-century English versions with a new interest in translation. The Latin Bible that Jerome (ancient biblical scholar and ascetic) translated in the fourth and fifth centuries became the unofficial Roman Catholic Bible. At the time of the Council of Trent in 1546, the Catholic Church had not yet authorized an edition of the Vulgate. The Council of Trent declared the Louvain edition the official church edition of the Bible.[3] But even the Louvain edition lacked full sanction of the highest ecclesiastical authority; nevertheless it was considered an authoritative edition.

Then in 1590 Pope Sixtus V attempted to publish a new edition to satisfy all ecclesiastical authorities. The new edition was named the Sixtine edition of the Vulgate Bible. But when Clement VIII ascended the throne early in 1592, he ordered all copies of the Sixtine Bible withdrawn. The Sixtine edition was

Lewis Lupton (1909–96)

"An artist with brush and pen as well as words and wisdom" (James I. Packer).

Early one afternoon I arrived with close friend and fellow collector Brian Hill at the London home of the late Lewis "Luppy" Lupton. Lewis was the author of a series of personally illustrated and highly researched books titled *The History of the Geneva Bible*. Mrs. Lupton greeted us, and for the remainder of the day she nostalgically recalled stories of her husband's work. My excitement peaked when I was able to purchase the remaining eighteen volumes of Lewis's work as well as a 1548 edition of Erasmus Paraphrases containing Lewis's handwritten marginal notes.[4]

First and foremost an artist, "Luppy" Lupton was born in 1909 in Fulham, London, and earned a seven-year scholarship to study at Sheffield Art School. From 1934 until the outbreak of World War II he was employed at a London art studio. During the war years he exhibited oil paintings in the Royal Academy and designed posters for the Ministry of Food and Power. He was also commissioned to paint scenes of "This England" on the boarded-up windows of bombed offices along the Strand. In the 1950s he designed exhibitions, including "The Faith of Britain" and "The Bible Speaks to the World."

Gaining a reputation as an illustrator in *The Evangelical Magazine* and for Scripture Union, Lewis spoke at the Puritan Conference at Westminster Chapel in 1959. After hearing the lecture, world-renowned preacher and scholar Dr. Martin Lloyd-Jones urged Lewis to publish his work. Soon after, Lewis self-published the twenty-five-volume *History of the Geneva Bible*, listing the publisher's name as "Fauconberg Press," which was later changed to "Olive Tree." The first seven volumes of his work were typeset, but beginning with volume eight Lewis personally hand-wrote each book, each page taking a day to write. In 1996 while in the process of preparing volume 26 on Cranmer, Lewis passed away.

Pictured in front is Fulke's *Counterblast* against the Roman Catholic Rheims New Testament. The Bishops' Bible and the Rheims were set side by side in the text of *The Counterblast* to portray the weaknesses of the Rheims. Stacked in the back are the Rheims New Testament (1582), the Douay Old Testament (1610), and the Bishops' Bible (1577). Photo: M. Brake.

viewed as a revised Louvain edition, and the clergy had grown accustomed to the wording in their prayer books and service manuals (based on the Louvain Bible). Clement VIII ordered that another official edition be published by the Vatican Press, and this version has since been known as the Clementine Bible.

The common English men and women had no access to a Catholic Bible in the vernacular, and the popularity of the Geneva Bible for English Protestants put pressure on Rome for an English Bible. While the priests were not happy about giving the commoners access to a Bible that allowed private interpretation, they were forced to support a translation that provided Catholics with Catholic doctrine. The first English translation of the Roman Catholic New Testament (called the Rheims—an alternate spelling, used in the original edition, is "Rhemes") was published in 1582 at the English College of Rheims in France. As with the Protestants under Queen Mary, the

Douay-Rheims was a product of exiles fleeing persecution—this time from Protestant Elizabeth.

Gregory Martin led the new translation work, assisted by William Allen, Richard Bristow, and William Reynolds. The men met at the English College of Rheims in France and began their work on the New Testament in 1578. The translators translated from the Latin Bible (not the Greek), but they also drew from the English Geneva Bible and Coverdale's edition of the New Testament Diglot (a bilingual version published by Francis Regnault in 1538 that placed his English translation side by side with the Latin text). The Rheims New Testament adopted some of Coverdale's readings, for example: "the Son of man hath not where to lay his head" (Matt. 8:20), and "I see men as it were trees, walking" (Mark 8:24).[5] From the Geneva Bible, the Rheims adopted "the wicked generation" (Matt. 12:45) and "whited tombs" (Matt. 23:27).

Because of financial difficulties, the Old Testament was not published until 1610 after the college was moved to Douay, France. Scholars generally agree that the end product of both the Old and New

The Bishops' Bible served as the English basis used in the work of creating the King James Version. The 1568 (in the center) was the first edition; the 1572 edition (on the left) was a major revision; and the 1602 edition (on the right) was circulated among the King James translators to use in their work.   Photo: M. Brake.

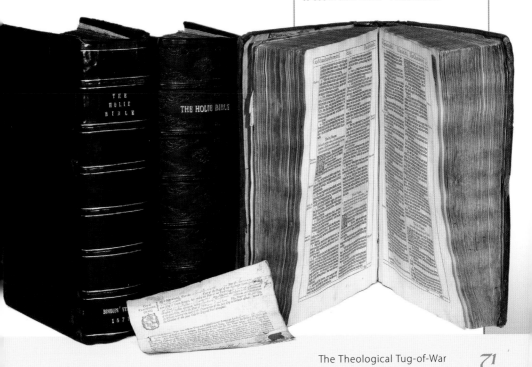

Testaments, known as the Douay-Rheims Bible, is substantially a good translation. Though lacking in vernacular expressions and normal English word order, it includes notes that support Roman Catholic theology.

The Bishops' Bible: The Anglican Church's Translation

Only five of the bishops who had been appointed during Edward VI's short reign (1547–53) survived Mary's reign (1553–58). Her appointments of bishops reflected her own Roman Catholic convictions, and public use of the Bible was banned in England for five years. But Queen Elizabeth's

The objects of Mary's anger included her Protestant cousin, Lady Jane Grey, and her sister Elizabeth, who were sent to the Tower of London. Protestants, seeing the handwriting on the wall, fled to the continent. In 1554 the Heresy Bill was restored, which signaled the beginning of a period of intense Protestant persecution.[6]

During Mary's reign, she gained the title "Bloody Mary." It is estimated that during her rule three hundred people were burned at the stake (a popular method of persecution). Approximately one-third of those were clergymen and two-thirds were Protestants living in London and the South of England, with about one-fifth of those being women. Thomas Cranmer (archbishop of Canterbury), Hugh Latimer (English Reformer), Nicholas Ridley (bishop of London), and others felt the flames of Mary's fires. The numbers were overshadowed by those who suffered religious persecution in Europe during the Spanish Inquisition.

While Mary undoubtedly deserved her title, much of what we have heard of her has been handed down by the Protestant zealot and church biographer John Foxe. Many scholars believe he exaggerated Mary's persecutions. While we may not know the extent of Mary's total responsibility, she stands today as a true villain of Protestant Christianity.

ascension to the throne of England in 1558 brought church reform. Men and women everywhere could once again read the Bible without fear of reprisal.

Matthew Parker, an unassuming scholar, filled the powerful theological seat of the archbishop of Canterbury. Educated at Corpus Christi College in Cambridge, Parker served as chaplain to Henry VIII's queen, Anne Boleyn. His reserved nature and quiet Reformed ideas enabled him to escape the wrath of Mary and suited him for the task of becoming a cofounder of Anglican doctrine and thought.

Prior to the rule of Elizabeth and Parker's leadership, no Bible, not even the Geneva version, was universally accepted. Religious authorities condemned Tyndale's version, and Coverdale's Bible and the Great Bible were

Before 1800, the number of folds the printer's sheet was divided into determined the size of the book. Pictured from left to right are a folio KJV (1634), quarto (4to) KJV (1648), octavo (8vo) Latin Bible (1739), duodecimo (12mo) Greek NT (1551), and 24mo KJV (1653).   Photo: A. Sanchez.

rejected because they were not translated from the original languages. The Matthew's and Taverner's versions fell short of general acceptance because they were associated with Tyndale, a supposed heretic.

The majority of the clergy in England did not embrace the popularity of the 1560 Geneva Bible. Although they recognized the superiority of the translation, church leaders considered the Calvinistic notes offensive. Recognizing the inadequacies of the Great Bible, the English church bishops, under Matthew Parker, suggested that an official translation be undertaken that could complete the task previously given to Coverdale.[7] Even Cranmer wanted the mission of translation put into the hands of the bishops or the church hierarchy. The Geneva Bible was eventually published in England as a small octavo edition completed in 1575 and a folio edition completed in 1576.[8] If an English publisher had quickly moved to produce the Geneva Bible, the Bishops' Bible may never have been undertaken.

In 1563 Archbishop Parker was selected as the chief editor for the official translation of the Bishops' Bible. Although it is unknown who translated the various sections of Scripture, the following scholars were assigned the task: William Alley, bishop of Exeter; Richard Davies, bishop of St. Davids; Edwin Sandys, bishop of Worcester; Andrew Pearson, canon of Canterbury;

Andrew Perne, canon of Ely; Robert Horne, bishop of Winchester; Thomas Bentham, bishop of Lichfield; Edmund Grindal, bishop of London; John Parkhurst, bishop of Norwich; Richard Cox, bishop of Ely; Edmund Guest, bishop of Rochester; Gabriel Goodman, dean of Westminster; and Giles Lawrence, professor of Greek, University of Oxford.

The newly commissioned Bishops' Bible was prepared in accordance with Archbishop Parker's specified principles. The translators used Stephanus's Greek New Testament (1550), Pagninus's Latin (1528), and Sebastian Münster's Hebrew (1539). They omitted any marginal notes that might cause offense.[9] The translators' reliance upon the original languages testifies to the quality of their scholarship. While the Bishops' Bible was never widely accepted by laypeople, educated Anglican clergy preferred it. The translators' fear that the work might be rejected appears to have dissuaded them from producing a truly revised text that conformed to the standard language of the day. Additionally, Parker's theological persuasion caused him to reject superior readings in the Geneva text. As a result, although an improvement on the Great Bible, the Bishops' Bible fell short of the Geneva Bible in quality and simplicity. Yet even with its faults, many editions of the Bishops' Bible were published from 1568 to 1617,[10] and it exerted historic influence

As bishop of London, Edmund Grindal translated the Minor Prophets. He later became archbishop of Canterbury. Photo: Original art, L. Lupton.

when it was chosen as the standard reference tool for the King James Version.

The Bishops' Bible, published by Richard Jugge, was the most beautifully illustrated and superbly printed edition in a long history of remarkable folios produced in the sixteenth century. Adorned with finely carved woodcuts, the Bishops' Bible stands as a masterpiece of printing. Its ornate embellishment demonstrated that with the war for biblical legitimacy at an end, publishers were now concentrating on aspects of fine printing and elaborate illustrations to enhance the Scripture's readability.

In an attempt to gain the crown's approval, the translators sent Queen Elizabeth a copy of the Bishops' Bible on September 22, 1568. The cover page displayed a prominent portrait of the queen, which was a distinguishing feature of the first edition. Even though the Bishops' Bible was never officially licensed as the authorized Bible and did not gain Queen Elizabeth's approval, both church and state enthusiastically endorsed the version.[11]

The Convocation of Canterbury in 1571 ordered a copy of the Bishops' Bible to be placed in every cathedral and, whenever circumstances made it possible, in every church. Each bishop was encouraged to keep a copy of the new translation in his house for use by servants and strangers.[12] Parker, as chief translator, insisted the New Testament be printed on the thickest paper available so it would stand up to heavy use. But the Convocation of Canterbury could not stir public sentiment. While the Bishops' Bible had achieved the goal of a standard translation for the English-speaking church, the nation responded to the Bible's publication passively,[13] as if they were in waiting. Little did they know that the Bible that would mark the world for centuries was about to be born.

4

Puritans, Petitions, and Plots

A Royal Battle for an English Legacy

Queen Elizabeth sat motionless and silent next to the fire in her room at Richmond Palace, the retreat she had fondly named her "warm, snug box." Her feet rested on pillows beneath a dress that had gone unchanged for days. A cloud of fear hovered over the courtiers scattered about the room. They could not voice what they knew was true. The queen was dying.

Near the door an attendant shifted her weight, and with the flicker of motion the queen's gaze faltered. "When will we have a successor to my throne? Do you think I will live forever?" she shouted. Her outburst carried a strength that belied the frailty of her frame and intellect over the past weeks. No sooner had the words fallen from her lips than her eyes closed once more, and again she lapsed into the prison of her mind, paralyzed and unable to make even the smallest decision of a royal monarch. After almost seventy years, Elizabeth I was losing the greatest battle of her life: her mind and body were collapsing beneath the weight of old age, failing health, unremitting fatigue, and unrelenting work.

Eventually the queen's condition worsened and she was carried to her bed. The moment had come for her to appoint the next ruler of England— a decision she had delayed until her final moments of life. Elizabeth knew too well the implications of naming a successor too soon, having herself been imprisoned in the Tower of London by her sister Mary.

In the silence of her bedchamber, the question was asked of her. Whom would she appoint to ascend the throne upon her death? With one final act of will, Elizabeth gathered her wits and spoke—the son of Mary Queen of Scots, James VI. "Who but our cousin of Scotland should sit on my throne?" The final vestiges of Elizabeth's spirit spilled out with the pronouncement. Her next words came in a whisper, as though she could see her end was near. "I pray you trouble me no more."[1]

On March 22, 1603, the Privy Council drafted a statement naming the successor to the throne of England. The next morning Elizabeth, the most powerful monarch in England's long and storied history and the last reigning monarch of the House of Tudor (Henry VII through Elizabeth I), fell asleep for the last time. James VI of Scotland and the House of Stuart was proclaimed King James I of England, France, Scotland, and Ireland.

James's mother, Mary Queen of Scots, was a committed Catholic, and she had ruled Scotland ineptly during a period of pro-Reformation sentiment. Her marriage ended when a suspicious house explosion took the life of her husband and James's father, Lord Darnley. Soon thereafter she married the Earl of Both-well, the man believed to be responsible for her first husband's death. Shortly after the marriage, her subjects turned against her, and she was imprisoned and forced to abdicate. Amid the upheaval in 1567, Protestant lords declared her son James VI king of Scotland. Eventually Mary fled to England, where she was imprisoned as an alleged accomplice in the murder of Lord Darnley. After several attempts by Catholics to place Mary on the English throne, Queen Elizabeth ordered her beheaded in 1587. Despite family ties, James refused to protest his mother's execution, and Catholic resentment against him mounted.

James had been brought up by the earl and countess of Mar, who raised him within the national Protestant Church of Scotland, which was the church embraced by the majority of the Scottish ruling class. Declared head of both church and state in Scotland in 1584, James soon began a long history of state interference with the church that extended to his reign in England. His enthusiastic claim of divine right to rule over the throne in both civil and spiritual matters ultimately mired his reign in deep conflict.

The Sovereign and the Scholar

King James knew the affliction of unrelenting pain. A sickly man, he was plagued with arthritis, gout, abdominal colic, and chronic illnesses that over-shadowed his walking, talking, and daily routines. Illness, however, did not affect his mind. James is regarded as one of the most scholarly and educated monarchs of his day. Fluent in French, Latin, and Greek, and having knowledge of Hebrew, Spanish, and Italian, King James authored *Paraphrase upon the Revelation; A Meditation Upon the Chapters XXV, XXVIJ, XXVIIJ, XXIX, and XV of First Booke of the Chronicles of the Kings; A Defense of the Right of Kings; Basilicon Doron;* and his famous *Counterblast against Tobacco.*[2]

James's lack of affection for papists is clearly demonstrated in his works titled *Basilicon Doron* (Kingly Gift) and *His Maiesties Instructions to His Dearest Sonne, Henry, the Prince.* Yet a small 1609 octavo edition of a Roman Catholic Latin Bible Clementine edition shows the coat of arms of James I stamped on the cover. Oddly, the title page is removed from this book and the introduction is in English—a page obviously inserted from another Bible. The details are particularly fascinating to me because this Bible is one from my personal collection. Inside the cover is a note from Bible scholar Paul Schmidtchen that presents the theory that this Bible belonged to James I, and he attempted to hide the fact that it was a Roman Catholic Bible from anyone who might stumble across it.[3] Whether or not the theory has merit, James was certainly fluent in Latin and as a biblical scholar could have made use of any Latin Bible.[4] The 1609 edition was produced after the Clementine edition of 1592, which was declared the official edition of the Vulgate, was issued by the Vatican, and remains the official edition today. Why James, a Protestant, retained a copy of the official Roman Catholic version is indeed puzzling unless the version was used for study purposes.

A more likely answer is that this particular Bible bearing King James's coat of arms simply belonged to a member of the royal family and was not necessarily the king's own copy. But the book's unique features do arouse speculation.

The lasting legacy of King James I was his contribution in the creation of the King James Version. Photo: King James I, *The Workes of the Most High and Mightie Prince, James* (1616), frontispiece.

James's ascent to the throne of England brought hope to previously persecuted Catholics and Puritans.[5] Catholics hoped James would follow the path of his Catholic mother, Mary Stuart. The Puritans rested their hope in James's Calvinistic education and thirty-seven years as head of the Presbyterian Church in Scotland. James, however, was not a man who lived to fulfill the hopes of others. He soon smothered the expectations of both groups as he sought his own agenda.[6]

The Unexpected Detour to a New Translation

James's participation in church affairs in Scotland spilled over into his inherited kingdom of England. In kingly fashion, he distributed knighthoods and promises as he traveled his triumphal route from Scotland to ascend

The Thousand Man March

The coach bearing the king's crest jerked to a halt. Men on horseback and on foot had converged on the road from the adjacent thickets. The royal bodyguards aimed their matchlock firearms at the hearts of those blocking their path as they awaited the signal from the king to shoot.[7]

Recognizing their peril, the intruders called out, "Your Majesty, Your Majesty, we come in peace. May you have a long life."

Muffled voices came from inside the coach, and an attendant moved swiftly into place. With a flourish, King James I emerged, dressed in regal cloak and hat. He raised his hand to calm the bodyguards and spoke sternly. "What are you ruffians up to?"

Removing his hat and bowing, the leader of the group stepped forward. "Your Majesty, be assured we are your loyal subjects. We have come to present you with a signed petition representing the sentiments of one thousand of your loyal Puritan ministers who would deem it the highest honor to speak to Your Majesty personally. We stand as their representatives, and this document presents our concerns about the state of the church in England."

The king motioned for the courier to bring the petition to him and glanced through the document. "I will take this under advisement once I arrive in London. Good day for now." With a sweep of his hand the king disappeared back into his coach. His entourage continued down the forested road to London as the band of Puritan petitioners was left to watch and wait.

the throne of England in 1603. En route he was confronted by Puritans who presented him with a petition for church policy reform that had been signed by one thousand Puritan ministers. The document, known as the Millenary Petition, was formally titled *The Humble Petition of the Ministers of the Church of England desiring Reformation of certaine Ceremonies and abuses of the Church.* Steeped in tones of political correctness and devotion, the document assured the king of the Puritans' unquestioned loyalty to him and best wishes for a long reign. Carefully worded, the paper articulated the hopes and dreams of those who had suffered under Queen Elizabeth and Bishops

Whitgift and Bancroft, Anglicans who had shown little sympathy for the Puritan cause.[8]

Anglicans were quite willing to support James's influence over the church, but they vehemently opposed the petition. They accused the petitioners of supporting the Scottish Reformation, which limited the monarchy and opposed certain rites and ceremonies such as: using a ring in marriage rituals, bowing at the name of Jesus, making the sign of the cross at baptism, reading the Apocrypha in services, creating excessive dress for clerics, giving sermons before communion, and following the practice of excommunication.

James was willing to abandon the Scottish form of religious expression, but he did not want a public display of euphoria from his subjects at the time of his ascension to the throne. He wanted to appear, at least outwardly, to seriously regard the concerns of the Puritans. In an act of shrewd diplomacy, James convened the Hampton Court Conference to negotiate between polarized requests for reform and to mediate a position between the Puritans and the Church of England.

The Anglicans continued to be troubled by the Puritans' bold action, fearing James would side with the Puritans. He had already abolished tithes that funded Anglican bishoprics from parish incomes. Although the Anglicans later persuaded James to reverse his decision on tithes, the environment of uncertainty warned the Anglicans of James's willingness to compromise at their expense. Yet neither group was certain of the king's commitment to their cause, and anxieties among both groups continued to mount.

Richard Bancroft, the powerful archbishop of Canterbury, opposed the views of the Puritans but was influential in supporting the new King James Version.   Photo: Original art, L. Lupton.

Bishop Bancroft

Lambeth Palace. 10 VI '69 LfL

The ongoing feud had reached a crescendo by the time the Hampton Court Conference convened in 1604 to discuss the alleged flaws in church policies and practices and to consider the complaints of the Puritans. The anti-Puritan atmosphere of the conference surfaced immediately. The powerful archbishop of Canterbury, Richard Bancroft, along with other bishops and six cathedral deans, including those of Westminster Abbey and St. Paul's Cathedral, joined a nineteen-member Anglican delegation, while only four Puritans were invited to represent their views.[9]

James, hailed as "a living library and a walking study," addressed questions on issues of papal power versus regal power, communion, amusements on Sunday, and the removal of images from churches. The king was critical of both the Roman Church and the Geneva Bible.[10] He disapproved of both for their positions on abuse of power as it related to the role of kingship.[11] His sentiments against the teachings on this subject in the Geneva Bible's notes were instrumental in James's decision to support the work of a new translation that was boldly proposed by John Rainolds, a distinguished Puritan representative.

Rainolds's suggestion may have been precipitated by his desire to seek authorization of his beloved Geneva Bible. Nevertheless, James recognized the political opportunity Rainolds was offering him: a way to foil the Puritans by publishing a translation free of their sectarian and objectionable notes. The timing was perfect. The Bishops' Bible, authorized by the Church of England, had not gained general acceptance. The Geneva Bible, while widely circulated, especially among the Puritans, did not carry the authorization of the English church. The need for a new translation seemed clear to James, and he appointed teams to begin the work of translation.

> James's aggressive actions rebounded in assassination plots in the early years of his reign.

The Puritans were disappointed with the outcome of the conference; they realized little reform would take place in the Anglican Church. They had hoped the conference would take seriously their call for wide reform addressing church polity. But even the promise of a new translation did not satisfy the Puritan conservative wing. They had hoped for a ratification of the Geneva Bible and had, instead, been surprised by the king's support of a new Bible version. Fifty-four men were assigned to the translation team that was heavily weighted with Anglican scholars, some more moderate in their beliefs than others. Once again the Puritans felt the political sting as they took on the work with justified concerns about the sheer imbalance in numbers.

In an effort to further underscore his disdain for being politically manipulated, James sent a message to English Catholics by pardoning all prisoners except papists and murderers and imprisoning a priest who had petitioned him to remove anti-Catholic laws. James's aggressive actions rebounded in assassination plots in the early years of his reign. The most infamous was the failed Gunpowder Plot of 1605. This Roman Catholic plan sought to blow up the House of Lords by concealing more than a ton and a half of gunpowder in thirty-six barrels hidden under coal and bundled branches in the cellars beneath Parliament. An informant who had only recently become James's loyal subject foiled the plot.[12]

King James signed a warrant for the arrest of Guy Fawkes, and after he and his fellow conspirators endured some months of torture, they all signed this letter of confession. The signatures of the other men are clear, but the signature of Fawkes appears in very faint letters on the right side across from the last sentence ending "named." The weak signature was undoubtedly a result of his torture. The letter pictured here is probably a high-quality facsimile.

After the Gunpowder Plot against King James failed, Lancelot Andrews became embroiled in a controversy over King James's imposed Oath of Allegiance. James was consumed by his fear that the pope could commission the murder of a king or prince for being disloyal to the Catholic Church. He insisted his subjects adhere to the oath that read, "I [name] swear that I do from my heart abhor, detest, and abjure as impious and heretical, this

The Foiled Plot

Guy Fawkes inhaled deeply, and the pungent odor of gunpowder filled his lungs. Ahead of him, Robert Catesby led the way with a single candle that flickered its way down the narrow tunnel. Fawkes could hear the labored breathing of the ten men following him. His back strained under the weight of the gunpowder that grew heavier with each step. But he dared not draw closer to Catesby and the candle. As engineer of the plot, Catesby had devised every detail with precision, but he could not give the men courage. Over the eighteen months it had taken them to bring their plan to fruition, fears had surfaced. Fawkes had known that fear would come to all of them eventually, and he had been the one to instill the confidence that brought each man to this place at this hour.

He smiled. The plot he and his co-conspirators had set into motion to blow up the king in St. Stephen's Chapel during the opening of Parliament would soon be realized. Within hours the king would be dead and every soul in the House of Lords with him. No one knew Fawkes and his friends had rented a house adjacent to Parliament and dug a tunnel to the cellar beneath. No one suspected they were filling the cellar with gunpowder.

Fawkes hefted the bag higher on his shoulder. *May the flames burn so bright that the pope himself sees the fires and rejoices.*

In the tunnel ahead, Catesby motioned to his followers to halt, pressed a finger to his lips, and pointed toward the halls of Parliament above them.

damnable doctrine and position, that princes which be excommunicated or deprived by the pope may be deposed or murdered by their subjects or any others whatsoever." When Cardinal Robert Bellarmine (under the alias Matthaeus Tortus) attacked the oath, Andrews wrote a vigorous rebuttal entitled *Tortura Tori*, gaining James's great favor over his support of the oath.[13] As the controversy subsided, Andrews became known for his scholarly piety and adherence to the Scriptures.

In the light of the flame, Fawkes saw fear sweep over the face of Thomas Percy, a co-conspirator. "What will happen if we are caught?" he hissed. "His Majesty will certainly stretch our necks or put us on the rack. Who knows but that the next sovereign might choose to strip all English Catholics of their homes and businesses or worse? Have we all gone mad?"

"Enough, Thomas! Silence." Fawkes strained to listen to the sounds overhead above his friend's whispered words. But it was too late; his heart dropped. In the distance he heard the sound of soldiers descending the stairways of St. Stephen's Chapel. He watched as eleven men retreated and scattered like roaches exposed to light. He struggled with the gunpowder strapped on his back as they fled through the tunnels and cellar rooms beneath the Houses of Parliament. Stumbling and unable to free himself of the weight, Guy Fawkes was caught, and the destiny of the saboteurs was sealed.

One man had changed the course of history and exposed the Gunpowder Plot by sending an anonymous letter to Lord Baron Monteagle. The anonymous author's identity has never been authoritatively established. But because of his efforts, Monteagle alerted the king and the plot was thwarted.

All participants in the Gunpowder Plot were apprehended and imprisoned in the Tower of London. At the personal request of the king, Guy Fawkes was tortured for months. He eventually signed a confession. Ultimately all participants were hanged, drawn, and quartered (hung until nearly dead, disemboweled, then beheaded, with the body divided into four parts).[14]

5

The Men and Their Mission

The Translation Work Begins

King James I convened the Hampton Court Conference in January 1604 in response to the concerns of the Puritans expressed in the Millenary Petition. The conference resulted in few concessions to the Puritans, but even while recognizing the king's reluctance to support their position, they remained in the Anglican Church rather than splitting off from it. One concession was made that had a huge impact on the English-speaking Christian world. Puritan John Rainolds, president of Corpus Christi College in Oxford, recommended a new English translation of the Bible, and as a result he became known as the father of the King James Version.

In addition to the fifty-four men Archbishop Bancroft appointed for the translation of the new version, James directed him to enlist anyone qualified to be included in the translation process in order to assure that no one party had too much influence and that every book translated would be the most accurate possible. This guaranteed that no English scholar would be without a voice in the new translation. Bancroft found the most highly trained scholars to fill the translation team—mainly church clergy, bishops, academics, and scholars of the English language. He had to do little convincing to bring the men into the group, in spite of the fact that stipends were not guaranteed.

The Cathedral of Winchester provided prebends for transla-tors. Photo: Original art, L. Lupton.

The final years of Elizabeth's reign had depleted the treasury, so the king could not possibly compensate the vast number of translators who had been appointed, although Oxford, Cambridge, and Westminster may have provided free meals and lodging for them. James decided the translators would be paid from positions as leaders in the churches. When church offices became available, translators were given first consideration to fill them. The result was, at least to a degree, the practice of simony—selling or showing preference in the distribution of church offices.

As mentioned earlier, the bulk of the translation burden fell on the fifty-four translators who were divided into six companies—two companies from each of the major teaching faculties and ecclesiastical leaders at Cambridge University, Oxford University, and Westminster Abbey.[1] From each of the six companies, two men were selected to review and edit the ongoing work of the translators. From those twelve men, three were chosen to oversee further review and editorial work.

These three men were John Harding, Edward Lively, and Lancelot Andrews. Andrews, an affable Anglican, became the chairman of the translation committee and the most influential of the translators. Because of his gracious demeanor toward the Puritans as well as Anglicans, all on the committee accepted him. Andrews had been present when Queen Elizabeth died, he preached at her burial, and then he participated in King James's coronation. He was known for meeting often with scholars to discuss the finer points of Hebrew and Greek grammar. And his mastery of fifteen languages made him a natural

The Cathedral of Ely was the seat of a powerful bishopric and responsible for awarding many prebends. Photo: Original art, L. Lupton.

The Bishop, the Parson, and a Night of Surprise

A poor parson happily received an invitation to dinner from the bishop of the wealthy districts of Winchester and Elysees. Curiosity stirred in this humble man of God, but curiosity was soon followed by apprehension. What could the newly appointed bishop of Winchester want from a poor preacher? Had he committed an offense?

The parson was further intimidated on the day of the dinner when he was ushered into the dining room. Before him the table groaned beneath the weight of delicacies, some the parson could not even identify. He had not been invited to dinner; this was a veritable banquet.

There was no clue for the parson during the polite dinner conversation. Following dessert, Bishop Lancelot Andrews pulled away from the table and stood. The parson knew the moment had come. The weight of the rich food suddenly gripped him, and he thought for a moment he might be ill.

Bishop Andrews's words fell with the ring of a gavel. "Parson, it is my pleasure to announce that you have been granted a prebend. The living stipend represents a significant change in your circumstances. This comes, of course, in recognition of your allegiance to the church."

The parson stammered out his thanks as the significance of the words rang in his ears. His wife and children would no longer know the sting of poverty. He rehearsed the words he would say to his wife as he scurried through the village and up the lane to his cottage.

A prebend meant that at last he and his wife would enjoy the financial security that had so long lain beyond their reach.[2] He had heard of Bishop Andrews's generous spirit. Now he knew firsthand the stories were true.[3]

choice for a more powerful position, where his skill in teaching biblical languages could flourish.

As ultimate overseer of the project, Miles Smith became the final authority and editor. He was responsible for the final editing, and then he and Thomas Bilson carried out the final check of the text before it was sent to the printer. Thomas Bilson also added the headings to the chapters, and Smith wrote the preface to the King James Bible.

Twenty-first-century readers are familiar with committee-produced modern versions; however, prior to the King James Version, translations were attributed to individuals, places of origin, or small groups. The Wycliffe, Tyndale, Coverdale, Matthew's, and Taverner Bibles were the work of individuals. The Great Bible (Coverdale), Geneva (Whittingham), and Bishops' (Parker) Bibles were the work of one man assisted by a small band of scholars. The 1611 King James translation took the name of the king who unofficially authorized its production, but committees produced the translation work. The contributors were men who were highly qualified to perform the task that has made the King James Version a household name for four hundred years.[4]

First Westminster Company (Genesis through 2 Kings)

The first appointed company of translators met in an edifice worthy of a major translation project: the Jerusalem Chamber at Westminster Abbey in London.[5] At this time in history, Westminster Abbey was a center of administration where court proceedings meted out justice to British citizens. The large, prestigious abbey compound housed Parliament, the king's council, and a vast number of living quarters for court servants. Westminster Abbey was the site of many great historical events, coronations, and burials of state officials, including Queen Elizabeth. When Henry VIII dissolved the monasteries years before, Westminster was named the seat of a bishopric and designated a cathedral. Under Elizabeth's reign it was made a college and became independent of episcopal power, falling under the authority of its own dean. During most of Elizabeth's reign, Gabriel Goodman, one of the translators of the Bishops' Bible, served as the dean of Westminster.[6] His death in 1601 paved the way for a transfer of power to the stately, handsome, and capable Lancelot Andrews.

Lancelot Andrews (d. 1626):[7] director of the First Westminster Company, dean of Westminster (1601), bishop of Ely (1609), bishop of Winchester (1618)

Educated at Pembroke Hall, Cambridge University, Andrews became closely connected with Queen Elizabeth and preached at her funeral. He also

Lancelot Andrews was bishop of Ely and director of the First Westminster Company of translators. Photo: Original art, L. Lupton.

became aligned with King James and held the lead translation role.[8] Early in his academic career he championed Puritan causes, especially the strict observance of Sunday, but after he became chaplain to Archbishop Whitgift, he severed his ties with the Puritans.

One of the most able preachers of his day, Andrews was called "an angel in the pulpit." Conversant in Latin, Greek, Hebrew, Chaldean, Syriac, Arabic, and nine other languages, he was the most able linguist in Christendom. At his funeral he was remembered as follows: "He was, as all our English world knows, a singular preacher, and a most famous writer." His mouth was likened to a weapon: as stones in a dog's teeth to his adversaries.[9]

John Overall (d. 1619): dean of St. Paul's Cathedral (1691) and bishop of Lichfield and Coventry (1614)

Educated at Trinity College, Cambridge University, Overall was weak in Hebrew but fluent in Greek and Latin. These language strengths may have increased his influence since much of the translators' discussion was in Latin.[10] Overall had quickly found favor with Elizabeth, who tolerated his Arminian theology. He was a member of the Court of High Commission and attended the original Hampton Court Conference at the invitation of King James. But he later lost favor with the king because of his views of kingship expressed in *Convocation Book*—rules articulating the governing relationship between church and state in which Overall stated that legitimate revolutions result in people's obedience to new rulers. James, of course, suppressed the book and attacked Overall in his own book, *The True Law of Free Monarchies*, which stated that kings were chosen by God and were to be obeyed.[11]

In his later years, Overall married Anne Orwell (1604), one of the most beautiful women of the day. Anne was "carried off" by John Selby just prior to the publication of the King James Version in 1611, but she was found and returned to Overall, where she remained for the rest of their lives.

Hadrian à Saravia (d. 1612): prebendary of Westminster, Canterbury, and Lichfield and bishop of Norwich

Born to Belgian and Spanish parents, Saravia was educated at the University of Leyden and received a Doctor of Divinity from Oxford. He was a soul mate with Lancelot Andrews and one of the high-level Protestant apologists sharing with Andrews his view of the divine right of kings. His acceptance by the English people led him to retire in the land where he had become master of Southampton Grammar School. Saravia was the oldest member of the translation team, and his abilities in Hebrew and rabbinical traditions have been challenged, but his scholarship in Latin and general linguistics is unquestioned.

Richard Clark (d. 1634): fellow at Christ's College, Cambridge University

As an accomplished preacher and writer, Clark occupied a pulpit at Canterbury. His only published works were from his sermons.

John Layfield (d. 1617): rector of St. Clement Dane's Church, London

Layfield's marvelous description of his journey to the West Indies demonstrates his English language abilities. His travels quite possibly took place with Queen Elizabeth's buccaneers.[12] Words like *apparel, attired, nakedness,* and *boring ears* that found their way into the King James Version are the same words he used to describe West Indies sites. While these terms are certainly not direct proof of Layfield's influence, they do point to his ability in descriptive language.

As an architect, Layfield may have influenced the description of the tabernacle in the Pentateuch. Olga Opfell, author of *The King James Bible Translators*, suggests that Exodus 26:4 may be a direct reference to Layfield's influence: "And thou shalt make loops of blue upon the edge of the one curtain from the selvedge in the coupling; and likewise shalt thou make in the uttermost edge of *another* curtain, in the coupling of the second."[13]

Robert Tighe (d. 1620): archdeacon of Middlesex and vicar of All Hollows, London

Educated at Oxford and Cambridge, Tighe was known for his ability as a linguist and administrator.

Geoffrey King (d. unknown): Regius Professor of Hebrew, Cambridge University

The term *regius* refers to a professorship founded by a monarch. King's anti-Catholic feelings were well known and encouraged by most. He was one of the Westminster Company who had a good grasp of Hebrew.

Richard Thomson (d. 1613): fellow at Clare Hall, Cambridge University

Thomson was chosen as a translator in the Westminster Company while earning a living from Cambridge. An articulate advocate of Arminianism, he was known as a philologist (student of linguistics and literature) and a heavy drinker. Critics claimed he seldom went to bed sober, which begs the question as to why such a drunkard was allowed on the translation team. The answer may lie in his knowledge of Hebrew, which was sorely needed in the First Westminster Company.

William Bedwell (d. 1632): vicar of Tottenham High Cross Church

While John Layfield traveled west, Bedwell was fascinated by the east. An Orientalist and Arabic scholar educated at St. John's College, Cambridge University, he wrote a dictionary in Arabic and a lexicon in Persian. His profound ability in other languages helped in the translation of words encountered in the Hebrew Bible that descended not from Hebrew but from related languages.

Francis Burleigh (d. unknown): fellow of Chelsea College, Cambridge University

Burleigh was competent in the study of Greek and Latin, and as a recipient of the Thomas Watts scholarship award (named after a former archdeacon of Middlesex), he possessed a reputation in classical studies.

First Cambridge Company (1 Chronicles through Song of Solomon)

Among the most prestigious universities in Britain, Cambridge chose its greatest scholars to translate 1 Chronicles through Song of Solomon. The First Cambridge Company scholars were a Hebrew language group. The company met at the University of Cambridge, an institution dedicated to training men for the church, on a beautiful campus that provided a fitting backdrop for translation work. The school was a hotbed for Reformers, martyrs, exiles, and Puritans, even though the established hierarchy at Cambridge had opposed the Millenary Petition signed by the Puritan ministers.[14]

Oxford was known for Catholic leaning during the reigns of the Tudors, and Cambridge was known for producing Reformers, many of whom fled from Cambridge to Geneva during the reign of Queen Mary. When Protestant Elizabeth took the throne, many of the exiles returned to Cambridge. Beginning with Thomas Cartwright's message in 1570, crying out for a holier Church of England, returning exiles were dubbed *Puritans*. These Reformers ranged from radical to moderate in their attempts to purify the Anglican Church. More moderate Puritans were represented at the Hampton Court Conference in 1604.

Edward Lively (d. 1605): director of the First Cambridge Company and Regius Professor of Hebrew at Trinity College, Cambridge University

After teaching Hebrew for thirty years, Lively, considered one of the greatest of England's linguists, died before the King James translation was complete. His method for discovering meaning in a text was to collate all verses that used the same phrase. He then evaluated the contexts and drew conclusions about meaning. Lively's thirteen children attributed his death to his constant struggles with creditors and subsequent lawsuits.

John Richardson (d. 1625): Regius Professor of Divinity at Cambridge University, later vicar of Algarkirk in Lincolnshire, and finally vice-chancellor of Cambridge

Born in the same year as William Shakespeare (1564), the year of the Great Plague, Richardson became a renowned teacher of Greek and Latin.

As a fellow at Emmanuel College, his responsibility was to assist in the management of rental properties.

Laurence Chaderton (d. 1640): master of Emmanuel College

Although Chaderton grew up in a Roman Catholic family during Protestant Queen Elizabeth's reign, he had no interest in becoming a priest. His disappointed father threatened to disinherit him if he did not study law. Instead, Chaderton's desire for a university education led him to matriculate in Christ's College, Cambridge, where he was soon converted to Protestantism. While he often sided with the Puritans, Chaderton never spoke against the Anglican Church.

Francis Dillingham (d. unknown): fellow at Christ's College, Cambridge University

Fluent in several languages, Dillingham was an exceptional linguist. Although single, Dillingham was known for extolling the virtues of married ministers.

Thomas Harrison (d. 1631): vice master of Trinity College, Cambridge University

Probably a Puritan, Harrison was renowned for his poetry, although none has surfaced bearing his name. His poetic skill was important because his company translated the book of Psalms and other poetic books. He was also knowledgeable in interpreting Hebrew idioms.

Roger Andrews (d. after 1618): master of Jesus College, Cambridge University

A brother of Lancelot, Roger defined the spirit of nepotism and took full advantage of his brother's fame and power, moving up in the church by following his brother from position to position. He is said to have made a small contribution to the translation of Psalms.

Robert Spalding (d. unknown): fellow at St. John's College, Cambridge University

Following Lively's death shortly after the beginning of the translation work, Spalding took his place among the translators.

Andrew Bing (d. 1652): fellow at Peterhouse, Cambridge University, and later archdeacon of Norwich, 1618

Gathering various ecclesiastical offices, Bing made a good living as a teacher and preacher. He outlived all of the translators and even lived to see the beheading of King James's son, Charles I.

First Oxford Company (Isaiah through Malachi)

Oxford University is known for its beautiful campus marked by spiraling towers, numerous quadrangles with carved stonework, abundant trees, small gardens, and beautifully manicured lawns. Its library, restored by Thomas Bodley, was the favorite of King James.

Of all the companies of translators, the First Oxford Company may have been the most able and qualified to translate their portions of Scripture. All of the translators were fellows of colleges, four were heads of colleges, four were experts in oriental languages, and three held the title Regius Professor of Hebrew.

John Harding (d. 1610): director of the First Oxford Company, Regius Professor of Hebrew, and president of Magdalen College, Oxford

During Harding's tenure, a great debate raged over whether angels and saints could know the thoughts of the human heart. The debate focused on whether people could pray to saints or angels. Harding opposed the arguments for the case. His claim to fame was his position as a former chaplain to Lady Jane Grey.

John Rainolds (d. 1607): president of Corpus Christi College, Oxford

A staunch Reformer, Rainolds held to the proposition that the authority of Scripture is greater than the authority of the church. His father, also named John, remained a Catholic his entire life. Even though Harding was the director of the company, Rainolds soon became de facto

John Rainolds, a Puritan divine who called for a new translation at the Hampton Court Conference. Photo: Original art, L. Lupton.

director. His integrity was diminished when he aligned himself with King James and Bancroft in supporting the idea that the ministry of the Church of England was in direct descent from St. Peter. His support of royal and apostolic authority was a conveniently timed position in light of His Majesty's royal visit to Oxford in August 1605.

Thomas Holland (d. 1612): Regius Professor of Divinity and rector of Exeter College, Oxford

Holland agreed with Harding and argued against the concept that saints and angels had knowledge of the thoughts of the human heart. Queen Elizabeth expected him to lead the college to denounce its Puritan leanings and support the Church of England. But Holland continued to insist, even in public, that bishops were not superior to presbyters.[15]

Richard Kilby (d. 1620): Regius Professor of Hebrew and rector of Lincoln College, Oxford

In addition to his scholarly abilities in debating and his language expertise in Hebrew and Latin, Kilby was an able preacher known for his spiritual sensitivity. He became the official director of the company following Harding's death in 1610.

Miles Smith (d. 1624): final revisionist of the project, Brasenose College (originally named Kings Hall), Oxford, prebendary of Hereford and Exeter Cathedrals, and bishop of Gloucester

Miles Smith was the final revisionist of the Bible translation project. Photo: Original art, L. Lupton.

Smith was a scholar in classical and oriental studies (Chaldean, Syriac, Arabic, and Hebrew). His contribution to the King James Version is perhaps greater than any other from among the translation teams. His responsibility was to edit the entire Bible once it was completed by the various companies as well as to write the preface to the new version.

Richard Brett (d. 1637): fellow of Lincoln College, Oxford, and rector of Quainton, Buckinghamshire

Brett is one of the few commoner translators who entered Hart Hall (which later became Hertford College) rather than a college. (At that time, these halls of residence did not have the same status as colleges, but later most became colleges.) Brett became a scholar in classical and eastern languages, including ancient Ethiopic (Ge'ez).

effigy Quainton

Richard Brett, rector of Quainton and translator. Photo: Original art, L. Lupton.

Richard Fairclough (d. 1645): fellow of New College, Oxford, and rector of Bucknell, Oxford

Because he was only twenty-two years old in 1604, Fairclough's participation in the translation team has been questioned.

William Thorne (d. 1630): fellow of New College, Oxford, and Regius Professor of Hebrew, Oxford

While certainly qualified to participate in the translation of the Old Testament, Thorne's place on the committee is disputed.

Second Cambridge Company (the Apocrypha)

John Duport (d. 1617): director of the Second Cambridge Company, master of Jesus College, Cambridge, and prebendary of Ely

Duport is known for applying his academic training to a career of gathering prebends. During this period of church history, wealthy benefactors, churches, and universities filled vacant parish pulpits by making ministerial appointments. Frequent changes in parish appointments were a sign of upward mobility and one's connectedness to people of influence. Patrons could fill vacancies with the ministers of their choice, and congregations had little say regarding their spiritual leaders. If parishioners disliked the teaching of their pastor and decided to go to another church, they were still required to pay tithes to the church they left. Prebends could also be bought and sold, and because they were often owned by unbelievers and unscrupulous men, corruption was frequent. Duport gained a number of prebends as he moved upward in his career.

William Branthwaite (d. 1620): fellow of Emmanuel College and master of Gonville and Caius

Most men who participated in a fellowship at Emmanuel married and took up the work of evangelizing. Instead of resigning the fellowship as most did, Branthwaite continued to teach Greek. His knowledge of Greek made his work on the Septuagint Apocrypha extremely important.

Jeremiah Radcliffe (d. 1612): fellow of Trinity College, Cambridge University

Jeremiah's brother Edward, who was a physician to King James, was the more prominent of the two siblings. Very little is known of Jeremiah's work except that he collected consecutive prebends.

Samuel Ward (d. 1643): fellow and master of Sidney Sussex College and royal chaplain

Along with Richard Fairclough, Ward was one of the youngest of the King James Version translators and was considered a "vast scholar." Reminiscent of Martin Luther in his long-winded confessions, Ward often bemoaned his desire for advanced church offices, his inattention at church services, his gluttony, and his inability to think of God as his last remembrance of the day. Ward's translation work did not end with the 1611 edition. He also assisted in the Cambridge revisions of 1629 and 1638 along with John Bois and even assisted Bishop James Ussher in his study of genealogies. Ussher's genealogies (not to be confused with the genealogies placed in a separate section of the original 1611 King James Version) were placed in the margins of the text, and they were first included in the printing of the King James Version beginning with the 1701 edition. They are perhaps most noted for dating creation at the year 4004 BC.

Andrew Downes (d. 1628): Regius Professor of Greek at St. John's College, Cambridge University

Downes is responsible for the resurrection of Greek studies at St. John's College, where he held the position for thirty-eight years.

John Bois (d. 1643): fellow of Clare Hall, Cambridge University, and dean of Canterbury

An extraordinary scholar and student of Andrew Downes, Bois excelled in advanced Greek. He soon distinguished himself as a notable Greek scholar with disciplined study habits, often awakening at 4:00 a.m. and studying until 8:00 p.m. Bois, an editor of the King James Version, has become well known because he recorded notes in the margins of his Bishops' Bible that give a glimpse into his thinking during the translation process. Bois also worked with Samuel Ward in revising the King James translations of 1629 and 1638.

Robert Ward (d. unknown): fellow of Kings College and prebendary of Chichester Cathedral

Little is known about Ward except that he was a qualified Greek scholar.

Second Oxford Company (Matthew through Acts and Revelation)

The Second Oxford Company was perhaps the most prestigious of the translation groups. The four deans, two future bishops, and one archbishop were experts in the Greek language, and they were working on perhaps the most important portion of the Scriptures. Christ Church College, Oxford, was the most respected college of the day and is still considered one of the most beautiful. Oxford began its reign of honor when it was founded by Cardinal Wolsey, Lord Chancellor of England, as Cardinal College. After Wolsey fell from grace, Henry VIII refounded the college in 1532 as King Henry VIII's College. In 1546 the king broke ties with Rome and refounded the college once again as Christs Church, under the Church of England.

Thomas Ravis (d. 1609): director of the Second Oxford Company, dean of Christ Church College, bishop of Gloucester, bishop of London, and chaplain of Archbishop Whitgift

At the age of only fifteen years, Ravis was admitted to study at Christ Church College. In 1604 he was one of the six deans called by James I to Hampton Court to verbally subdue the Puritans. He was an astute, disciplined scholar who stood ready to issue harsh judgments on those who disagreed with him.

Sir Henry Savile (d. 1622): warden of Merton College, provost of Eton College

Entering Brasenose College, University of Oxford, at the age of merely twelve years, Savile was appointed fellow of Merton College when he was sixteen. By age twenty-one he had firmly established himself as a leading scholar. He was widely published in the writings of the Greek fathers, and his knowledge of the Greek language went unquestioned. Queen Elizabeth used him as a Greek tutor, and he was later elected warden of Merton College. After a long period beseeching the queen, he was awarded the position of provost at Eton College.

Henry Savile was one of England's finest scholars and a competent translator. Photo: Original art, L. Lupton.

McClure sums up Savile's life as "that magazine of learning, whose memory shall be honorable among the learned and the righteous forever."[16]

George Abbot (d. 1633): dean of Winchester, vice-chancellor of Oxford, bishop of Coventry and Lichfield, bishop of London, and archbishop of Canterbury

Abbot was one of the greatest scholars in Elizabethan England. Committed to a strong Reformed theological position, he supported the Puritan

He Aimed at a Stag but Bagged a Keeper

The fall air was crisp beneath clouds slung low over a forest rich with game. The morning held the promise of fresh venison as men stealthily moved through the woods in search of a prize multipoint buck. For a time they tracked prints into the thickening foliage until the markings disappeared up a streambed. Then, for what seemed like hours, they backtracked through the dense underbrush, arguing among themselves as they wandered in circles.

Dejected and deflated, the small band plopped to the ground and stretched out to ponder their fate. They were lost and exhausted. But as they rested in the silence, a rustle stirred in the brush.

One man raised his head. "A stag." In an instant he leaped to his feet. An arrow sped through the air and disappeared into the bushes with a thud.

"I got him." The man's face flushed with pride, and he rushed into the brush to claim his prize. But when George Abbot parted the bushes, he discovered that in his haste to bag the big one, he had bagged the gamekeeper who set up the hunt for his hunting party.[17] Horror washed over him. He was archbishop of Canterbury, and he had just killed a man.

Abbot's life took a dramatic downward turn in 1621 when this tragic accident occurred. He was accused of manslaughter by his enemies, and his critics insisted he be defrocked, but the king exonerated him. The controversy raged for many years until a commission of bishops, judges, and lawyers ruled Abbot not guilty. Although he was never deposed from his position, he lost all influence. Following the ascension of King Charles, Abbot lost the final vestiges of his power.

cause even as a loyal subject to the king. Perhaps because of his Puritan leanings, he was not invited to Hampton Court but was quickly chosen as a translator of the new version. The death of Richard Bancroft in 1611 led to Abbot's installation as archbishop of Canterbury.

Abbot's most controversial act was enacting a 1615 statute calling for the inclusion of the Apocrypha in every copy of the King James Version. While Protestants do not generally accept the Apocrypha as Scripture today, some denominations still include it in their Bible translations.

John Harmer (d. 1613): Regius Professor of Greek and warden of St. Mary's College, Winchester

A strong supporter of the Puritan Geneva Bible, Harmer was invited to participate in the King James revision based on his knowledge of Greek. His name appears twice in the notes left behind by John Bois (Second Cambridge Company), suggesting he may have been one of the team of twelve (two from each group) who made the final revisions of the whole Bible in Stationers' Hall, London, in 1610.[18]

John Perne (d. 1615): fellow of St. John's College Oxford, Regius Professor of Greek, vicar of Wafting in Sussex, and canon of Christ Church

Perne's scholarship and importance were recognized when he was selected to give an oration in Greek welcoming the king on his royal visit to Oxford in 1605.

Giles Thomson (d. 1612): fellow of All Soul's College, dean of Windsor, and bishop of Gloucester

Little is known of this renowned preacher except that he participated in the debate over the knowledge of the thoughts of a human's heart by angels and saints.

Richard Edes (d. 1604): dean of Worcester

Edes was chaplain to King James and an accomplished orator. He was chosen as one of the translators of the new version, but he died before the translation began. Either Aglionby or Montague replaced him when he died.

John Aglionby (d. 1609): principal of St. Edmund Hall

Aglionby was an expert on the Greek fathers, an accomplished linguist, and an effective preacher. His contribution to the translation was well known.

James Montague (d. 1618): dean of Worcester, bishop of Wells and Bath, and bishop of Winchester (1616)

Montague may have succeeded Aglionby when he died. He was also the editor of King James's folio work, *The Workes of the Most High and Mightie Prince, James.*

Ralph Ravens (d. 1615): rector of Great Easton, Essex

Ravens may have served as a translator, but some believe his name was on Bishop Burnet's list of translators in error. But a document that traces the history of St. John's College indicates Ravens served in this company.[19]

Lenard Hutton (d. 1632): prebend in Christ Church and canon of Christ Church

Hutton's participation in the Second Oxford Company has been questioned. Because of his scholarship, he was chosen to officiate at the opening of the Bodleian Library in 1602, so King James may have sought Hutton's participation as one of the "scholars throughout the land."

Second Westminster Company (Romans through Jude)

Churchmen of the seventeenth century possessed excellent academic qualifications; clergymen did not discard the academic for the practical. The well-trained minister embraced language studies, classics, and historical studies. Academic acumen was the foundation for greater ministry for God's kingdom.

One academic shortcoming these translators faced in working on the books of Romans through Jude was that in the seventeenth century Greek language studies did not recognize that Koine Greek formed the New Testament rather than classical Greek. It was not until Adolf Deissmann discovered papyri in Egypt in the nineteenth century that New Testament Greek was demonstrated to be the common (Koine) language of the day.

Buckden Palace, residence of Bishop Barlow, director of the Second Westminster Company of translators and author of *Summe and Substance*. Photo: Original art, L. Lupton.

William Barlow (d. 1613): director of the Second Westminster Company, dean of Chester, and bishop of Rochester

Barlow was the writer of the official report from the Hampton Court Conference, *The Summe and Substance of the Conference*. After its publication in 1604, the Puritans attacked the document's content as anti-Puritan.

In his capacity as chaplain to Archbishop Whitgift, Barlow was asked to comfort the Earl of Essex while he was imprisoned in the Tower of London. In a sermon the following Sunday at St. Paul's Cross, Barlow reported the Earl of Essex had acknowledged his guilt and repented of his treason.[20] As a result, Barlow found great favor with both Queen Elizabeth and King James.

John Spencer (d. 1614): president, Corpus Christi College, Oxford, and editor for Richard Hooker

Corpus Christi College was founded in 1516 by Richard Fox, bishop of Winchester, for the purpose of teaching Latin and Greek studies. The college had never had a married president until 1568, when Queen Elizabeth appointed William Cole president of the college. Cole had been a participant in the translation of the Geneva Bible while in exile from Queen Mary, but that did not lessen the controversy over his appointment as the first married president of the college.

Cole was replaced by John Rainolds in 1598, who was also a married man. By the time Spencer became president of this historic and important university in 1607, the controversy over having a married president had died down.

Roger Fenton (d. 1616): fellow of Pembroke Hall, Cambridge University, and prebendary of St. Paul's Church

A skillful preacher, Fenton was admired by all. The story is told that Fenton prepared a funeral sermon for a friend whose death appeared to be imminent. Fenton seemed disappointed the friend survived, and in fact, the friend preached at Fenton's funeral in 1616.

Michael Rabbett (d. 1630): vicar of St. Vedast, London

Thomas Sanderson (d. 1614): rector of All Hallows the Great, London, and archdeacon of Rochester

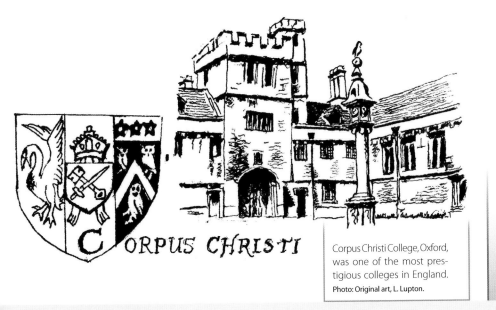

Corpus Christi College, Oxford, was one of the most prestigious colleges in England.
Photo: Original art, L. Lupton.

Ralph Hutchinson (d. 1606): president of St. John's College

William Dakins (d. 1607): vicar of Trumpington and junior dean at Trinity College

Both Hutchinson and Dakins died early in the translation process.

Many consider the Elizabethan and Jacobean periods the historical apex of the English language. Greek and Hebrew study also culminated during this era, which contributed to scholarship and the eventual success of the King James Version. Historical and cultural circumstances converged to bring the world's finest scholars, the most gifted linguists, and the most experienced biblical writers of the time to the work of translating the Bible for the King James Version.

Robert Barker, the king's printer, supplied each company with unbound leaves of the Bishops' Bible to assist them in the work of translation. These unbound sheets were used to record corrections and alterations to the Bishops' text. The sheets were then passed on to the revisers-editors for another round of editing. In addition to these leaves, editors were supplied additional reference tools: Tyndale's work (New Testament, Pentateuch, historical books, and Jonah), the Matthew's Bible, the Coverdale Bible, the Great Bible (Whitchurch), and the Geneva Bible.

The translators were challenged with the task of ensuring the accuracy of a new Bible while still reflecting the work of previous translations. By the seventeenth century, Hebrew studies had come to maturity and were being taught in most universities as well as preparatory schools. Hebrew grammars were easily obtained, and Hebrew Bibles were accessible. While former translations were primarily revisions of previous works, the Geneva Old Testament was a translation from the Hebrew and served as a primary source for and influence on the King James Version.

Passages from the Old Testament as listed below show marginal alternative readings that provide a glimpse into the decision-making process of the translators as they might have sat around the table speaking Latin during their company sessions.

Passage	Text reading	Marginal reading	Comments
Genesis 2:22	made a woman	Heb. *builded*	
Genesis 3:7	aprons	Or, *things to gird about*	The Geneva used "breeches" but mentioned in the margin, "things to gird about them to hide their privities."
Genesis 7:11	windows of Heaven	Or, *floodgates*	All versions used "windows."
Genesis 22:14	Iehouah-jireh	That is, *The LORD will see, or provide.*	Note: LORD is all in large capitals.
Exodus 2:10	Moses	That is, *Drawen out.*	
Exodus 17:15	IEHOUAH Nissi	That is, *The LORD my banner*	Note: LORD has the first letter in large capital and the remainder in smaller capitals. This reflects the change of the spelling from Genesis 40 onward.
Leviticus 11:42	creeping things	Heb. *Doth multiply feet*	
Joshua 10:12	sun, stand thou still	Heb. *be silent*	
1 Samuel 16:12	a beautiful countenance	Heb. *fair of eyes*	

Contemporary biblical studies scholars David Price and Charles Ryrie point out that the unevenness of the original Greek text in the Epistles made translation work difficult. To address this issue, the Second Westminster Company depended more on the Bishops' Bible than any of the other translation groups and incorporated more freely the readings from the Rheims New Testament of 1582.[22] The use of the Rheims New Testament is borne out by Ward Allen's analysis of Bois's notes inserted on his copy of the Bishops' Bible where he recorded frequent readings taken from the Rheims.[23]

William Shakespeare: Translator of the King James Version?

Is it possible that the most recognized figure in literary history played a part in the translation of the King James Version? To some the suggestion might seem possible, perhaps even likely. And popular lore swirls with a fascinating tale of Shakespeare's involvement in the King James translation. But what facts does history contribute?

In 1604 when the Hampton Court Conference was in session, William Shakespeare had already written many of his works and was one of the most widely regarded and acknowledged poets and playwrights of his time. James I is said to have enjoyed Shakespeare's comedies *The Merry Wives of Windsor, Measure for Measure,* and *Twelfth Night.* Scholars suggest the Geneva Bible was a likely source for quotes in Shakespeare's literary works; however, citations from the Bishops' Bible, the Geneva Bible, the Great Bible, and perhaps even the Douay-Rheims Bible were all used in various Shakespearean plays.[24] Many of the Bible translations of the period were so similar that it is difficult to determine which one Shakespeare used. He quoted more from the Psalms than any book except, perhaps, Matthew. When he quoted the Psalms, it was most likely from the Psalter (part of the prayer book, generally the Great Bible version), which was frequently bound with the Geneva Bible.

A fascinating theory links Shakespeare with the translation of Psalm 46. The theory suggests that if you count forty-six words from the beginning of the psalm, you arrive at the word *shake,* and if you count forty-six words from the end of the psalm, you arrive at the word *spear*. Shakespeare was forty-six years old at the time the psalm was translated. The coincidence suggests to some a veiled reference to the psalm as a work of William Shakespeare. No documentation exists, however, that William Shakespeare had anything to do with work on the King James Version.

An ongoing debate exists over Shakespeare's religious affiliation. Some scholars maintain he was a closet Roman Catholic. Evidence to support their case includes the fact that Shakespeare's parents, especially his mother, remained Catholic for the duration of their lives. His use of Scripture in his plays, however, followed the Reformed Bible translations. It appears that although he was reared Roman Catholic, his theological views were either muted by his lack of interest or concealed because of open hostility toward Catholics by royal supporters of the predominant Puritans and Anglicans. Furthermore, Shakespeare was buried in a well-known Anglican cemetery. The ongoing disputes of modern Shakespearean scholars demonstrate the difficulty of arriving at any solid conclusion in the quest to unearth Shakespeare's personal religious beliefs.[25]

> If Shakespeare had been Catholic, he certainly would not have been asked to translate a Protestant Bible.

If Shakespeare had been Catholic, he certainly would not have been asked to translate a Protestant Bible. And even though he may have been a schoolmaster in his earlier years, most scholars agree he knew little or no Greek—a prerequisite for translation work. He was not a churchman, and all other translators were important figures in the English church tradition. Perhaps neither a practicing Catholic, Puritan, or Anglican, Shakespeare undoubtedly did not participate in the translation of the King James Bible.

Beauty in the Seemingly Insignificant

So how did a collection of academic scholars not accustomed to literary endeavors achieve the remarkable and enduring qualities attributed to the King James Version? None of Bancroft's rules for translation mention style or beauty of language, yet the King James Version is characterized by a metrical, lyrical style: "Come vnto me all yee that labour, and are heauy laden, and I will giue you rest. Take my yoke vpon you, and learne of me, for I am meeke and lowly in heart: and yee shall find rest vpon your soules. For my yoke is easie, and my burden is light" (Matt. 11:28).

Alfred Pollard attempts to explain the natural process that led to the long-recognized literary quality of the King James Version in *Records of the English Bible*:

> Whether the wonderful felicity of phrasing should be attributed to the dexterity with which, after meanings had been settled and the important words in each passage chosen, either the board of twelve or the two final revisers put their touches to the work, or whether, as seems more likely, the rhythm, first called into being by Tyndale and Coverdale, reasserted itself after every change, only gathering strength and melody from the increasing richness of the language, none can tell. All that is certain is the rhythm and the strength and the melody are there.[26]

While analytical answers for the reasons behind the beauty of the King James Version may be elusive, readers need only experience the poetry and passion of the Psalms or the artistry of the book of Isaiah to understand the magnetic majesty of this enduring translation.

The King James translators were not without doctrinal preconceptions, political aspirations, and personal flaws. While they were chosen for their scholarship, certainly political and church affiliations played a vital role in their selection. Their spiritual character was often commendable, but they were also unmistakably human. Accumulating prebends often led to charges of favoritism and corruption. Some translators possessed questionable morals, some were drunkards, and one was even accused of murder. Those who participated in the work wielded varying degrees of influence. Some died before the translation began or before it was finished. Others made only minimal contributions, and still others bore the brunt of the load. Their legacy stands as an example of the combined efforts of a diversified body of gifted yet flawed believers uniting to accomplish a task for the greater good of the kingdom of God.

The Principles and English of the King James Version

King James chose fifty-four highly qualified translators from among England's finest scholars in the production of the King James Version.[27] Because the men were handpicked, James was able to control the balance between Anglican and Puritan influences. A division of six companies emerged that took responsibility for translating various books: two from Westminster (Genesis through 2 Kings and Romans through Jude), two from Cambridge (1 Chronicles through Song of Solomon and the Apocrypha), and two from Oxford (Isaiah through Malachi, Matthew through Acts and Revelation). Upon completion of the initial translation, a twelve-man committee comprised of two delegates from each of the companies met to revise the total work. Miles Smith, a Calvinist, contributed the introduction and Thomas Bilson, bishop of Winchester, added the headings to chapters.

> Each highly qualified scholar brought specific language expertise that contributed to the clarification of words, passages, and the development of explanatory marginal notes.

Each highly qualified scholar brought specific language expertise that contributed to the clarification of words, passages, and the development of explanatory marginal notes. They created their work from the original languages, assisted in their efforts by past translations, the juried judgments of other scholars, argumentation, and the process of rechecking their work at various stages throughout the process. The King James Version translators were linked in a team effort from start to finish, and the controlling principles of their work stand as a model for collaborative scholarship.

Perhaps the most distinctive element of the King James Version is its lyrical and stylized language. The average Bible reader today is likely to believe the King James Version was translated into the language of its time: the early-seventeenth-century language of the people. But the translation of the KJV was conducted according to controlling rules and principles established by Archbishop Bancroft, one of which required use of the Bishops' Bible as the primary reference source, thereby guaranteeing that the King

James Bible would use the sixteenth-century English found in the Bishops' Bible.

King James had appointed Richard Bancroft, then bishop of London, to the archbishopric of Canterbury upon the death of Archbishop Whitgift in 1604. Bancroft was a staunch defender of the faith and an especially tenacious supporter of the Anglican Church. His long-standing feud with the Puritans made him a natural choice to lead the translation process and suited him well to devise the overarching principles of translation. His fifteen rules for translation clearly reveal bias against the Puritans and inevitably led to a translation that favored the Church of England. It is noteworthy that none of his principles suggest seeking an inerrant translation or even one dependent upon the work of the Holy Spirit. Translators were simply charged with making a good English translation better by applying a mechanical and logical approach to their work.

Bancroft's rules were set forth in *Rules to Be Observed in the Translation of the Bible*.[28] The first of his principles controlled the use of archaic language.

Principle One: The ordinary Bible read in the Church, commonly called the Bishops' Bible; to be followed, and as little altered as the Truth of the Original will permit.

As they worked within the parameters of Bancroft's rules, the translators were committed to translating each Greek word with an English equivalent. Among other things, this decision forced them to use forms of certain personal pronouns found in the Bishops' Bible that were already becoming archaic, such as *thou, thee, thy,* and *ye,* even though the more popular form, *you,* had already come into use. By contrast, the Geneva Bible word choice was more representative of the contemporary English of the day since it was written by those in exile during Mary's reign.

Principle Two: The names of the Prophets and the Holy Writers, with the other names in the text to be retained, as nigh as may be, accordingly as they are vulgarly used.

The Puritans preferred to translate the meanings of words and names rather than the transliteration (e.g., Adam = "red earth [man]" and Timothy = "fear God").[29] But principle two required the King James translators to retain names rather than use transliteration. For example, the KJV uses *Adam* where the Puritan Geneva Bible retains the word *man*.

Principle Three: The old ecclesiastical words to be kept, viz., as the word *church* not to be translated "congregation."

The introduction in the King James Version declares that the practice of translating used in the Puritan Geneva Bible is insufficient: "Lastly, we have . . . avoided the scrupulosity of the Puritans, who leave the old ecclesiastical words, and betake them to other, as when they put 'washing' for 'Baptism' and 'congregation' instead of 'Church.' "[30] The Puritans preferred to use the meaning of a word rather than the transliteration, but principle two guided translators to use the word *church* for the Greek term that meant *congregations*.

The Puritans believed this translation principle supported the Catholic view by translating, for example, *presbyteros* as *priest* and *ecclesia* as *church*. The former eliminated the need for priestly functions, and the latter presupposed an institution that requires a structure to support it. The Puritans vehemently rejected the idea of any *priestly* authority

The 1602 folio edition of the Bishops' Bible was handed out in sections to the various companies of the King James translators.

assigned to the elders of the *church*, even though those words are legitimate translations of the Greek terms. This principle stood in direct conflict with the teaching of the Puritans.

Principle Four: When a word has divers signification, that to be kept which hath been most commonly used by the most of the Ancient Fathers, being agreeable to the propriety of the place and the analogy of the faith.

The church of the early seventeenth century often sought the authority of ancient writers as a way to support their interpretation of Scripture. Similarly, modern scholars seek sources that support their ideas rather than expressing opinions without the authority of scholars who preceded them. This principle indicates the translators' desire for an authoritative understanding of the text in seventeenth-century terms.

Principle Five: The division of the chapters to be altered, either not at all, or as little as may be, if necessity or required.

The new version was to continue the tradition of chapter divisions used by the Bishops' Bible and earlier English versions. Alterations were to be considered sparingly.

Principle Six: No marginal notes at all to be affixed, but only for the explanation of the Hebrew or Greek words, which cannot without some circumlocution so briefly and fitly be expressed in the text.

The translation principles were established to prevent the Puritans' undue influence and to provide a system of checks and balances against the doctrinal positions of the Geneva Bible that concerned the king. Certain biblical texts and marginal notes of the Geneva Bible ran contrary to the position of the Anglicans and King James himself, implying that the church held authority over governmental powers. King James hated the Geneva Bible's Calvinistic notes and considered it a threat to his authority as king of England and Scotland. Therefore, the King James Version would include no marginal notes unless the words of the original were so ambiguous that an extended note was necessary for clarity. Words deviating from earlier translations were chosen for their beauty, cadence, and sound rather than simplicity of expression.

Principle Seven: Such quotations of places to be marginally set down as shall serve for the fit reference of one Scripture to another.

This principle ensured that the reader would see the interrelationship of the Old Testament with the New Testament and vice versa by placing cross-references in the margins. For instance, the fulfillment of Old Testament prophecy in the New Testament, quotations of Old Testament passages in the New Testament, and New Testament references to Old Testament events were referenced in the margins.

Principle Eight: Every particular man of each company, to take the same chapter or chapters, and having translated or amended them severally by himself, where he thinks good, all to meet together, confer what they have done, and agree for their parts what shall stand.

The King James Version represented a giant step forward from principles of past translations when King James organized a group of scholars to do the work. Beginning with principle eight, procedures were adopted that guaranteed a community agreement for the work of each company. Each person on the team translated, without collaboration, as he saw fit. The team then met to discuss the various ways of stating the text and then decided which wording was best or, in some cases, what compromise in wording best represented the text in question. This principle resulted in a text that was a genuine community translation. A letter from Lancelot Andrews, a leading Anglican bishop and translator of the King James Version, refers to the fact that a specific time was set apart for added review of the translation work: "But that this afternoon is our translation time."[32]

Principle Nine: As one company hath dispatched any one book in this manner they shall send it to the rest, to be considered seriously and judiciously, for His Majesty is very careful in this point.[33]

Each company was responsible to supervise the work of every other company. Since each company of translators represented a disparate school of thought, this principle theoretically protected the version from any one group's bias.[34] James was particularly concerned about keeping the Puritans from gaining any direct influence on his favorite kingship doctrines. Companies loyal to His Majesty could be counted on, but those under the influence of John Rainolds, the Puritan, needed to be kept from wandering away from Anglican influence. Reviews were sent to the king after each book was finished. It is clear from the reference to the king in this principle that James, while not officially authorizing this version, had an unquestionable influence on it.

Principle Ten: If any company, upon the review of the book so sent, doubt or differ upon any place, to send them word thereof; note the place, and withal send the reasons, to which if they consent not, the difference to be compounded at the general meeting, which is to be of the chief person of each company, at the end of the work.

The King James translators were all scholars, and yet every level of their work was checked, debated, and even criticized by peer editors. In some cases an original reading was ignored by the editors and another reading was chosen. The work was a humbling experience, but at the same time the process guaranteed excellence in translation.

This principle specifies the method of proceeding when a company disagreed with the translation of another company, and the method assured that no sectarian interpretation went unnoticed. The company in disagreement forwarded their suggestions to the general meeting of the twelve translators (composed of two members from each company) with their arguments in support of their findings. At every stage of the work, the King James Version was reviewed again and again.

> Bancroft encouraged other clergy to look at the translation and to forward suggestions to the companies.

Principle Eleven: When any place of special obscurity is doubted of letters to be directed, by authority, to send to any learned man in the land, for his judgment of such a place.

Upon completion of the reviews, if a reading or word was not completely satisfactory, members could inquire of other qualified scholars outside the committees. The principle indicates that Bancroft was striving to assure the king that every scholar's expertise would be sought for the translation of difficult words and passages to ensure the highest quality result.

Principle Twelve: Letters to be sent from every bishop to the rest of his clergy, admonishing them of this translation in hand; and to move and charge as many as being skilful in the tongues; and having taken pains in that kind, to send his particular observations to the company, either Westminster, Cambridge, or Oxford.

Bancroft encouraged other clergy to look at the translation and to forward suggestions to the companies. But he was careful to approve only those who were "skilful" in the languages. Novices were not welcome to make suggestions.

Principle Thirteen: The directors in each company, to be the deans of Westminster and Chester for that place; and the king's professors in the Hebrew or Greek in either University.

This principle allowed direct appointments of the heads of each company. The king controlled the appointments of university deans, which assured that those who supported his favorite doctrines were prominently placed.

Principle Fourteen: These translations to be used when they agree better with the text than the Bishops' Bible: Tyndale, Matthew's, Coverdale, Whitchurch [Great Bible], and Geneva.

This rule of translation focused on the series of Protestant Bibles extending from Tyndale's New Testament (1525–26) to the Bishops' Bible (1568). The translators made efforts to follow the Bishops' Bible (although

How Was God's Word First Delivered?

The message of the New Testament was first delivered as spoken language. During Bible times it was the custom among Greeks, Romans, and Hebrews to first read a text aloud to an audience of friends or in private.[35] While the art of silent reading existed, reading was commonly done aloud. The implications from the New Testament bear this out in passages such as 1 Thessalonians 5:27, "I charge you before the Lord to have this letter read to all the brothers" (NIV). Evidence of oral reading of Scripture is also seen in Colossians 4:16, "After this letter has been read to you, see that it is also read in the church of the Laodiceans and that you in turn read the letter from Laodicea" (NIV). The oral tradition is also recorded in Revelation 1:3, "Blessed is the one who reads the words of this prophecy, and blessed are those who hear it and take to heart what is written in it, because the time is near" (NIV). The clear implication is that the letters of Paul were delivered orally.

In the first century, illiteracy was widespread. New Testament scholar Robert Stein, quoting ancient history scholars William V. Harris and Harry Y. Gamble, writes, "The figures that most often come up are that about 5 to 10 percent, at most perhaps 10 to 15 percent, of the population in Greek and Roman society could read. The percentage of Christians who could read in the first century was probably 3 to 10 percent."[36]

they often departed) and even the Geneva Bible. For instance, the historical books of the Bible favor the Bishops'. In spite of the king's strong statements against the Geneva Bible, it was given a place of prominence in the translation of the Prophets.

Although the Roman Catholic version, the Rheims New Testament, is not listed as a consulting source, Ward S. Allen states that in the translation of the Gospels, the King James Version contains more Rheims version readings than any other single version.[37] Of course the king's new version could not acknowledge the superiority of Roman Catholic readings over the Anglican Bishops' Bible, but even in the shadow of the failed Catholic

First-century believers were more hearers than readers, receiving messages through their ears rather than their eyes. Anyone learning a foreign language in the country where it is spoken quickly realizes the learning curve is quite different than when instruction takes place in a classroom. Paul Achtemeier writes, "There is considerable evidence that oral and written cultures existed side by side in the ancient world, particularly since writing tended to be used as a help to memory rather than as an autonomous and independent mode of communication."[38]

As a young missionary in Ethiopia learning Amharic, I soon discovered that those who had at one time learned a language from a book had difficulty learning a living language by means of listening and speaking. Teaching my first Greek language class using Amharic as the medium of instruction, I was amazed when students with fourth-grade educations recited their homework orally. Their lack of formal education did not prevent them from learning a language with little difficulty.

Scholars believe the King James revisers proofed, revised, and suggested alternate readings based on the sound of the text when it was read aloud.[39] If this is true, their methods may explain in part the reason behind the melody and cadence that make the King James Version easier to memorize than other translations.

Gunpowder Plot and James's hatred of the Catholics, the unnamed Roman Catholic Rheims still did influence the King James Version.

Adam Nicolson illustrates the influence of the many versions in the King James Version in a single verse from 2 Corinthians 1:11.

> You are also helping [Bishops' Bible] together [Geneva 1557] by [Bishops'] prayer for vs [Tyndale], that [Tyndale] for the [Geneva 1560] gift [Great Bible] bestowed vpon vs [Geneva 1557] by the meanes of many [Tyndale] persons [Great], thankes may bee giuen [Tyndale] by [Geneva] many on our behalfe [Tyndale].[40]

Principle Fifteen: Besides the said directors before mentioned, three or four of the most Ancient and Grave Divines, in either of the Universities, not employed in translating, to be assigned by the Vice-Chancellor, upon conference with the rest to the heads, to be overseers of the translations as well *Hebrew* as *Greek*, for the better observation of the fourth rule above specified.

The final translation principle assured readers that the Hebrew Bible, along with the Greek Septuagint, was consulted. Several Old Testament scholars on the committee were experts in the Septuagint, even though there is little evidence that the Septuagint was used instead of the Hebrew.[41]

The obnoxious, aggressive, and opinionated Puritan Hebrew scholar Hugh Broughton was denied a position on any of the translation committees, most likely because his persuasive and belligerent personality threatened Anglican translators. In a characteristic outburst at the completion of the King James project, the volatile Broughton blasted the version as a damnable translation lacking any solid Hebrew language understanding.

It is unfortunate that Bancroft's controlling principles, established at the outset of the translation process, limited the King James Version to an improvement of a sixteenth-century English translation that would satisfy all theological views rather than the creation of a new, original translation. While the King James Version achieved great historical influence and literary excellence, not one translation rule touched upon the structuring of literary style, readability, or elegance of thought. Through the work of a diverse, disheartened, yet devoted group of men, the King James Version was crafted into the most literal yet literal-lyrical Bible translation ever produced.

6

Tracing the Path

The Role of the Original Languages in the King James Version

Two young seminarians sat in a coffee shop debating a New Testament exegetical difficulty. Placing his cappuccino confidently on the table between them, the younger of the two leaned forward and invoked the wisdom of his ultimate authority: the Greek New Testament. He confidently explained the nuances of the Greek text supporting his case and then smiled as he lifted his cup for a sip.

Across the table his colleague countered with a brief comment. "I see you've chosen a Greek text that supports your position. I, however, believe a reading from a different Greek text most accurately represents the original meaning of this passage. It would appear your argument is not as airtight as you would like to believe."

Silence hung in the air for several moments before the conversation turned to which of several Greek New Testament texts most closely represented the original manuscripts delivered by the apostolic community. Several cups of coffee later, the two friends parted company with their questions unresolved and with a list of new questions for their seminary professors on the subject of textual criticism.

Textual Criticism and the Guiding Principles for the King James Version

Textual criticism focuses on the identification and removal of manuscript errors that occur when an original copy is duplicated. The King James Version translators did not use the tools nor face the challenges of modern textual critics for one simple reason: in 1611 only one Greek New Testament existed. It was a work edited in 1516 by humanist and Catholic theologian Erasmus of Rotterdam, and all printed biblical texts of the time stemmed from it. Manuscript text *types* were unknown and therefore irrelevant in the seventeenth century.

King James's translators had been charged with improving upon the existing Bishops' Bible. So how did their attitudes toward the existing Greek and Hebrew texts available to them shape their translation decisions? The answer provides modern readers of the King James and other versions a context for understanding translators' commitment to produce Bibles that communicate first-century accuracy to the current generation and generations to come.

As discussed in the previous chapter, translators of the King James Version were bound by strict principles. Although these principles did not direct the translators to use a specific Greek text, we know they were limited to the Byzantine text, a text-type found in the largest number of surviving manuscripts but not necessarily the oldest manuscripts. Text-types are *families* of similar manuscripts that circulated in specific regions that shared a common language. Understanding the story behind the Byzantine text-type and its dominance as a Greek New Testament reference tool is integral to understanding the story of the King James Bible.

The original writers of the Bible wrote on leather skins or papyrus rolls in Hebrew and Aramaic (Old Testament) and Greek (New Testament). These manuscripts no longer exist. Time, flood, fire, and acts of destruction all contributed to their disappearance. In spite of the meticulous care of the hand-copiers, occasional errors crept into the manuscripts. Boredom, fatigue, and distractions contributed to a lack of concentration during their work. Errors multiplied when successive copyists duplicated and added to the mistakes of those before them. As subsequent copies were made, older copies disappeared, eliminating the possibility of checking and correcting existing copies. Subsequently, extant manuscripts came to include errors in spelling, poor penmanship, omissions, and insertions. The tale of textual criticism turns back the pages of time, showing how the search for the *true* text unfolded from manuscript to manuscript to printed Bible. Tracing the journey helps us understand why differences exist among modern English Bible translations.

More than sixty years passed between the printing of the Gutenberg Bible and Erasmus's Greek New Testament. During this time the church was limited to reading and studying the papal-authorized Latin Vulgate. Even the English translation of John Wycliffe (1382) originated from the Latin Vulgate. Until the middle of the fifteenth century, Greek was little known in the West. But the fall of Constantinople in 1453 and conquest of the Turks forced many Greek scholars to flee to the West. Subsequently, Greek teaching had been introduced in a large number of Western institutions by the turn of the sixteenth century.

Bible translations in other spoken languages were of little threat to the Vulgate, but a New Testament in Greek would mean an ultimate critical examination of the Vulgate. Progress in producing a Greek New Testament, however, was slowed by the official status and popularity of the Latin Vulgate. Fifty years lapsed before the political climate would tolerate a rival text to the Latin. Fanned by the winds of Reformation, Greek scholarship spread, bringing with it church receptivity to a Greek New Testament.

Opened and unidentified scroll and papyrus fragments from third- to sixth-century manuscripts. The upper right-hand fragment is on leather from Psalm 89:31–35.

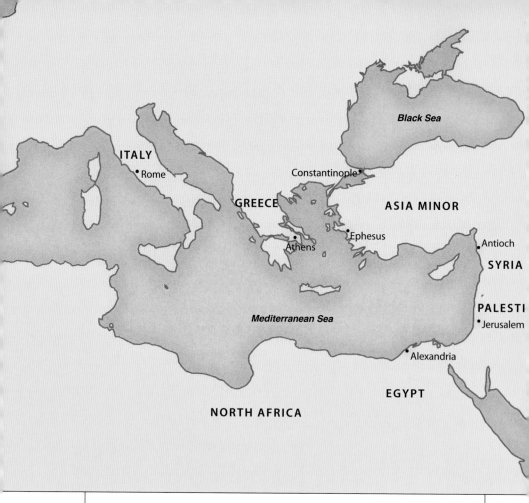

Original Geographical Distribution
of New Testament Books

The New Testament is a collection of twenty-seven individual books gathered into one book we call the New Testament. The writers sent their Gospels and Epistles to various provinces throughout the Roman world, as depicted in this map.

Asia Minor* (Greek): John, Galatians, Ephesians, Colossians, 1 and 2 Timothy, Philemon, 1 Peter, 1, 2, and 3 John, and Revelation; possibly Matthew, Luke, Acts, James, and 2 Peter

Greece** (Greek): 1 and 2 Corinthians, Philippians, 1 and 2 Thessalonians, and Titus

Rome (Latin): Mark and Romans; possibly Luke, Acts, 2 Peter, and Hebrews

Palestine (Greek): Possibly Matthew, James, and Hebrews

Egypt/North Africa (Coptic): None

*Antioch in Asia Minor was the center of Christianity, therefore it is natural that a majority of the Gospels and Epistles originally came to this region.

**Greek was the lingua franca at this time in history.

Geographic Roots of the King James Version

New Testament textual critics Kurt and Barbara Aland observe that by AD 180 the greatest number of Christian churches existed in Asia Minor and along the Aegean coast in Greece.[1] History records that all of the early church councils were held in Asia Minor, which is further evidence of a large concentration of Christian churches in that region. The city of Antioch was home base for Paul, Mark, Barnabas, Silas, Peter, Matthew, and Luke, and these church leaders were likely all in the region at the same time.

For the first three hundred years of church growth, congregations in Asia Minor and Greece exerted the greatest force in Christianity. By AD 325 the church was centered in Asia Minor, and it was there that the majority of New Testament documents circulated. Because of the Antioch church's leadership role for the Gentile church, it may be there that the first copies of Scripture were produced, and it may also have served as an important copying and dissemination center.

Under normal circulation patterns, biblical autographs would have benefitted their areas of origin most; however, these books were written to be circulated to churches throughout the Christian empire. Colossians 4:16 reads, "Now when this epistle is read among you, see that it is read also in the church of the Laodiceans, and that you likewise read the epistle from Laodicea" (NKJV). As the church grew along the western coast of Asia Minor (modern Turkey) and Greece, the need for copies of the Scripture undoubtedly increased, and the supply of copies multiplied, crisscrossed the region, and were compared and edited. The gospel spread from Ephesus and Laodicea, where the church was centered, and found an eager audience throughout the region. And the growth continued, as evidenced by John as he addressed seven churches in Asia Minor (Rev. 1:11) less than fifty years after the gospel was first presented (ca. AD 95).

As Christianity spread throughout the Roman Empire into North Africa, Egypt, and Rome, the New Testament documents were translated into Latin, Coptic, Syriac, and other languages. The various Greek text-types following the texts circulating in their areas were translated into local languages. As Christianity expanded, these manuscripts migrated beyond

Avid Bible collector Vince Savarino copied this modern manuscript of the Gospel of Mark by hand, using as his example third-century books found at Nag Hammadi (northern Egypt). Photo: B. Bahner.

the Greek-speaking churches in Antioch, Asia Minor, and Greece and developed into local texts referred to as text-types or families. While texts were passed among provinces, especially from Rome to North Africa and Constantinople, scribes copied from texts within the local areas where the documents were more plentiful.[2] At that time early Christians were not concerned with the fine points of modern textual criticism: Greek exegesis, textual exactness, and the minute accuracy of their various documents. Early Christians viewed every text as God's Word; the idea of differences in texts causing different interpretations may not have occurred to them.

When the King James translators were working in the seventeenth century, scholarship had not yet revealed that three distinct text-types or families existed. The Coptic Church had developed in Alexandria, and Coptic replaced Greek as the lingua franca (a language used to communicate between persons not sharing a mother tongue). In the Roman Empire, the Roman Catholic Church had gained prominence, and Latin replaced Greek. In Asia Minor (modern Turkey) and Greece, the Eastern Orthodox Church had become dominant, and Greek continued to be the primary local language. The resulting historic and language influences are reflected in modern textual criticism's three text-types: Alexandrian (Egypt), Western (Roman Empire), and Byzantine (Asia Minor and Greece).[3]

Underlying the three text-types is the central question of textual criticism: If the three text-types represent local *families* of manuscripts, which text-type best represents the original? A second and related question concerns the method behind the prioritizing or weighting of text-types. Most scholars today defer to the oldest extant manuscripts known as *Vaticanus* and *Sinaiticus* from Egypt. Scholars who support the oldest text-type reason that the most reliable text is represented by manuscripts *closest to the original*.[4] Another small group of scholars argues that the most reliable text is the one found in the later witnesses but constitute *the majority of extant manuscripts*.

Since Greek was in use longer than Coptic or Latin among these early Christian communities, one would expect to find more extant Greek manuscripts in the Eastern Empire, especially among later manuscripts. Prior to the fall of Constantinople, only a few Greek manuscripts were scattered throughout Europe. But when the Turks invaded the eastern capital in 1453, Greek scholars fled to Europe,

The invention of movable type and the printing press enabled the supply of printed copies of the Bible to meet the demand. This is a working replica model of the Gutenberg Press. It was built by Joe Hellstern and is housed at the Dunham Bible Museum at Houston Baptist University. Photo: C. Brake.

taking Greek New Testament manuscripts with them. These manuscripts were, of course, the Byzantine text. It logically follows that when Erasmus subsequently chose five manuscripts for his translation, his chances of securing the Byzantine text-type far outweighed his chances of locating a Western or Alexandrian manuscript.

The first printed Greek New Testament reflected the efforts of an overanxious printer named Johann Froben. Froben sought the Greek scholar Erasmus to edit a Greek New Testament. Erasmus based his work on a small number of incomplete manuscripts. The result was an incomplete Greek text with a few readings translated from a Latin manuscript. Nevertheless, once Froben printed Erasmus's imperfect New Testament, it remained a standard throughout the history of Greek New Testaments.

Two basic Greek texts exist, usually identified as (1) the *critical text* and (2) the *Textus Receptus* or *Byzantine text*. The King James Version is based on the *Textus Receptus* (or Byzantine text). Most other modern translations (NIV, NASB, NEB, NRSV, etc.) are based on the critical text. The term *Majority Text*

Textual Criticism and the King James Translators

Large numbers of existing manuscripts and the variances between them have created the science of textual criticism. Textual critics consider two areas when determining the best reading of the manuscripts: external and internal evidence.

External evidence refers to the weight given to the manuscript or family of manuscripts. This requires assigning weight to the age of the manuscript, the geographical location of its production, the scribe producing the manuscripts, and his habits in copying a text.

Internal evidence has to do with the quality of the writing of the document. This includes tendencies of the scribe to make unintentional mistakes, copyist harmonies, and intentional (either doctrinal or emendation) changes.

Textual criticism evaluates the processes that have taken place over the course of generations of New Testament manuscript copying. Principles of textual criticism that are taken for granted today developed after the King James translators completed their work.

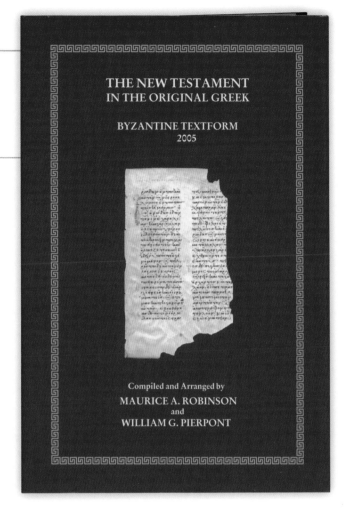

THE NEW TESTAMENT IN THE ORIGINAL GREEK

BYZANTINE TEXTFORM 2005

Compiled and Arranged by
MAURICE A. ROBINSON
and
WILLIAM G. PIERPONT

refers not to any single manuscript but to the compilation of readings supported by most of the extant Byzantine text-type manuscripts. The *Textus Receptus* and the Majority Text are more closely related to each other than they are to the critical text.[5] At first glance, a disconnect exists between the Greek manuscripts used by Erasmus in his printed text (*Textus Receptus*) and the Greek manuscripts identified today by many scholars as the oldest extant manuscripts (critical text). A closer examination, however, reveals how the texts are related.

The Printed Greek Text of the King James Version

The first printed Greek New Testament rolled off the press in 1514 as part of a massive Polyglot (multilanguage) Bible. This comparative work in Hebrew, Aramaic, Latin, Greek, and other languages was the work of Cardinal

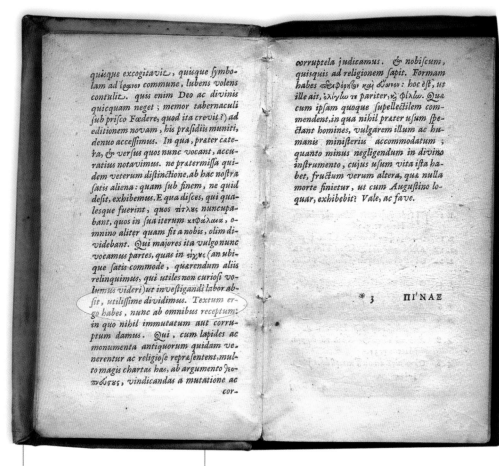

quifque excogitavit, quifque fymbo-
lam ad ἐργον commune, lubens volens
contulit. quis enim Deo ac divinis
quicquam neget ; memor tabernaculi
fub prifco Fœdere, quod ita crevit?) ad
editionem novam, his præfidiis muniti,
denuo acceffimus. In quâ, præter cæte-
ra, & verfus quos nunc vocant, accu-
ratius notavimus. ne prætermiffa qui-
dem veterum diftinctione, ab hac noftra
fatis aliena: quam fub finem, ne quid
defit, exhibemus. E quâ difces, qui qua-
lesque fuerint, quos τίτλες nuncupa-
bant, quos in fuâ iterum κεφαλαια, o-
mnino aliter quam fit a nobis, olim di-
videbant. Qui majores ita vulgo nunc
vocamus partes, quas in ςιχες (an ubi-
que fatis commode, quærendum aliis
relinquimus, qui utiles non curiofi vo-
lumus videri)ut inveftigandi labor ab-
fit, utiliffime dividimus. Textum ergo habes, nunc ab omnibus receptum:
in quo nihil immutatum aut corru-
ptum damus. Qui, cum lapides ac
monumenta antiquorum quidam ve-
nerentur ac religiofe repræfentent, mul-
to magis chartas has, ab argumento ϑεο-
πνέυςες, vindicandas a mutatione ac
cor-

corruptela judicamus. & nobifcum,
quisquis ad religionem fapit. Formam
habes ἀυτόφρητον καὶ ἀΐδιον: hoc eft, ut
ille ait, ὀλίγω τε pariter, κ, φίλω. Qua
cum ipfam quoque fupellectilem com-
mendent,in qua nihil præter ufum fpe-
ctant homines, vulgarem illum ac hu-
manis minifteriis accommodatum ;
quanto minus negligendum in divino
inftrumento, cujus ufum vita ifta ha-
bet, fructum verum altera, quæ nulla
morte finietur, ut cum Auguftino lo-
quar, exhibebit? Vale, ac fave.

* 3   ΠΙ'ΝΑΞ

The text underlying the King James Version (Erasmus and Stephanus from the
sixteenth century) is often referred to as
the *Textus Receptus*. The Elzevir Greek New
Testament published in 1633 coined the
term *Textus Receptus* when in the introduction it used the Latin expression: *"Textum
ergo habes, nunc ab omnibus receptum"*
(therefore you have the text that is now
received by all). So technically speaking,
the term *Textus Receptus* was not coined
until the seventeenth century.

Francisco Ximenes de Cisneros and several
highly qualified scholars and was printed in
Complutum, Spain.

The style of this edition, which became
known as the Polyglot Greek New Testament,
followed the handwritten letter formations of the
eleventh and twelfth centuries. The manuscripts
used in its production are unknown, but in the
dedication to Pope Leo X, Cisneros expressed
his indebtedness to him for sending manu-
scripts from the Apostolic Library. The famous manuscript *Vaticanus* (written
about AD 325–50 and considered by many modern scholars to be the most
important manuscript in existence) was thought to have been in the Vatican

collection before 1475. Why the cardinal did not cite such a seminal work as part of his document is a mystery, although he may have been concerned about textual differences.

The Polyglot text itself shows no dependence on *Vaticanus,* and any actual manuscript used by Cisneros remains unknown.[6] Some suggest the manuscripts he used at the University of Complutum were sold to a pyrotechnic to make fireworks in celebration of the arrival of a dignitary,[7] but this is highly unlikely. The librarian at the time was an astute scholar, and it is doubtful he would have allowed such a horror. It is more likely the manuscripts were sold or lost.

Whatever manuscripts were used, the text varies little from the text produced by Erasmus, and those manuscripts are known. Most probably Cisneros's manuscripts were secured from a collection held by friends or other familiar sources. At that time the overwhelming numbers of available manuscripts would have been from the same text represented in Erasmus's text.

> The first published Greek New Testament was edited by Erasmus and published by Froben in 1516.

Did attention to scholarship strip Cisneros of the honor of publishing the first Greek New Testament? It seems likely. The translators producing the Complutensian Polyglot seemed more interested in completing an accurate text than in being the first to be published. The work retained the honor of being the first printed Greek New Testament (1514), but it was not published until 1521–22. Therefore, the first published Greek New Testament was edited by Erasmus and published by Froben in 1516.

Sixteenth-century printers were well aware of the economic advantages of being the first to publish a major work. Basel printer Johann Froben (1460–1527) received word that a Polyglot was in preparation in Spain. Aware that Erasmus was demonstrating great interest in the Greek New Testament, Froben enlisted him to quickly produce one. Some suggest that Erasmus may have already been preparing a Greek New Testament since he was in the process of producing a Latin text that was ultimately published with the Greek.

Seeing the opportunity, Erasmus immediately accepted Froben's offer. Arriving in Basel in the summer of 1515, he began the arduous work of editing the Greek New Testament. The project was completed in March of 1516. The pressure of a short deadline forced Erasmus to produce an imperfect and inferior edition. Using only a few actual manuscripts (two of which are preserved today in the library at Basel), Erasmus completed the New Testament. For the book of Revelation he borrowed a mutilated copy of a Latin manuscript from German humanist and scholar Johann Reuchlin, but the

A Trip to Ireland Resolves the Mystery

The debate has raged for centuries regarding the reliability of Erasmus's decision to place 1 John 5:7 in his 1522 third edition Greek New Testament. When I purchased a 1516 Erasmus Greek New Testament without the 1 John 5:7 verse, I personally was drawn into the drama.

Erasmus's 1522 New Testament includes the verse "For there are three that bear record in heaven, the Father, the Word, and the Holy Spirit: and these three are one" (1 John 5:7). This passage makes a clear statement about the Trinity; it is Scripture's most doctrinally direct statement about the trinitarian Godhead.

Tradition says Erasmus did not want to include the reading in his Greek New Testament because the verse could not be found in his Greek manuscripts. He challenged his harsh Roman Catholic critic Stunica to produce a Greek manuscript that contained the passage. If Stunica could find such a manuscript, Erasmus would include the verse in his third edition. In time Stunica produced a manuscript containing the stated text—Codex Montfortianus. Keeping his word, Erasmus included 1 John 5:7, and it became a permanent part of the printed Greek text and ultimately part of the English New Testament, including Tyndale's translation, all sixteenth-century English translations, and the King James Version of 1611.[8]

When I found myself the owner of a 1516 Erasmus Greek New Testament, my curiosity piqued regarding the inclusion of this verse. Nowhere had I read or heard that *Codex Montfortianus* had ever been examined to verify if it had been altered in any way, perhaps at the hands of Stunica himself. As I researched I discovered that the manuscript dated to around 1520. Some scholars suggest commentary and text were so incomplete that the task of producing an accurate rendering was almost impossible. Ever resourceful, Erasmus translated portions of Revelation (22:16–21) from the Latin Vulgate back into Greek.

Because of his limited sources, Erasmus's work included incomplete and questionable texts; several scattered throughout the New Testament appear to be translations from the Latin. This is probably the case in Acts 9:5–6 where Erasmus's English translation reads, "It is hard for thee to kick against the pricks, and he, trembling and astonished, said, Lord, What wilt thou

the possibility that Franciscan Friar Roy had translated the reading back into the Greek from the Latin Vulgate. Was it possible Stunica had the manuscript prepared for Erasmus? The Complutensian Polyglot does include the 1 John 5:7 reading in a slightly different form, and it was included in a 1576 Luther Frankfurt edition and in some Wittenberg editions until 1596. But no other Greek manuscripts have come to light that include the reading.

Could an examination of *Codex Montfortianus* solve the mystery? I had to see for myself.

The manuscript was housed at Trinity College in Dublin, and my adrenalin pumped as I maneuvered through the city's cobbled streets. The atmosphere of the college was all I hoped it would be: a stately entrance, long antique tables, and rooms exuding antiquity. I approached the librarian and presented my credentials as a legitimate student of the New Testament. Not only did the research assistants grant me access to the manuscript I sought, they also allowed me into the private antiquities room.

The assistant set the manuscript on the table in front of me. Putting on my cotton gloves, I took a deep breath. The answer to my question would be revealed with a few careful turns of pages.

I was surprised to discover the leaves were in good condition for a book over 480 years old, but the beginning pages were faded. Slowly, surely, I found the page I'd traveled so far to examine. Did the handwriting reveal any attempt to insert the verse from the Latin Vulgate? No! Nothing in the handwriting indicated any type of insertion. The verse showed no line variation, no change in ink color or penmanship. In fact, the whole page appeared to have been copied without errors. I saw no evidence of textual tampering whatsoever. Now I knew! [9]

have me to do? And the Lord said unto him . . ." (KJV).[10] This reading occurs in the Latin but not in the Greek manuscript used by Erasmus. In his annotations accompanying this 1516 edition, Erasmus confesses this phrase is not in the Greek codex he is using, and yet he includes it entirely.[11] It may surprise or even disturb some Protestants to know that such a quotable passage as Acts 9:5–6 was taken from the Roman Catholic Latin Vulgate.

Erasmus's Greek New Testament met with mixed reviews. Some received the work with enthusiasm while others condemned him for taking liberties with the Latin Vulgate. Erasmus's publication of a Latin New Testament side

Displayed are Greek New Testaments that followed the *Textus Receptus*. Open in front is a 1551 Stephanus with 1550 Stephanus sitting on the open page. In the back from left to right: 1598 Beza, 1516 Erasmus, 1589 Beza, and 1565 Beza, and 1528 Pagninus Latin (no significance here but first to have verse divisions in margins). Photo: M. Brake.

by side with the Greek was viewed as a direct assault against the venerated Vulgate. Had he published the Vulgate New Testament instead of his own translation, his critics may have accepted his work more readily. Erasmus's first 1516 edition did not include the famous *Comma Johanneum* passage that cites the three heavenly witnesses in 1 John 5:7. His critics viewed this with suspicion as well because the reading appears in the Vulgate. Erasmus's most vocal critic was Lopez de Stunica, the prime editor of the Complutensian Polyglot New Testament, who especially insisted on the inclusion of 1 John 5:7. Many of Stunica's criticisms were legitimate, and he called into question editorial errors he believed needed correction, but many of Erasmus's other critics accused him of heresy without providing any constructive criticism.

Aware of the weaknesses in his edited New Testament, Erasmus quickly produced revisions. According to scholars, Erasmus's third edition of 1522 differed from his preceding editions in 118 places. Many of these changes corrected his Latin translations into Greek.[12] His fourth edition of 1527 shows evidence that it consulted the Complutensian Polyglot. In 1535 another edition was printed, but it varied in only five places from the 1527 version.

By the time Erasmus produced his 1535 edition, Christianity was far more concerned with theology than with textual criticism or analysis. The text was well established, and no one cared to emend it. The world was contending with the struggles of the Reformation and was less focused on the investigation of textual purity, so manuscript authority went unchallenged for many years.

During the Reformation, Martin Luther used Erasmus's 1519 second edition to produce his translation into the vernacular German language. English Reformer William Tyndale, on the other hand, used Erasmus's famous third edition in the production of the first English printed translation of the New Testament. Even though eighteenth-century textual critics began to question it, the text of Erasmus (*Textus Receptus*) remained the dominant text until 1881.

The King James translators used the 1588–89 or 1598 Beza New Testaments,[13] which were essentially the same as Erasmus's third edition (1522), the 1550 Stephanus, the 1565 Beza, and the 1633 Elzevir editions. Darlow and Moule, famous for their cataloging of printed English Bibles, mention that the 1598 Beza edition differs from the 1550 Stephanus third edition in forty-nine passages and from the 1588–89 Beza edition two times. They also suggest, but without documenting examples, that "No other Greek Testament agrees so closely with the text which underlies the English New Testament in the King James Bible."[14]

Stephanus and Beza Greek Texts

During this time, however, printed Greek New Testaments remained popular. In 1546 and 1549 Robert Stephanus printed two small editions of the Greek New Testament based upon both Erasmus and the Complutensian. His testament was not a critical edition, which is one that compares the text with other manuscripts, but both of his early editions (along with Colinaeus's edition completed in Paris in 1534) noted minor variant readings. This opened the door for future critical examination. In 1550 Stephanus issued a beautiful royal folio that relied almost exclusively on Erasmus, shifting acknowledgment of Complutensian readings to the margins. As a result, Erasmus's text took precedence, and Stephanus's popular 1550 folio quickly became the standard text.

The annotations to his Bibles in French and Latin provoked severe attacks; consequently, sometime after the publication of his folio edition, Stephanus secretly fled Paris for Geneva, where he published a small edition using verse divisions in 1551. The story is related that as he escaped on horseback over miles of rough terrain, he placed a mark in the text every time the horse bounced. These marks became verse divisions. This story accounts for the fact that verse divisions sometimes seem to be placed arbitrarily rather methodically or thematically. A more likely explanation, however, is that verse divisions were inserted for convenient reference in light of Stephanus's plan to publish a concordance, as well as the ease in comparing the three columns published in Stephanus's Greek text edition of 1551 (the Latin Vulgate, Erasmus's own Latin text, and the Greek).[15]

Robert Stephanus's prominence as a printer assured the acceptance and dominance of Erasmus's text for the next several generations, especially in England. Later it came to be known as the aforementioned *Textus Receptus* (1633).

French and other European printers recognized the business benefits of printing the Greek New Testament and entered the market. Jean Crispin reprinted Stephanus's 1550 folio in Geneva in 1553, altering Stephanus's folio in only five or six minor places. He also printed the variant readings of the 1550 edition without acknowledging their sources. William Whittingham, brother-in-law of John Calvin, used either Stephanus's or Crispin's edition in what is now the famous 1557 Geneva New Testament, the first English version to use verse divisions.[16]

It was only a matter of time before an edition of the Greek New Testament captured the minds of scholars and theologians. Theodore Beza, Calvin's successor as leader of the Calvinist tradition in Geneva, published five major editions of the Greek New Testament (1565, 1582, 1589, 1598, and 1642) and several additional minor editions. Beza had access to the famous *Codex Cantabrigiensis* (more popularly known as Beza) and *Codex Claromontanus*. But he cited them in his marginal notes rather than in the text itself, which was essentially the text of Stephanus. Occasional departures were not made on the basis of textual authority but were a reflection of arbitrary choices and Beza's theological persuasion. Luke 2:22 reads: "And when the days of *her* purification according to the Law of Moses were accomplished" (emphasis added). Very little manuscript evidence exists for *her* in Greek or Latin.[17] The correct reading from the manuscript evidence is *their*. Beza chose *her* from the Complutensian Polyglot. Unfortunately, the reading of *her* found its way into the King James Version as well.[18] This word choice suggests that the true *Textus Receptus* is not the Stephanus edition of 1550 but the text of Theodore Beza. In any case, theologians and New Testament scholars now had Greek texts from which to study and teach.

> The impact of Beza's various editions can be measured by their popularity among Protestants during his lifetime.

The impact of Beza's various editions can be measured by their popularity among Protestants during his lifetime. His work cemented the acceptance of the text first published by Erasmus, resulting in its unchallenged position among scholars and the clergy. The Beza edition—either 1589 or possibly

1598—became the Greek text used by the translators of the 1611 King James Bible.

John Eadie, a nineteenth-century biblical scholar, suggests the King James translators were free to choose from various editions of the Greek New Testament and even from the Latin Vulgate. He believes they used the 1589 Beza edition but were also free to use Stephanus's folio of 1550.[19] In eighty-one places the translators agreed with Beza over Stephanus, in twenty-one places they agreed with Stephanus over Beza, and in twenty-nine places they used Erasmus, the Vulgate, or the Complutensian Polyglot. When they could not decide, they provided the alternative reading in the margin.[20] By the time the King James translators began their historic task, Erasmus's basic text with all its faults (and the slight variations that would come in the editions of Stephanus and Beza) was firmly entrenched as the standard Greek New Testament text. The following chart identifies selected textual New Testament readings preferred by the translators.

Text	KJV 1611	Beza Greek Text 1589	Stephanus 1550
Matthew 21:7	"they set him thereon"	"they set him thereon" (*epekathisan epano*)	"he sat thereon (cloaks)" (*epekathisen epano*)
Mark 9:40	"he that is not against us"	"he that is not against us" (*humon*)	"he that is not against you" (*hamon*)
Luke 2:38	"Jerusalem" Margin: "or, Israel"	"Jerusalem" Note: "or, Israel"	"Jerusalem" Margin: "or, Israel" after Beza's note
Romans 7:6	"*That* being dead wherein"	"or, being dead to that" (*apothanontos*)	"or being dead to that" (*apothanontes*)
Romans 8:11	"by his spirit that dwelleth in you" Margin: "Or, because of his spirit"	"because his spirit indwelling in you" (*enoikountos*)	"through his indwelling spirit" (*enoikoun*)

Among seminarians, Erasmus's, Stephanus's, and Beza's texts are commonly understood to be what is signified by the term *Textus Receptus*. Bonaventure Elzevir and his nephew Abraham Elzevir (sometimes erroneously referred to as brothers), printers in the Netherlands, initiated the term *Textus Receptus* in the second edition of their small publication of 1633. In the introduction they declared the text they were printing was the "universally accepted text free of alterations and corruptions" (*"Textum ergo habes, nunc ab omnibus receptum"*). These enterprising printers were not as concerned with the purity of the text as they were with the marketability of a self-described universally recognized text. They recognized the advantage of promoting their product as superior over other texts. Subsequently, the term *Textus Receptus* attached itself to this text, which was basically a close reprint of Beza's 1565 edition, and that term still applies today.

The Elzevirs were interested in the commercialization of the Greek text; however, they were also dedicated to producing a first-rate product. Their efforts are evidenced in their first edition of 1624. This volume was not only beautifully printed, but it also standardized the wording of the text that had fluctuated in preceding editions. Because of the work produced in the Elzevir editions, the biblical text remained consistent for a hundred years without being exposed to further alterations.

The Post–King James Greek Text Comes under the Scholars' Scalpel

After three hundred years of dominance, would anyone challenge the authority of the *Textus Receptus*? In 1831 German professor Karl Lachmann took up the challenge when he published a small edition of the New Testament that dared to abandon the *Textus Receptus*. The only indication of Lachmann's choice was a small section at the end of the work where he listed the places he had abandoned the *Textus Receptus* and the alternate readings he had inserted. Some speculate that his lack of notice regarding his choice indicates his awareness of the unpopularity of his undertaking. His second edition (1842) explains his theory and rationale for the textual alterations and justification for his alternate readings. Few took his work seriously. Because Lachmann had not provided explanations, critics wondered what text he had followed. If they had analyzed his work, they would have discovered that he followed a variety of New Testament printed texts, not any single edition. [21]

Lachmann set aside the printed text that had been followed since Erasmus. He wished to print the Greek New Testament in a form that represented the transmission of the majority of the most ancient documents available. He believed recreating a first-century text was impossible, so instead he attempted to produce a text that would date to about the fourth century rather than the text as it came from the pen of the apostles.

Two men influenced the church's ultimate departure from the Greek text used by the King James translators.[22] In 1881 B. F. Westcott and F. J. A. Hort published a two-volume work culminating a twenty-eight-year project. They produced a text using the sources and methodologies developed by their predecessors, Lachmann, Griesbach, and Tischendorf. Although Westcott and Hort's text is considered a critical text, they did very little collating and editing of manuscripts, instead relying heavily on *Codex Vaticanus*. Volume one of their work consists of their critical text without a critical apparatus (information at the bottom of a page or in a margin that identifies variant readings among the extant Greek New Testament manuscripts). Volume two includes an introduction and explanation of their theory of textual criticism.[23]

The Greek text had finally reached a state that prepared the way for departure from the King James Version and the introduction of modern translations. Westcott and Hort's major contribution was their development of the history of the early transmission of the New Testament text. They believed they could arrive at the apostles' original written text through examination of all extant witnesses. They classified all manuscripts into various families; family authority was far more important than numbers of manuscripts supporting any particular reading. According to Westcott and Hort, the primary family was the neutral text best represented by *Codex Vaticanus*.

History sometimes demonstrates that a failure can be a success. Such was the case when Hermann von Soden (1852–1914) produced a valuable textual-critical work in 1902–13 often referred to as "a magnificent failure."[24]

Do Differences in Greek Texts Affect Meaning?

Many scholars acknowledge that the variances in readings among extant manuscripts make very little difference in Bible doctrine. Passages do exist, however, in which a particular reading does influence exegetical meaning. One such instance is the reading of 1 Corinthians 15:51, "Behold, I tell you a mystery: We shall not all sleep, but we shall all be changed." *Vaticanus* (Alexandrian family) and the vast majority of Greek texts (including the Byzantine family) read as above. But *Sinaiticus* and a few other manuscripts (A, C, F, and G) read, "We shall all sleep, but we shall not all be changed." Beza (D) adds to the variants: "We shall rise but not all be changed." Manuscript P 46 reads, "We shall not all sleep nor shall we all be changed." The Western text (Vulgate and others) reads, "We all will rise but we shall not all be changed." The differences in each of the readings points to a divergent doctrinal view. The difficulty arises when the textual evidence is not decisive. How much theology influences the decision on the reading? Which text is best? This is where all your hermeneutical and textual critical principles must be applied.

Von Soden sent a number of research students and scholars to libraries in Europe and the Near East to examine a great number of previously unexamined partial or complete manuscripts. Upon investigating the documents, von Soden devised a new system of nomenclature to designate the age, contents, and characteristics of each manuscript. He identified three text-types as follows.

1. The Koine (K) type was produced by Lucian of Antioch (d. AD 312) and became the text of the Byzantine Church.
2. The Hesychius (H) text-type represented the Egyptian text as in *Vaticanus* (B) and *Sinaiticus* (א). This is the text-type used by Westcott and Hort and by most modern textual critics.
3. The Jerusalem (I) text-type was derived from Eusebius of Caesarea (c. 263–339), the bishop of Caesarea in Philippi and a textual critic. This was the text von Soden believed was his greatest contribution, but it is generally not accepted today.

In von Soden's view, the three text-types originated in a lost archetype that was corrupted by the second-century theologian Marcion, who was excommunicated by the early Christian church as a heretic. If Marcion's corruptions could be eliminated, the original text could be discovered. Scholars today have found von Soden's theory inadequate.[25] But his work is far from a failure; its research unearthed an enormous number of readings supporting the *Textus Receptus* text-type and the value of the text underlying the King James translation. Von Soden's work provides a primary source for collating many of the known manuscripts of this family.

The Greek text was of no concern to the common, churchgoing person in Britain; the nuances of original languages held significance only for translators who could read the ancient biblical texts and for the translators of the King James Version. Modern textual criticism did not significantly affect English Bibles until the Revised Version of 1881–85. Since that time textual criticism has been the wind in the storm as modern translators have argued for or against the dominance of modern versions over the King James Version and the Greek text on which it was based.

The Old Testament Texts of the King James Version

Tracing the textual support for the Old Testament books is a bit mysterious. The list of principles did not specify that any particular Hebrew or Septuagint edition be followed, but the Complutensian Polyglot with the Latin, Greek, and Hebrew would have been available to the translators. Modern textual criticism did not exist, and the variants among these versions were few and apparently of little consequence. The eighteenth-century textual critic F. H. A. Scrivener notes that the Complutensian sheds light on some passages.[26] The most popular Hebrew Old Testament editions of the time were the Pagninus (1528), Munster (1539), and Antwerp Polyglot, edited by Arias Montanus, which is an interlinear Latin translation of the Hebrew text (1572).

The Apocrypha and the King James Version

Translators prior to the King James Version had included the Apocrypha in their work.[27] But how would the controversial books fare in the new translation? It is clear from King James's own writings that he did not accept the Apocrypha.[28] Nevertheless, Anglican Archbishop Richard Bancroft made the decision to include the apocryphal books in the new version in spite of Puritan opposition and the king's opinion. Because they were not considered inspired by God, the translation in these books is much freer than the translation of the canonical books. In fact, the translation principle that each original word must have a direct English equivalent was abandoned on occasion.

According to the principles, the translators were to follow the Bishops' Bible except when the original languages demanded change. Lewis Lupton mentions that in Samuel Ward's report to the Synod of Dort he decided if there were discrepancies, the Septuagint should be followed.[29] Sources for the Septuagint could include the Basel Bible (1545 or 1550), the Complutensian Polyglot (1517), or the Aldine Bible (1518). Many Old Testament passages reference the Septuagint.

The Latin Bible also influenced the production of the Hebrew Bible. The Latin editions of the Hebrew Bible produced by Hebrew scholar Immanuel Tremellius and his son Francis Junius (originally published in 1575–79 and revised in 1590) were the latest and most important Latin versions during the era of King James. Marginal notes in the KJV reflect the use of Tremellius's Latin edition.[30] In addition to Latin, Hebrew, and Greek, J. Diodati printed an Italian translation in 1569, *Cassiodoro de Reyna*, and a Spanish version in 1569, and pastors in Geneva produced a French translation in 1587–88. As Westcott points out, "All these versions have an independent value, and when the King James revisers speak of their pains in consulting 'the Spanish, French, and Italian translators,' there can be no doubt that it is to these they refer."[31]

Modern Defenders of the Greek Text of the King James Version

Would abandoning the text underlying the King James Version—the *Textus Receptus*—bring about the demise of one of the world's greatest literary treasures? It would seem so. But in the late eighteenth century the *Textus Receptus* had its champions, as it does today.

While the following men defend the Greek text used by the King James translators, their theories of textual criticism, their data, reasons, and resultant text represent a spectrum of opinions on the issue.[32] Their text, however, is close to the text first published by Erasmus in 1516 that was used as the basis for the King James Version. Nevertheless, most textual critics supporting the basic text followed by the King James translation fall into one of the categories listed below.

> **John Burgon**: The textual theory of Burgon is linked to the doctrine of preservation. God inspired the Bible, and therefore he obligated himself to divinely preserve it. Burgon believed God did this through the Byzantine family of manuscripts. Since the Alexandrian family was not a part of the manuscript tradition until the nineteenth century, Burgon reasons the great Reformation was built on the *Textus Receptus*.

Zane Hodges, Arthur Farstad: The Majority Text represents the best theory because it is the only way to account for the vast majority of extant manuscripts. Under normal transmission processes, this also is the only way to account for the dominance of the Byzantine text. Textual critical practice also relies on majority reading support.

Maurice Robinson, William Pierpont: As stated by William McBrayer, "The 'Byzantine Textform' best represents the text of the early church. The emphasis in textual criticism is the history of the transmission of the text. The result of the transmission process produced a textform that is represented in the vast number of surviving Greek manuscripts. This view stresses that the overwhelming spread and dominance of the Byzantine text suggests it is closest to the original New Testament. The sharing of manuscripts between churches resulted in a gradual practice of correcting the local texts with manuscripts that were circulating among churches. This kind of comparison and correction restored the original autographs of the New Testament and eliminated scribal alterations."[33]

Harry Sturz: The Greek manuscripts of the Byzantine family must at least at times be considered for preserving the New Testament. Sturz attempted to refute

On top of the stack on the left side is the first Greek New Testament in octavo (1524), published by Cephaleus in Strassburg. Standing in the white vellum binding with red label is the first edition of Erasmus's Greek New Testament (1516). In white on the far right is the first edition of Erasmus's *Annotations* (1516). The book on top of the stack on the left side in white vellum depicts the 1633 *Textus Receptus* by Elzevir.   Photo: M. Brake.

the Westcott-Hort claim that distinctive Byzantine readings were not found in the early manuscripts of *Vaticanus* and *Sinaiticus* or in the early fathers, which was proof of the lateness of the Byzantine text, making it an inferior text.[34] Papyri supply evidence that distinctive Byzantine readings were not created in the fourth century but were in existence before the end of the second century, and therefore Byzantine readings merit consideration.

The King James translators of the early seventeenth century worked during a pre–textual-critical age. Textual variants played a minor role in their work. They took the printed Greek texts before them, assumed they were inspired, and exercised their gifts, producing a Bible version that was as accurate as humanly possible. Their efforts resulted in a version that has withstood not only the scrutiny of scholarship but also the test of time.

7

Rejection, Rewriting, and Revision

The Process of Translation

Michael Rabbett strode back and forth in the Lady Chapel of Westminster Abbey, hands clasped behind him, eyes following the inlaid detail of the Cosmati marble beneath his feet. Each step clicked against the stone floor louder than the first. "How dare the bishop not accept my translation in Romans 6. The wording is certainly better than the outdated expressions in the Bishops' Bible."

Rabbett glanced above him to the niches in the walls where the statues of ninety-five saints gazed down upon those who gathered to worship. Over the past months the Lady Chapel had become Michael Rabbett's favored place to pace out political frustrations regarding his translation work for King James. And while the chapel's beauty was compelling, Rabbett had returned again and again to stand beneath the penetrating presence of the statues.

Focusing on the faces of the saints, he named them, and the anger ebbed from his body. Today, as most days, he needed to hear the silent sermon they preached. Each of the ninety-five had struggled and carried sorrow, and all had been devoted. Passion for truth drove them.

Morning devotions called. The translation process was difficult, but it must move forward. He returned to his work—committed again to bring his best efforts and no less.

The Translation Process

While the above illustration is fictional, it is based on historical data. The King James translators undoubtedly experienced tensions as people of differing doctrinal, economic, and social backgrounds came together to pursue a shared goal. The translation process called for each man to work individually to make improvements to the Bishops' Bible and then pass his revisions on to others for approval or adjustment. The process ensured no translator could claim any particular reading as his own. The project was truly a team effort.

The intricate, labor-intensive work could not be executed quickly. Translators struggled to fulfill the obligations of their ministries, families, and professions. Yet they accepted the additional work, sometimes without reward.

With Archbishop Bancroft's principles established, the translators selected, the printer chosen, and the official approval given, work on the King James Version began in 1604. The first rule established for the translators required that they use the 1602 Bishops' Bible as their guide. According to Bible historian Lewis Lupton (and supported probably in part by a Bodleian manuscript), the king's printer, Robert Barker, made forty copies of the 1602 Folio Bishops' Bible for distribution to the translation teams. While it is difficult to substantiate the actual Bishops' Bibles that were available, Lupton refers to a record of unknown origin. He acknowledges the lack of support but believes it to be true. He writes:

> It is recorded, we know not where, that Robert Barker, the king's printer, printed forty "Church Bibles," that is folio sized Bishops' Bibles of his latest 1602 edition, for the six companies of translators. They were delivered unbound in quires that is to say in sections of twenty-four folio sheets folded once, each containing four pages of type. Thus when a translator was at work, whether alone or with others, his basic tools were his folio sheets, 20″x15″ (50x37cm) on which, no doubt, alterations were made.[1]

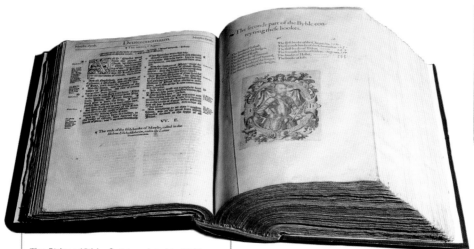

The Bishops' Bible, first translated in 1568, was supported by Anglican Church clergy. Here it is opened to a portrait of the Earl of Leicester, Queen Elizabeth's favorite loyal subject. Photo: M. Brake.

Historians speculate that one of the forty copies served as the manuscript eventually sent to the printers. Perhaps each company used three of the manuscripts to prepare the text for the general committee of twelve (two translators from each of the six companies); the remaining twenty-two copies became working copies for the six companies. Some of the surviving working copies were bound in a Bishops' Bible in the Bodleian Library labeled as Bibl. Eng. 1602 b.I.[2]

According to scholars, in the task of making a good translation better, the translators deemed a large percentage of the wording in the Bishops' Bible acceptable. The translators also consulted the Geneva Bible (the first complete Bible translated from the Hebrew Old Testament), the Tyndale New Testament, the Matthew's Bible, the Great Bible, and the Coverdale Bible.[3] The Roman Catholic Rheims edition influenced the King James Version translators as well, but not in a significant percentage.[4] As might be expected, the Latin and Hebrew Bibles of Munster and Pagninus were available as references, and the 1589 and 1598 editions of Beza's Greek New Testament[5] were the primary sources for the New Testament translation. Since only two alternate readings exist between them, it is difficult to determine which one was used. The King James translators, however, faced an enormous task since Hebrew studies had advanced considerably from the time earlier translations had been completed.

Ward Allen and Edward Jacobs's study of an annotated Bishops' Bible found in the Bodleian Library gives a glimpse into the details of the translation process. Each scholar worked alone on assigned portions of Scripture, recording comments and textual changes on the Bishops' Bible sheets. The translators within each company met weekly to compare findings. Once the books were completed, they were submitted to other groups for further comment. Outside specialists were also consulted to offer suggestions. This routine was in place from 1604 to 1608. When the work was complete, the king called for the general committee of twelve, composed of two translators from each of the six companies, to assemble at Stationers' Hall in London in 1609. This committee made final decisions on the revisions.

Modern scholars' interest in the methodologies and thought processes of the King James translators was reinvigorated when in 1858 Gustavus Paine found "Notes by John Bois" in the Bodleian Library. The work was later published by Ward Allen.[6] Of the twelve representatives who edited the final copy, only Bois, Andrew Downes, and John Harmer are known. Bois's notes reveal the committee's struggle and conscientious attempt to discuss meanings, offer alternatives, review grammatical differences, and compare words with their roots.[7] Bois's notes provide examples of the translators' specific choices: At 1 Corinthians 13:11 Bois suggests, "I understood, I cared as a child, I had a child's mind, I imagined as a child, I was affected as a child." The King James Version reads, "I spake as a child, I understood as a child, I thought as a child."[8] At Hebrews 11:1 Bois reads, "Is a most sure warrant of things, is a being of things hoped for, a discovery, a demonstration of things that are not seen." The KJV uses, "Now faith is the substance of things hoped for, the evidence of things not seen."

The principles used for selecting one individual reading over another by the revisers are not known. But the final determinations on wording suggest the original companies arrived at the best possible renderings. Although Bois fulfilled his responsibility to challenge, question, and offer alternative readings, in most cases he agreed with the companies' original suggestions. When Bois offered suggestions that strayed from the companies' findings, his suggestions, in most cases, were not adopted in the final revision. In at least one verse the revisers' alternate reading was inserted: in 2 Corinthians 7:1 the term suggested by Bois, "perfecting holiness," was retained in the King James Version. Since Bancroft's principles required that the translators retain

Bishops' Bible readings whenever possible, it stands to reason that few individual or creative readings were deemed acceptable.

After the translators invested four years in the production of the initial draft (1604–8), the general committee spent an additional nine months completing revisions of the second draft. Then Miles Smith and Thomas Bilson added finishing touches. Scholars attribute Bilson (probably along with Smith) with contributing new chapter titles and page headings. In deference to the king, Bilson penned the dedication, "To the most high and mighty Prince James." Smith wrote the preface, "The Translators to the Reader," which includes Scripture quotations from the Geneva Bible that reflect his Puritan tendencies. Smith and Bilson's editorial work completed the task of the King James Version.

Soon thereafter, however, clouds of controversy gathered on the horizon. After Bilson and Smith completed their final task as editors, translators complained that Bancroft had made an additional fourteen changes to the text. While these changes are undocumented, one suggested alteration in

The Challenge of Reaching Back

Language is best acquired through induction into the culture and exposure to the people who speak the language. Native language speakers provide insight into figures of speech, common expressions, strange word order, and often unreasonable language usage. Some experts suggest that in order to become truly bilingual one must be immersed in the language before reaching the age of twelve.

The King James linguists faced a barrier in their study of biblical languages: they were sixteen hundred years removed from the Greek language used during the time of the New Testament and more than two thousand years removed from the Hebrew of the Old Testament. Much information regarding biblical culture had been lost over this period of time. In spite of the translators' credentials, this vast distance from the original languages limited their perspective and made the translation of ancient Greek and Hebrew that much more challenging.

Acts 1:20 seems to change the wording of a text that associates the office of bishop with the curse placed on Judas—a thought that would have been beyond distasteful to Smith and Bilson.[9]

The translators had completed their work, but a central question remained: Would their years of work on the King James Version be accepted by the general public if they struggled to accept it among themselves?

Features and Curiosities

One curious feature of the King James Version is its use of paragraph markers and commas. Paragraph markers are distributed throughout the Old Testament and continue through the New Testament. In the book of Psalms, for example, the chapter titles include large beginning capital markers, but small paragraph markers appear where the italicized title indicates that words have been used in the text that do not appear in the Hebrew. Paragraph markers in the New Testament appear to be placed randomly in the text. They do not always follow the chapter titles but sometimes correspond to the numbered verses in the title. They end at Acts 20:36. The logical question the modern reader might ask is why they stop at the end of that passage. Was their placement the responsibility of the editors or the printer? The Second Oxford Company translated Matthew through Acts and Revelation, but because the book of Revelation includes no paragraph markers, their placement seems to have been the responsibility of the printers.

The text of the Old and New Testaments in the King James is heavily peppered with commas. For example, what appears to modern readers to be an excessive use of commas can be seen in a passage from Isaiah 9:6.

> And his name shall be called
> Wonderful, Counselor,
> The Mighty God,
> The Everlasting Father,
> The Prince of Peace.

In this passage, the comma does not belong after "Wonderful." On the other hand, a missing comma causes some ambiguity in Luke 23:32, "And there were also two other malefactors led with him, to bee put to death." A comma belongs after "two other," perhaps clarifying that only two of the three parties present were malefactors; Jesus was innocent. In verse 33 the meaning is made clear when the passage goes on to say, "There they crucified him [Jesus], and the malefactors." What appears today to be an excessive use of commas was common in the seventeenth century. Even Shakespeare was guilty of what we in the twenty-first century would view as overuse.

Culturally related wordings also appear in the King James Version that reflect the time gap between seventeenth-

The Bishops' Bible of 1602 (left) and the Geneva Bible of 1560 (center) were highly influential in the creation of the King James Version, while the Rheims (right) played only a minor role.

Photo: A. May.

century and modern readers. For instance, Matthew 16:13 reads, "Whom do men say that I, the Son of man, am?" A preferred reading today is, "Who do people say the Son of Man is?"

The Influence of the Latin Vulgate and the Geneva Bible

The Latin Vulgate played a surprisingly important role in the King James Version. Sixteenth-century debates between Gregory Martin (a Roman Catholic) and William Fulke (a fiery Protestant) had brought attention to the importance of the Latin Vulgate even before the King James Version was initiated.[10] English translations in the sixteenth century were based on Erasmus's and

Beza's Greek texts. By the seventeenth century, Greek and Hebrew were well entrenched in the schools of England and Europe, but Latin studies occupied much of the curriculum of theological schools.[11] Continued interest in Latin assured that the King James Version translators would consult the Rheims edition of the Roman Catholic Latin Vulgate and other Latin versions.

Despite King James's rule that the Bishops' Bible be the guiding English translation, the Geneva Bible's popularity among the laity and even some of the translators guaranteed its influence as well as the influence of the Rheims New Testament. Several phrases appear to be taken from the Geneva New Testament for the King James translation of the Sermon on the Mount (the spellings within versions vary slightly with different printings):

Text	KJV	Geneva
Matthew 5:11	Blessed are ye, when *men* shall reuile you, and persecute *you*, and shal say all manner of euill against you falsly for my sake.	Blessed shall ye be when men reuile you, and persecute you, and say all maner of euill against you for my sake, falsely.
Matthew 5:13	Yee are the salt of the earth: but if the salt haue lost his sauour, wherewith shall it bee salted? It is thenceforth good for nothing, but to be cast out, and to be troden vnder foote of men.	Ye are the salt of the earth: but if the salt haue lost his sauour, wherewith shall it be salted? It is thenceforth good for nothing, but to be cast out, and to be troden vnder foote of men.
Matthew 5:39	But I say vnto you, that yee resist not euill: but whosoeuer shall smite thee on thy right cheeke, turne to him the other also.	But I say vnto you, Resist not euill: but whosoeuer shall smite thee on thy right cheeke, turne to him the other also.
Matthew 6:7	But when yee pray, vse not vaine repetitions, as the heathen *doe*. For they thinke that they shall be heard for their much speaking.	Also when ye pray, vse no vaine repetitions as the Heathen: for they thinke to be heard for their much babbling.
Matthew 6:19	Lay not vp for your selues treasures vpon earth, where moth and rust doth corrupt, and where theeues breake thorow and steale.	Lay not vp treasures for your selues vpon the earth, where the mothe and canker corrupt, and where theeues digge through and steale.

The King James Version also seems to reflect the Rheims in the same passage:

A Visual History of the King James Bible

Text	KJV	Rheims
Matthew 5:18	For verily I say vnto you, Till heauen and earth passe, one iote or one title, shall in no wise passe from the law, till all be fulfilled.	For amen I say unto you, till heaven and earth pass, one jot, or one tittle shall not pass of the law, till all be fulfilled.
Matthew 5:25	Agree with thine aduersarie quickly, whiles thou art in the way with him: least at any time the aduersarie deliuer thee to the iudge, and the iudge deliuer thee to the officer, and thou be cast into prison.	Be at agreement with thy adversary betimes, whilst thou art in the way with him: lest perhaps the adversary deliver thee to the judge, and the judge deliver thee to the officer, and thou be cast into prison.
Matthew 5:47	And if yee salute your brethren only, what do you more *than others*? Doe not euen the Publicane so?	And if you salute your brethren only, what do you more? do not also the heathens this?
Matthew 6:2	Therefore, when thou doest *thine* almes, doe not sound a trumpet before thee, as the hypocrites doe, in the Synagogues, and in the streetes, that they may haue glory of men. Verily, I say vnto you, they haue their reward.	Therefore when thou dost an alms-deed, sound not a trumpet before thee, as the hypocrites do in the synagogues and in the streets, that they may be honoured by men. Amen I say to you, they have received their reward.

In some passages the King James Version emends the Bishops' version in favor of the Geneva or Rheims, as illustrated in the following chart:

Text	KJV	Bishops'	Geneva	Rheims
2 Corinthians 5:13	For whether wee bee besides ourselues, *it is* to God: or whether we bee sober, *it is* for your cause.	For yf we be to feruent, to God are we to feruent: Or yf we kepe measure, for your cause kepe we measure.	For whether we be out of our wit, we are it to God: or whether we be in our right minde, we are it vnto you.	For whether we be transported in mind, it is to God; or whether we be sober, it is for you.
Galatians 6:1	Brethren, if a man bee ouertaken in a fault, yee which are spirituall, restore such a one in the spirit of meeknesse; considering thy selfe, least thou also be tempted.	Brethren, yf a man be taken in any fault, ye which are spiritual restore such a one in the spirite of mekenes, consideryng thy selfe, lest thou also be tempted.	Brethren, if a man be suddenly taken in any offence, ye which are spiritual, restore such one with the spirit of meekenes, considering thy selfe, least thou also be tempted.	Brethren, and if a man be overtaken in any fault, you, who are spiritual, instruct such a one in the spirit of meekness, considering thyself, lest thou also be tempted.

Text	KJV	Bishops'	Geneva	Rheims
1 Timothy 6:15	Which in his times he shall shew, *who is* the blessed, and onely Potentate, the King of kings, and Lord of lords.	Which in his tymes he shall shewe that is blessed and prince only, the kyng of kynges, and Lorde of Lordes.	Which in due time hee shall shewe, that is blessed and Prince onely, the King of Kings and Lord of Lordes.	Which in his times he shall shew who is the Blessed and only Mighty, the King of kings, and Lord of lords.
Hebrews 4:11	Let vs labour therefore to enter into that rest, lest any man fall after the same example of vnbeleefe.	Let vs studie therefore to enter into that rest, lest any man fall after the same ensample of disobedience.	Let vs studie therefore to enter into that rest, lest any man fall after the same ensample of disobedience.	Let us hasten therefore to enter into that rest; lest any man fall into the same example of unbelief.
2 Peter 1:1	Simon Peter, a seruant and an Apostle of Iesus Christ, to them that haue obtained like precious Faith with vs through the righteousnes of God and our Sauiour Iesus Christ.	Simon Peter, a seruant and an Apostle of Iesus Christe, to them which haue obteined lyke precious faith with vs, thorowe the ryghteousnes of our god and sauiour Iesus Christe.	Simon Peter a seruant and an Apostle of Iesus Christ, to you which haue obteined like precious faith with vs by the righteousnesse of our God and Sauiour Iesus Christ.	Simon Peter, servant and apostle of Jesus Christ, to them that have obtained equal faith with us in the justice of our God and Saviour Jesus Christ.

The translation work of the King James Version required a monumental effort and meticulous attention to detail. The first draft required nearly four years and the second draft an additional nine months. Little did the translators know that orchestrating the details of printing would delay the completion of the project two more years.

8

Masterpiece from the Mayhem

The King's Bible Goes to Press

S ilence hovered over London's deserted, misty streets. Neighborhood residents burrowed deep in their beds enjoying the luxury of the last hour before dawn, unaware of the furious activity a few doors down the street. Inside Northumberland House, typesetters loaded presses while members of the printers' guild turned the huge handles that pressed plates and paper to the inked typesets. As sheets came off the printing presses, large folio pages were quickly hung to dry on ropes stretched from wall to wall.

Pages Roll off the Presses

Like most citizens enmeshed in the activities of daily life, London residents were unconcerned about the king's printing project. Over the next four centuries, however, nearly every household in the English-speaking world came to possess a copy of this printed book. Today children memorize it; pastors quote it at weddings and cite it at funerals; its words resound from pulpits on a global scale. Presidents swear their allegiance on it, and courts use it as the standard for truthfulness. Its language has woven its way into common expressions, becoming part of the fabric of society. The King James Bible

not only changed Bible reading but influenced society for the next four hundred years.

Printing books was a formidable challenge in the seventeenth century. Today we enter manuscripts into computers and print on demand, but this was obviously not the case in the era of James I. Not only was the printing of a large folio Bible a massive undertaking, but the task required royal approval before production could be initiated. From the time of Henry VIII and the Great Bible, printers were required to gain royal sanction for printing and distribution, and this sanction was still necessary under the rule of King James I.

Christopher Barker began printing the Geneva Bible as early as 1576 when he used an imprint called "Tygers Head," based on the coat of arms of his patron, Sir Francis Walsingham.[1] The coat of arms appeared as decorative printers' initials placed in the Psalms of 1634 (Psalm 35, initial letter *P*; Psalm 1, initial letter *B*) and 1640 (Psalm 1, initial letter *B*). Christopher had also printed many editions of the Bishops' Bible. In 1589 he was named the queen's exclusive printer. After Christopher's death in 1599, the appointment passed on to his son Robert, who became the king's printer in 1603 when Elizabeth died and James I ascended the throne.

In 1609, having acquired the exclusive, royal authority to print Bibles, Robert Barker began work on the King James Version. Mystery surrounded the actual printing process. What manuscript copy was used? How many copies were printed? How many printing offices participated? How many printing presses were used? Who proofread the printed pages? How much did the King James Bible originally cost per copy? Unfortunately, history is reluctant to reveal the answers.

The Barker printing shop was located in the Northumberland House, Aldersgate, in London. It was later moved to the Hudson House in Black-friars when Barker's weakened financial position forced him to take three partners to share the expenses of the project: John Bill and John and Bonham Norton.[2] Acquiring the position of the queen's printer had come at a price. In 1610 Barker had paid 3,500 pounds for exclusive printing rights for the King James Version. Adjusting for inflation (which can be calculated in a number of

Christopher Barker (1529–99) and Robert Barker (d. 1645) dominated the printing business as the queen's and king's official printers. This painting depicts the site of their memorial at the location of their print shop.   Photo: Original art, L. Lupton.

different ways), this number is approximately equivalent to just over a million dollars today. An approximate figure for a print run of 20,000 copies (a reasonable estimate of the print run for the first edition KJV) bound in leather at 2011 prices would be $75 per copy multiplied by 20,000 copies, for a total cost of about $1.5 million dollars. However, some suggest only 1,500 copies were printed, a normal run of this nature. This would place the cost at a more reasonable estimate at $112,500, still a large sum by seventeenth-century standards.

> While printing could be risky and highly competitive, it could also be quite lucrative.

While printing could be risky and highly competitive, it could also be quite lucrative. A number of presses were in operation at the time. Lewis Lupton writes that in 1580 Anglican Archbishop Whitgift authorized an inventory documenting that Christopher Barker owned five presses. During that same period, twenty-three other licensed printers worked fifty-three presses.[3]

The printing began in 1611 and presented numerous challenges. Large folio editions bound in black leather were the norm for first-edition Bibles. Two large folio pages, each 17 x 11½ inches, were printed on one side and allowed to dry before the pages were printed on the reverse side. Some historians suggest the pages were printed on the verso or reverse side before the paper fully dried, which caused wrinkles and made alignment of the pages difficult.

Setting up the press was time consuming and labor intensive. Individual letters were molded and formed, then placed in *cases* with slots that held a single letter. For storage purposes, capital letters were placed in upper slots and small letters in the lower slots—thus the terms *uppercase* and *lowercase* letters. Each double page of the King James Version consisted of fifty-nine lines per column set in double columns with ruled margins. To produce a printed page, a printer turned a large handle connected to a huge screw, thereby lowering a heavy platen onto the paper. This motion pressed oil-based ink onto metal letters that had been set into and secured in a wood frame. In order to assure the best possible print quality, the printers' metal letters were discarded after approximately sixty uses.

The proofing process was tedious. Proofreaders compared the first copy that rolled off the press against the first page of the original manuscript; they then made corrections before the print run of that page began. Proofing may have been done orally, with one individual reading to another as the proofreaders focused on word and spelling accuracy. But standards of proofing were often inferior to modern standards and were influenced by human error, exhaustion, urgency, and the pressure for profit.

The format of the manuscript copy placed in Robert Barker's hands as the template for the 1611 King James Version remains shrouded in mystery. Three formats seem possible.

The first option is that the printer was given a handwritten manuscript of the complete text of the new translation. This possibility is supported by a 1660 pamphlet that circulated in London claiming that certain printers possessed a handwritten copy of the Holy Bible in English.[4] If this was the case, the manuscript copy of the King James Version has disappeared—possibly destroyed in the great fire in 1666. The London fire raged for several days, sweeping through London, engulfing hundreds of acres of land, destroying thousands of homes, nearly a hundred churches, and most of the business community. When it finally ran its course, little of London remained.

A second possibility is that the King James translators delivered a fully annotated version of the Bishops' Bible. Some scholars suggest a strong likelihood that Barker possessed printed pages or pre-set trays still in stock from the 1602 Bishops' Bible, which would have been similar to approximately 80 to 90 percent of the text of the King James Version. In this case the printer's work would have been easier since he could replace words and phrases in the existing Bishops' Bible typeset with the new changes rather than have to set entirely new print trays for the King James Version.

The translators' original manuscript may have been unusable because it was too messy. This is evidenced in a manuscript numbered Bishops' Bod 1602, which can be traced back to the translators and is sloppy and difficult to read. An indecipherable manuscript would have made it very difficult for the printer to typeset the manuscript correctly. And after the translators' careful attention to detail, the proofreaders' work would have been subjective—sometimes to the point of guesswork.

Biblical scholar David Norton suggests a third alternative: an original, compiled manuscript in final form may have never existed. If an annotated Bishops' Bible, rather than a compilation of the translators' work, served as the manuscript provided to the printer, then the first copy that came off the press was used as the *original* King James Version printer's copy and served as the template for all subsequent editions (i.e., 1613 folios and 1612 quartos and octavos). Translators Smith and Bilson may then have added editorial comments along with the chapter headings and page summaries.[5] This theory provides a possible accounting for the variances in the 1612 and 1613 editions, where both the "he" and "she" reading occurs in Ruth 3:15.

Scholars still debate the various theories regarding the method by which the translators' manuscript was passed on to the printers. But no matter the theory or weight of evidence behind it, no manuscript has yet surfaced that represents the translators' fully revised text for the King James Version. Unless history one day reveals new documentation, scholars, historians, and Bible students searching for a clear picture of the printing process for the King James Version will be disappointed.

Piecing Together the Printing Process

It is difficult to assess how many Bibles may have been printed in Barker's first run. In 1540 Henry VIII ordered a Great Bible placed in every church in England; and while the King James Version was not directly appointed to be read throughout the kingdom, it was authorized for reading in British churches—a fact that argues for the version's broad acceptance at least by Anglicans. Charles Ryrie suggests as many as 20,000 copies were printed.[6] Adam Nicolson, author of *God's Secretaries*, proposes that 20,000 copies of the 1540 Great Bible were printed at a cost of ten shillings each or twelve shillings if the copies were bound;[7] however, he is quick to point out that no record has been found establishing with certainty the number of copies of the KJV printed or the cost per copy. Barker's legendary financial difficulties, which led him to unhappy unions with business partners, seem to suggest that a first printing of 20,000 may be an excessive estimate. Since a new printing began soon after 1611, it is questionable that an initial run of 20,000 copies would have sold out that quickly. As mentioned earlier, a run of 1,500 may be more realistic. No organized attempt to destroy Bibles and Barker's printing of Geneva Bibles at the same time would argue for a smaller run than 20,000. After all, there are only about 150 copies that survived.[8] Yet in spite of Barker's financial struggles, he published a smaller, more conveniently sized quarto edition of the KJV in 1612, adding further mystery to the number of his first print run.

When modern scholars examine existing copies of 1611 King James Bibles, they find it challenging to reconstruct the exact printing and collation process. They have discovered that, among other things, reprinted pages (corrected pages) from one edition often appeared in later editions. But how did this occur? We do know that printers did not immediately bind books as they came off the press. Leftover pages were stored until the market demanded additional printed Bibles. Then when orders were received, individual pages were taken from shelves, collated, bound, and sold. Remaining pages from one edition were often bound with subsequent editions since the printers were more concerned with convenience than with maintaining a *pure* translation. To add to the confusion, print-shop formats of the period commonly set presses page-for-page. Barker often used formats that began and ended at exactly the same point: large, black-type folios (page folded once), Roman-type quartos (page folded twice), and Roman-type octavos (page folded three times). This practice allowed pages to be inserted into Bibles from one typeset run to another, creating a high risk for mixed copies—pages from one edition or corrected edition of the Bible inserted into another edition.

A second, seventeenth-century printing practice most likely accounts for at least some of the mixed readings scholars have identified. Proofreaders corrected pages as they came off the press, literally while the presses were still rolling; as a result, mixing corrected and uncorrected pages during the storing and collating stages was inevitable. And while the above-mentioned

When modern scholars examine existing copies of 1611 King James Bibles, they find it challenging to reconstruct the exact printing and collation process.

scenarios are undocumented and somewhat speculative, they are rooted in historical knowledge of printing practices of the day and provide an accounting for the mixed readings in both shorter passages and leaves (pages) of the folio editions of the King James Version.

Several additional complexities made matters even more intractable. Multiple editions of the Geneva Bible may have been in various stages of printing while the King James Version was being typeset and printed, exponentially increasing the possibility of mixing print runs. Paper jams, ink smears, and faulty workmanship were inevitable in the printing trade, and that produced inconsistent final numbers in individual-page print runs. Also, multiple presses most likely operated in multiple locations. If this was the case, how did Barker determine whose office was responsible for proofing and printing different portions of Scripture? Were multiple offices responsible for the same portions of Scripture? What system was orchestrated to implement consistency among multiple sites? And in a revealing observation that attests to the business pressures of Bible printing from the earliest days of the King James Version, Norton states that Barker often presold books before they were completely printed to pay for supplies and personnel costs. Thus it is impossible for us today to gain more than a clouded picture of what occurred during the 1611 printing.

Distinctions between "He" and "She"

One issue that has fascinated scholars for years is the inconsistency in wording between the so-called "He" and "She" editions of the King James. These terms have become synonymous with the first and second editions of the King James Version based upon the Ruth 3:15 reading: "And he went into the citie," found in one edition and, "And she went into the citie," found in the other. Scholars have generally determined that the *he* reading of Ruth 3:15 is the rendering of the first edition and the *she* reading is the rendering of the second edition.[9] The Bishops' Bible uses *she*, but surprisingly, both readings are supported based on underlying Hebrew manuscripts. Modern translations are divided on the reading: the New American Standard Bible reads *she*, while Today's New International Version reads *he*. One reason offered by scholars behind the two renderings in the Kings James is that the translators of the first edition mistakenly used the pronoun *he*.[10] When they discovered the error, they changed the wording to reflect the *she* reading of the Bishops' Bible. Later editions of the King James Version consistently render Ruth 3:15 as *she*.

The chart below identifies additional differences between the "He" and "She" editions of the 1611–13 King James Version.

Text	1611 "He Bible"	1611–13 "She Bible"
Exodus 14:10	The children of Israel lift up their eyes, and behold, the Egyptians marched after them, and they were sore afraid: and the children of Israel lift up their eyes, and behold, the Egyptians marched after them, and they were sore afraid: and the children of Israel cried out unto the LORD.	*The lines repeated were omitted in the "She" edition, but space was left on the following page so that the signature would read the same word for word.*
Exodus 38:11	hoopes	hooks
Leviticus 17:14	ye shall not eat	ye shall eat
Genesis 10:16	emorite	amorite
2 Chronicles 25:12	children of Judah	children of Israel
Esther 1:1	twentie	tweny
1 Esdras	Anocrynha	Apocrypha
Malachi 1:8	and if hee offer	and if ye offer
Matthew 26:36	Jesus	Judas
Matthew 16:25	his his (*repeated*)	his (*not repeated*)

Two general title pages exist for the 1611 edition. One is a copper engraving by Cornelius Boel that shows Moses standing in a niche on the left side of the leaf holding the Ten Commandments in his right hand and the high priest Aaron standing to Moses's left on the right side of the leaf (see p. 195). The tetragrammaton (four-letter Hebrew word representing the name of God) heads the page with the four Gospel writers on the four corners. The bottom depicts a large pelican with open wings. The other general title page is the same woodcut as the New Testament title page and appears in the 1602 Bishops' Bible (see title page in photo on p. 171).[11]

Scholars have speculated that the final "1" in the woodcut title date of 1611 has been altered from a "3" (1613), which is the date of the second edition. The theory is that a few 1611 Boel title pages were replaced by the 1613 title pages (perhaps the Boel title was destroyed or damaged) and then changed to read 1611. In my worldwide census of 1611 "He" Bibles, I found a copy of the 1611 woodcut title at Württembergische Landesbibliothek, Bibelsammlung/

A Collector's Plight

I was finally the owner of a 1611–13 (general title dated 1611 and NT title 1613) "She Bible"—an expensive acquisition, but the original binding, cover, and spine had made it well worth the sacrifice. The volume was the center of my collection until Maggs Brothers, rare book dealers in London, sent me a letter describing a 1538 Coverdale Diglot. This dual-language Bible had been printed in France by Francis Regnault and published by Richard Grafton and had come from the famous book collection of Sir R. Leicester Harmsworth.[12] The volume had been in the Maggs's basement since 1948, and they had only just discovered it.

As the only diglot of the three editions that had been under the super-intendence of Miles Coverdale (the other editions were pirated), the book was an extraordinary find. I immediately saw an opportunity to purchase one of the few books more rare than a 1611–13 King James Version. Ward Allen, Hargis Professor of English emeritus from Auburn University and the author of several works about the King James Version, informed me of the university's interest in purchasing my "She Bible" for their collection. With mixed emo-tions I agreed to sell it to Auburn so I could purchase the diglot. The decision ultimately proved to be a good one; I have had the opportunity to buy and sell several 1611–13 King James Versions over the intervening years but never another opportunity to purchase a Coverdale Diglot.

Nevertheless, I regretted saying goodbye to my "first love." A few years ago I approached Auburn to ask if they had any interest in selling my first 1611–13 King James Version back to me. To my disappointment, they politely declined. My first King James 1611 was one "She" I was forced to say farewell to forever.

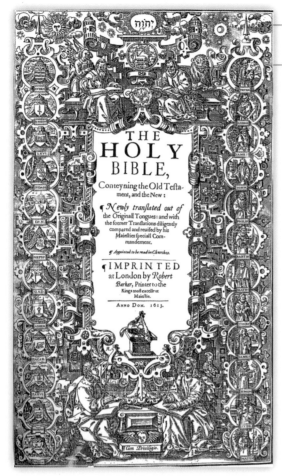

Bible Collection in Stuttgart, Germany, that was clearly altered from 1613 to 1611. On the other hand, a copy at Gruber Library in Chicago (Lutheran School of Theology) appears to be an unaltered, genuine woodcut 1611 title page.

Opposition to the London Bestseller

While modern-day scholars speculate about the specifics surrounding the Bible's production, history more fully documents the version's guarded reception by the people. The appearance of the first copies of the King James Version in seventeenth-century bookshops most likely did not produce long lines, and the new version did not hit the January 1612 *London Times* bestseller list. Decades passed before this new translation surpassed the popularity of the Geneva Bible or even the Bishops' Bible (not printed after 1606) and ultimately became the world's bestselling book of all time.

The King James Version's battle for popularity and endorsement as the standard version began immediately upon publication. Hugh Broughton and Andrew Willett, two well-established Hebrew scholars of the period, had been ignored by the translation assignment committee, and as might be expected, they became vocal critics of the new translation. Broughton was known for his aggressive temperament and antagonistic personality, and some speculate the translation committee may have passed him by because they feared his potential for intimidating the other translators as well as his inability to respond appropriately to challenges to his opinion. Broughton had sharply criticized the Bishops' Bible thirty years earlier, and in his critique of the King James Bible, he arrogantly condemned the work as totally erroneous and warned that the translators would answer for their corrupt work on the day of judgment. But Broughton's history of poor behavior had preceded him and tempered any influence his criticisms might have had.[13]

Nevertheless, the King James Version did not fall into the arms of an adoring and waiting public. In 1611 the Geneva Bible continued to be read as the popular Bible of the masses, and its influence was felt for years to come. At least nine editions had been published in 1599, and even many of the translators of the King James Version used the Geneva Bible. Once the King James Version had been authorized and released, James banned the printing of the Geneva Bible in England after 1616. The Geneva Bible, however, continued to be printed outside England until its last edition in 1644,[14] and Robert Barker printed several editions in 1633 but gave them the date 1599, which was the last year of his father Christopher's printing license. This way he avoided the ban on Geneva Bibles.

The death of James I in 1625 and the ascension of his son, Charles I, marked a new attitude toward the Geneva Bible in England. By this point the tension between Puritans and Anglicans had reached a crescendo. After Charles appointed William Laud as archbishop of Canterbury in 1633, Laud blamed the tension on the Geneva Bible with its Puritan-Calvinistic notes and lack of support for the divine right of kings—a position that threatened King Charles. According to King's College chair of theology, ministry, and education, Alister McGrath, Laud charged that the support of the Geneva Bible was unpatriotic and importing Geneva Bibles hurt English printers financially.[15] Laud used this excuse to block the importation of Geneva Bibles. In 1642, however, the notes from the Geneva were included in the first King James Bible printed abroad.

King Charles I (king of England 1625–49) was obsessed with the concept of the divine right to rule—a conviction that ultimately brought about his death. During his rule the influence of the King James Version grew while the popularity of the Geneva Bible waned. Photo: Original art, L. Lupton.

Followers of the popular Geneva Bible tenaciously took their stand. In his introduction to the King James Version, Miles Smith quoted from the Geneva Bible, and he continued to quote that version in his sermons. Other translators also continued to preach from the Geneva text well into the 1620s. In a sermon before King James I on February 26, 1623, at Whitehall, Sir Lancelot Andrews, one of the leading translators of the King James Bible of 1611, quoted from the Geneva Bible.[16] In contrast, however, the staunchly Calvinistic archbishop of Canterbury and King James Version translator George Abbot, who as a Calvinist seemed a likely candidate to prefer the Calvinistic Geneva Bible, almost immediately made frequent use of the KJV, as did the great preacher and poet John Donne.[17]

Because the king of England supported the King James Version, many people today assume it was named the official Bible of England. No evidence exists, however, to support this assumption. The title page statement, "Appointed to be read in the Churches," carries different implications than if the statement had read, "Authorized to be read in the Churches." In fact, several editions of the King James Bible omitted the phrase altogether (e.g., 1612 octavo, 1612 quarto, 1612–13 quarto, 1616 small folio). It is likely the phrase was included to indicate that the larger folio edition was appropriate for use from church pulpits. The church clergy probably assumed official sanction of the King James Version since the king's printer, Robert Barker, had published a translation initiated by the king himself, and King James fully supported the translation. Whatever the case, the so-called Authorized Version continued to be published. It grew in popularity, and its authority was soon established.[18]

Within time the King James Version gained a full share of the consumer market. By the end of its second decade of printing, the King James Version was established as the version used in nearly every household. Another ten years passed, however, before the KJV completely displaced the popular Geneva Bible. The University of Scotland began printing the King James Version in 1629, but it was not until 1633 that it was printed under the authority of the king's printers, and it was officially recognized by the church of Scotland in 1634. As the well-recognized Bible cataloger A. S. Herbert affirms, the Authorized Version continued to be printed in increasing numbers from 1616.[19] Sir Fredric Kenyon reports that between 1611 and 1640, 182 editions of the King James Version were printed, while during the same period 15 editions of the Geneva were printed.[20]

Once the King James Version gained acceptance, its rising popularity could not be halted. The new version ultimately triumphed for several reasons.[21] First, the scholars who translated the KJV gave considerable attention to literary as well as linguistic elements. Literary beauty made the text

Acquiring a Treasured "He"

The 1611 King James is the foundation of all Bible collections. Over the years I have bought and sold several first editions of the "He" King James Version of 1611. Each time I sold one, I deeply regretted it. And each time I found another, I could scarcely believe my good fortune, especially since the new purchase was almost always better than the one I decided to give up. Over the years I've unearthed these treasures at auctions, in private collections, and with the assistance of rare book dealers.

My love for Bible collecting drew me to England and the continent many times. Hours spent with friend and fellow collector Brian Hills were a high-light of many of my trips. Brian's knowledge of books fueled my desire as we searched historical shops, sipped tea, and perused books from his collection in his London home.

I was unprepared, however, when Brian called one afternoon and said he was ready to retire. Were there any books in his collection I'd like to have? With barely a thought, I booked my flight and braced myself for a bittersweet trip.

Brian first offered me his entire collection, and we mutually agreed on a price. But the all-too-familiar hitch struck again: I did not have the funds. I suggested that perhaps I could find an investor or something to sell when I got home. Brian graciously agreed to give me a few weeks to try.

Not wanting his friend to return home empty-handed, Brian let me borrow a 1611 "He Bible" he had bought several years earlier from Cambridge University. The 1611 bore the original covers with a brass center and corner pieces. It was beautiful, and it instantly became my favorite King James treasure. A week later I sent Brian my check—for the Bible only.

What could have been a disappointment turned out to be a happy ending for both of us. Although I was never able to raise the funds to acquire Brian's entire library, I was able to purchase three of his other Bibles. Not long afterward, Brian's collection went to a local museum, where he became curator of his own beloved collection.

appealing to a wide range of readers. Its flowing patterns and rhythmic style also made the text memorable. The translation was produced during Shakespeare's heyday, when the English language was venerated and at its apex.

Second, the King James Version found acceptance among English-speaking clergy and theologians. Because it did not contain notes like the Geneva Bible, clergymen representing a variety of positions embraced the King James.

Third, the new version won over its readers by sheer merit. Its faithfulness to the original languages and its fluid expression guaranteed its success. By the middle of the seventeenth century, the entire English-speaking world had embraced it as the Word of God. The King James Version dominated and for 270 years knew no peers. It was not until the English Revised Version of 1881–85 came on the scene that any version challenged its supremacy. That challenge, however, was more symbol than substance. A short time later the door of the twentieth century, with its plethora of new translations, stood ajar.

9

Maps, Margins, and Mythology

The Formatting of an English Treasure

W e all love beautiful books. When I received the first copy of my previous book, *A Visual History of the English Bible*, its visual design captured my eye: the cover, headers, sidebars, fonts, and graphics all work together to enhance the text. Before the book went to press, artists and editors made design choices that were intended to heighten reader interest as well as increase the book's readability. The same, of course, applies to the book you're holding.

The editors and printers of the King James Bible wrestled with similar decisions: What printing and formatting choices would stimulate interest in the new King James Version in light of the popularity of the Geneva Bible? What visual enhancements would improve readers' understanding of the new translation? And what elements of previous translations should be retained and new elements be implemented in order to most effectively communicate a clear message to readers of the day: "Come, turn these pages, for this is God's Word"? The formatting choices made for the 1611 King James Version reveal strategic decisions that address these very questions.

Formatting Choices for the First Edition

The King James translation team faced the dual challenge of not only producing an accurate translation but also overseeing format choices that would present God's Word in the most effective manner possible. Their choices encompassed several aspects of overall graphic design. One basic element of that design was the choice of typesetting: a strategically selected, well-proportioned, beautiful, black-letter font in double columns that communicates both authority and dignity. Words not represented in the Greek text were inserted in smaller roman type.

Additional formatting choices reveal the translators' focus on making the version user-friendly and understandable. Content summaries are placed on the top left side of each page. The name of the book is centered on the verso (reverse or left-hand) leaf, and the chapter number is centered on the recto (right-hand) leaf. In the apocryphal books, the summary headings have been replaced with the term *Apocrypha*. The word *Psalms* appears at the top of both pages of that book, centered over double columns. Chapter summaries appear at the beginning of each chapter, and marginal notes in both italic and roman type further explain the text. Signature letters (an intricate letter-number system of pagination) appear at the bottom righthand corner of the first three pages of the signature. The first word of the following page appears at the bottom righthand corner of each page as well.

The translators were attentive to the aesthetic elements of formatting as well. Each page of the King James Version is surrounded by a straight-line border.[1] Chapters begin with ornate woodcut initials (illustrations) that adorn the first letter of each chapter and capitalize the second letter. Most chapter initials throughout the book are decorated with a variety of vine motifs surrounding the first letter. In the book of Psalms, some initials occupy six lines, some seven lines, and some only four (Psalms 137, 141, and 145). Eight unusual initials are scattered throughout the Bible in no discernable pattern:

1. ten-line Neptune astride a horse (Matthew 1 and Revelation 1)
2. ten-line demonic face with bat wings (Hebrews 1)
3. ten-line nude Daphne (Romans 1)

A Visual History of the King James Bible

4. nine-line figure of two demons depicted with horns and pitchforks (2 Corinthians 1; Galatians 1; Philippians 1; 2 Thessalonians 1; Philemon 1; and 1 Peter 1)

5. seven-line Luke (Luke 1 and 1 Thessalonians 2)

6. seven-line apostle John (John 1)

7. nine-line monster, half man–half beast (2 Peter 1)[2]

8. seven-line figure of Pan playing a flute and dancing (Psalm 141; Wisdom of Solomon 1 from the Apocrypha; and 1 Peter 3).[3]

Other initials are used sparingly throughout the King James Version:

1. flying goose (Job 1; Joel 1; and others)

2. sitting angels (Daniel 1 and Zechariah 1)

3. deer at rest (Ecclesiasticus 29 from the Apocrypha)

4. woman carrying a jar (1 Corinthians 1; Ephesians 1; 1 Thessalonians 1; and Titus)

Many consider it a mystery why the King James translators, all ministers of the gospel, allowed pagan images to illustrate the initial letters of God's

Eight distinctive decorated initials in the 1611 King James Version are from top and left to right: ten-line Neptune astride his horse; ten-line initial of a demonic face with bat wings; ten-line nude Daphne; nine-line figure of two demons with pitchforks; seven-line Luke; seven-line John; nine-line monster, half man–half beast (apparently in some 1611 copies); and seven-line figure of Pan.

Word. While readers today might consider depictions of mythological images contrary to the biblical message, the translators likely did not view them as a threat to Christian belief. As scholars, their formal education had exposed them to the literature of the classics, which included mythology. In the final analysis it is more likely that Barker, the printer, was responsible for decisions regarding woodcut titles and initials. After all, he used many of these same initials in the four subsequent major folio editions he printed, most likely for convenience.

> Obviously, formatting issues encompassed more than just the text of Scripture.

While page numbering might seem a minor formatting consideration to twenty-first-century readers, the system used for the King James Version reveals much about printing in the seventeenth century.

The printing process for this Bible began with three double-folio leaves or sheets printed on both sides, with each single leaf carrying four pages of text; the leaves were then folded in half to form a quire (a gathering or section of varying length). Next, quires were gathered into larger groupings called signatures and numbered in the lower right corner of the recto (front or right-facing) side of each folio page. The signatures were placed in larger groupings called gatherings. Numbering of the first leaf began with a large capital letter (A) and a small Arabic numeral (1). When the alphabet was exhausted, a small letter (a) was added to the capital letter (A). The second folio leaf was numbered A2, and the next level was numbered Aa2. Signatures typically had three double folio leaves. Some signatures, however, fell short of the full three double-folio leaves. Signature B, for instance, consisted of only two leaves (4 pages of text). The total 123 quires of the 1611 King James Version were signed, including the introductory material, Old Testament, Apocrypha, and New Testament. The Bible had a total of 366 sheets of two leaves (double folios), which when folded in half gave 732 folio pages or a total of 1,464 pages that were printed on beautiful rag and linen paper.[4]

Obviously, formatting issues encompassed more than just the text of Scripture. The contents of the completed 1611 King James Version included the following in addition to the title page:

"Dedication to the most high and mightie Prince, James . . ." (3 pages)

The Translators to the Reader (1 page)

Kalendar (12 pages)

Almanacke for xxxix years (1603–41) with notes of the Golden number (1 page)

To find Easter forever (1 page)

Table and Kalendar, expressing the order of Psalms . . . (5 pages)

Genealogies (34 pages plus title)

Map (2 Pages)

Names and order of the books (1 page)

Old Testament text (A–Jiii 2)

Apocrypha (Jiii–Ccccc)

New Testament title (1 page)

New Testament (A2–Aa3).[5]

The translators were careful to include church-tailored resources, including a religious calendar, almanac, chart on how to find Easter, the order of Psalms, and lessons for morning and evening prayers. The introductory materials make it clear the new 1611 version was intended for use in Britain's churches.

One additional design element and perhaps the translators' most revealing formatting decision is reflected in their choice of the folio size for the first edition. The folio represents the largest Bible of the day, and folios were reserved for pulpit use. Since the work of the translation team had been overseen by King James himself, the folio size represented the King James Version as a Bible issued under the king's authority to be used in churches throughout Britain. Smaller formats for personal use were then issued after the foundational folio first edition.

The first edition of the King James Bible most likely sold out quickly in light of the fact that the English church had endorsed it. To keep inventory costs low, printers assembled copies as they were sold. Proofreaders made copy corrections (called reprints) on a page-by-page basis during the printing process. But the uneven print numbers produced during each run due to ink smears and paper jams required that individual pages be printed as needed. Printers conscientiously attempted to produce new pages with word-for-word precision; however, by the time single pages were printed and complete copies assembled and bound, no two Bibles were identical.

Formatting Distinctions between the First and Second Editions

Details that might appear insignificant to the twenty-first-century casual observer—title page formats, spelling inconsistencies, and graphic design choices—actually reveal much about the correlation between the first and second editions of the King James Bible. The 1613 second edition almost certainly attempted to keep each page identical to the 1611 edition. Interestingly, the second edition usually bears a 1613 general title that precedes the introductory sections and Old Testament but a 1611 date on the New Testament title page—although some 1613 general title dates have been changed to 1611. The mixed dates suggest that some copies printed in 1611 were sold in that same year, while the rest were sold in 1613. English language scholar David Norton thinks that about one-third of the 1611 KJV printing was destroyed in a fire, including the pages of Judges 13 through Ezekiel 20. If so, these pages had to be reset and reprinted.[6]

The 1611 King James Version helped stabilize the English language and is often thought of as the literary work that launched the modern English period. The new version, however, did not reflect advances in spelling. Variant spellings of the same word are often seen on the same page. Terms like *she*, *he*, *be*, and *me* often double the final *e*. Some scholars suggest the additional letter was added to help prevent excessive hyphenation of words at the ends of sentences, however, analysis of the texts does not provide clear support for this theory.

Nuances in spelling can help to determine a Bible's edition. The 1611 first edition spells "LORD" with all capitals of the same font size through the first thirty-nine chapters of the book of Genesis. From Genesis 40 through the remainder of the Old Testament, the word is spelled "LORD" in all capitals but with the "L" in a larger font. The 1613 second edition consistently uses the "LORD" spelling. This print detail in Genesis easily identifies a version as a 1611 first edition or a 1613 second edition.

Scholars debate whether the 1613 printing should be viewed as a second edition or an extension of the first printing. Pollard writes, "The so-called second issue is an entirely distinct and separate edition, save that a few leaves of the original edition, of which an excessive number had been printed by some mistake, are sometimes found used in it."[7] The second edition may have gotten underway shortly after the first in 1611, but the printing was not completed until 1613. This timing factor explains the general title date of 1613 and the New Testament title date of 1611.

Grammatical Structures of the King James Version

Almost any reader of the King James Version today will notice obsolete or unfamiliar terms and expressions. And yet we understand certain historically rooted words today that are not commonly used in conversation because they became threaded into our culture through the King James Bible. Even the 1611 version attempted to help readers understand unfamiliar words by inserting marginal comments. Note the following:

Reference	Text in 1611 edition	Marginal reading 1611	Modern meaning	Cambridge 1999*
Exodus 26:24	coupled	twinned	linked	coupled
Malachi 3:14	ordinance	observation	standards	ordinance
1 Corinthians 2:4	enticing	persuasible	persuasive	enticing
2 Timothy 3:3	false accusers	makebates	slanderers	false accusers
1 Timothy 6:5	perverse disputing	gallings one of another	conflict, constant friction	perverse disputings
Acts 22:5 and Mark 6:21	estates		those in authority, council	estate
Exodus 35:22	tablets		beads, pendants	tablets
1 Chronicles 12:19	advertisement		consultation	advertisement

*Cambridge Press's modern edition of the King James Version which retains the text of 1769.

During the translation of the King James Version, Jacobean language was still in flux; consequently, the 1611 translation shows the grammatical variations of two overlapping eras. Because the seventeenth-century translators lived and worked in an era that rode the shifting tides of language, they somewhat capriciously applied various rules of grammar. For instance, they used both forms of past tense: *clad* and *clothed*, *shone* and *shined*, *awoke* and *awaked*, *got* and *gotten*, and *built* and *builded*.

Today we can see the progression of time between seventeenth-century spelling and modern spelling.

Reference	Spelling in 1611	21st Century KJV 1994	Cambridge 1999
Exodus 16:1	moneth	month	month
Leviticus 27:13	fift	fifth	fifth
Deuteronomy 1:11	moe	more	more
1 Kings 18:5	lese	lose	lose
Matthew 17:20	unpossible	impossible	impossible
Acts 28:13	wee fet a compass	we followed a circuitous course[8] (distance along open water)	we fetched a compass

Many seventeenth-century forms ending in *ie* were changed to *y* in modern English, while the seventeenth-century *i* and *u* appear in modern English as *j* and *v*. The seventeenth-century *e* was often added to words such as *sonne*, *starres*, *arke*, *hee*, *shee*, and *bee*. But the most widely noticed inconsistency may be in the application of the singular and plural forms of *you*, *ye*, *thou*, *thy*, and *thee*. For instance, in the introduction to the King James Version, "To the Reader," the original translators used *you* in "You are risen up in your father's stead; as your fathers did, so do you"; however, the actual KJV text in Numbers 32:14 and Acts 7:51 uses the word *ye*.

Speed's Engraved Map

The introductory material of the King James Bible included a double-page map originated by John More and completed by John Speed in 1611. The city of Jerusalem, the table of showbread, the altars, and other implements used in

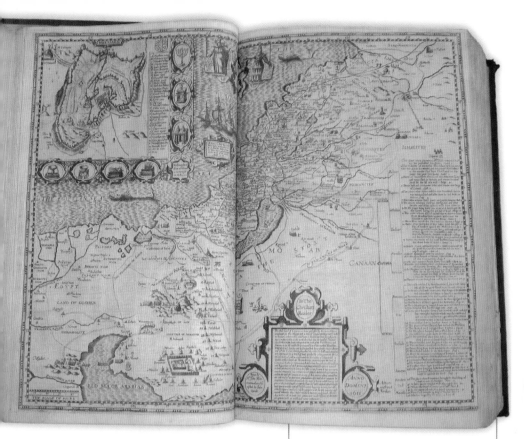

the temple are depicted in the corner of the map, which traces the journey of the Israelites from Egypt to Canaan. Speed's map appears in all the folio editions except the 1640 edition (to date none have been found that include the map).

Two distinct editions of Speed's map of Canaan exist, printed from two different plates, both dated 1611. Features of the map believed to be printed first include the following:

1. The seas are stippled (i.e., multiple dots make an appearance of gray shadowing).
2. No author name or signature is included.
3. An original copperplate was used to reproduce the map.

Features of the map believed to be printed second are as follows:

1. The seas are shaded using fine lines to make the gray shadowing.
2. The author's name, Renold Elstrack, is printed on the lower right corner of the right page, next to the circle with the names More and Speed.
3. The map was reproduced using a letterpress, a method of printing from a raised, inked printing surface.

The strongest evidence suggests that the map with Elstrack's name is probably the second one printed because it appears in the folios dated 1613, 1617, and 1634. Copies of the 1611 first edition exhibit different title pages, maps, and "To the Christian Reader" verso leaves (one blank and one with the royal coat of arms).

The Genealogies

Readers of the 1611 King James Version may find the lengthy genealogies in the introductory material somewhat amusing, beginning with the impressive title, "The Genealogies Recorded in the Sacred Scriptures

King James's coat of arms appears in some copies of the first edition, while other copies include only a blank leaf without the coat of arms. These details suggest the copies with the blank leaves are earlier. Once pages bearing the coat of arms were inserted, it is unlikely that they would ever have been removed.

The thirty-six-page genealogy from Adam to Christ in the King James Version is ornately presented in detail as the work of the Spirit of God in history.

According to Every Familie and Tribe, with the Line of Our Sauiovr Jesvs Christ obserued from Adam, to the blessed Virgin Marie. By J. S. Cum Priuilegio." The genealogies were first published in the 1611 KJV and were included in subsequent editions. Translator John Speed authored the work; however, Hebrew scholar Hugh Broughton, who had been excluded from the King James translation team because of his volatile personality, was given responsibility for gathering genealogies from the Old Testament. He submitted his work to John Speed for inclusion with the introductory material. Reflecting on Broughton's postpublication tirade against the King James Version, readers today might wonder if Broughton's public condemnation of the new Bible included the genealogies he helped produce.

Speed retained the patent for the genealogies and the map of Canaan for ten years. Francis Fry records twenty-three formatting changes or stylistic alterations in the genealogies in the folio editions,[9] most of which reflect minor differences. Very few printings included the introductory genealogies after the 1634 and 1640 folio editions.

1611 leaf of Matthew 1 with the heading, "The genealogie of Christ." The title initial verse 1 represents Neptune and sea horses. Verses 4–5 show inconsistent spelling of begate and begat. Both spellings also appear in verse 6 and in a note at verse 11. Verse 6 also uses both the ampersand and the word and.

The facsimile text reads:

1 The genealogie of Christ from Abraham to Ioseph. 18 Hee was conceiued by the holy Ghost, and borne of the Virgin Mary when she was espoused to Ioseph. 19 The Angel satisfieth the misdeeming thoughts of Ioseph, and interpreteth the names of Christ.

THE booke of the *genera-tion of Iesus Christ, the sonne of Da-uid, the sonne of Abraham.

2 *Abra-ham begate Isaac, and *Isaac begate Iacob, and *Iacob be-gate Iudas and his brethren.

3 And *Iudas begate Phares and Zara of Thamar, and *Phares begate Esrom, and Esrom begate Aram.

4 And Aram begate Aminadab, and Aminadab begate Naasson, and Naasson begate Salmon.

5 And Salmon begat Booz of Ra-chab, and Booz begate Obed of Ruth, and Obed begate Iesse.

6 And *Iesse begate Dauid the

11 And Iosias begate Iechonias and his brethren, about the time they were caried away to Babylon.

12 And after they were brought to Babylon, *Iechonias begat Salathiel, and Salathiel begate Zorobabel.

13 And Zorobabel begat Abiud, and Abiud begat Eliakim, and Eliakim be-gate Azor.

14 And Azor begate Sadoc, & Sadoc begat Achim, and Achim begat Eliud.

15 And Eliud begate Eleazar, and E-leazar begate Matthan, and Matthan begate Iacob.

16 And Iacob begate Ioseph the husband of Mary, of whom was borne Iesus, who is called Christ.

17 So all the generations from A-braham to Dauid, are fourteene gene-rations: and from Dauid vntill the ca-rying away into Babylon, are foure-teene generations: and from the cary-ing away into Babylon vnto Christ, are fourteene generations.

18 ¶Now the *birth of Iesus Christ was on this wise: when as his mother Mary was espoused to Ioseph (before they came together) shee was found

Doctrinal and Exegetical Issues in the King James Version

Not all King James Version readings are embraced today as the best possible renderings. Even though most observers agree that the King James Version admirably represents seventeenth-century scholarship and its translators attempted to be faithful to the text, a number of passages can be called into question. Of course, some modern readers still argue that the choices of the King James translators are more accurate than those offered in alternate renderings.

1611 leaf with the heading "Joseph imprisoned . . . is prosperous."

The beginning of each chapter features a content outline; the beginning initial occupies five lines and the second letter is capitalized. Genesis 39:23 is the last time "LORD" appears in capital letters all of the same size. Beginning with chapter 40 and following, the word is "LORD," using an initial capital letter followed by smaller capitals. Genesis 40:5 begins with a paragraph marker, which is not used after Acts 20:36. The verso or back side of the leaf pictured above includes a summary of the leaf in the heading, and the book title is centered. On this leaf the phrases "Joseph imprisoned" and "is prosperous" appear above the text.

The facsimile text reads:

Ioseph imprisoned,   Genesis.   is prosperous.

sephs hand: and he knew not ought he had, saue the bread which he did eate: and Ioseph was a goodly person, and well fauoured.

7 ¶And it came to passe after these things, that his masters wife cast her eyes vpon Ioseph, and shee said, Lie with me.

8 But he refused, and said vnto his masters wife, Behold, my master wot-teth not what is with mee in the house, and he hath committed all that he hath, to my hand.

9 There is none greater in this house then I: neither hath hee kept backe any thing from me, but thee, be-cause thou art his wife: how then can I doe this great wickednesse, and sinne a-gainst God?

10 And it came to passe as she spake to Ioseph day by day, that hee hearke-ned not vnto her, to lie by her, or to bee with her.

11 And it came to passe about this time, that Ioseph went in to the house, to doe his busines, and there was none of the men of the house there within.

12 And shee caught him by his gar-ment, saying, Lie with me: and he left his garment in her hand, and fled, and got him out.

13 And it came to passe, when she saw that hee had left his garment in her hand, and was fled forth;

14 That she called vnto the men of her house, and spake vnto them, say-ing, See, he hath brought in an Hebrew vnto vs, to mocke vs: he came in vnto me to lie with me, and I cried with a loud voice.

15 And it came to passe, when hee heard that I lifted vp my voice, and cri-ed, that he left his garment with mee,

and put him into the prison, a place, where the kings prisoners were bound: and he was there in the prison.

21 ¶But the LORD was with Ioseph, and shewed him mercie, and gaue him fauour in the sight of the kee-per of the prison.

22 And the keeper of the prison com-mitted to Iosephs hand all the priso-ners that were in the prison, and what-soeuer they did there, he was the doer of it:

23 The keeper of the prison looked not to any thing, that was vnder his hand, because the LORD was with him: and that which he did, the LORD made it to prosper.

CHAP. XL.

1 The Butler and Baker of Pharaoh in prison. 4 Ioseph hath charge of them. 5 He inter-preteth their dreames. 20 They come to passe according to his interpretation. 23 The ingratitude of the Butler.

AND it came to passe after these things, that the Butler of the King of E-gypt, and his Baker, had offended their lord the King of Egypt.

2 And Pharaoh was wroth against two of his officers, against the chiefe of the Butlers, and against the chiefe of the Bakers.

3 And he put them in ward in the house of the captaine of the guard, into the prison, the place where Ioseph was bound.

4 And the captaine of the guard charged Ioseph with them, and he ser-ued them, and they continued a season in warde.

Facsimile 1: Apocrypha — I. Esdras

The 1611 leaf of the Apocrypha shows the title page to Esdras. The Apocrypha was commonly included in most King James Versions until the turn of the nineteenth century. The headline of the leaf at Baruch 26:11 reads "Ecclesiasticus" instead of "Baruch," and the headline at 1 Esdras 4 reads "Anocrynha" instead of "Apocrypha." Only six or possibly eight paragraph markers appear in the text of the Apocrypha: 1 Esdras 2:8; 3:13; 4:13; 8:25; 2 Esdras 6:11; and 1 Maccabees 9:23. In some copies only two additional paragraph markers appear in 1 Maccabees 6:43.

1611 leaf with the heading "Boaz talketh with . . . Ruths kinsman." Ruth 3:15 contains the much-debated phrase, "he went into the citie." The spelling *he* or *hee* and *she* or *shee* appear on the same page and even in the same verses (Ruth 3:13, 15, 16, 17). The chapter summary renders the spelling as *she*, perhaps because that was the common spelling in 1611. Similar spellings are seen with *me* and *mee* in Ruth 4:4 and 4:9. Smaller and roman style letters are used for words that do not appear in the original language text; for example, Ruth 4:7, *the maner*, and 3:11, "*Wee are*." On the recto or front side of the leaf, the heading includes the leaf content summary but centers the chapter number between the border lines.

The margins contain alternate translations suggested by use of the Hebrew language, cross-reference verses, or additional English readings. The bottom of the leaf provides the first word of the following page ("to"), as well as the signature number, which orders and identifies the leaves and book sections for the printer ("Bb 2").

Text	KJV	Tyndale	Geneva	Bishops'	NET[10]
1 Thessalonians 5:22	Abstain from all appearance of evil	Abstain from all suspicious thing	Abstain from all appearance of evil	Abstain from all appearance of evil	Stay away from every form of evil.

The terms *appearance* and *suspicious* suggest semblance without reality. The term *form*, however, represents the text more precisely and suggests that abstinence is from all forms of evil.

Text	KJV	Tyndale	Geneva	Bishops'	NET
Romans 11:25	That blindness in part is happened to Israel, until the fullness of the Gentiles be come in.	That partly blyndnes is happened in Israhell, until the fullness of the gentiles be come in.	That partly obstinacle is come to Israel, vntil the fulnesse of the Gentiles be come in.	That partly blyndnesse is happened in Israel, vntyll the fulnesse of the gentiles be come in.	A partial hardening has happened to Israel until the full number of the Gentiles has come in.

In comparison, the term for *blindness* in Mark 3:5 is translated as *hardness* in the King James Version, the Geneva Bible, and the Bishops' Bible. "Israel has been hardened until the full number of Gentiles has come in."

The King James Version heading used in Isaiah 52:53, "The deliuerance of the Church," suggests replacement theology—a position that teaches that the New Testament church replaces Israel as God's chosen people and fulfills God's promises to Israel. This doctrine has divided theologians for generations. The issue under scrutiny, however, is not the validity of replacement theology but whether the translation team approved the headings' theological position when they authorized inclusion of the headings authored by Thomas Bilson, the translator responsible for all of them.

Text	KJV	Tyndale	Geneva	Bishops'	NET
Galatians 6:11	Ye see how large a letter I have written unto you with mine own hand.	large a letter	large a letter	large a letter	what big letters

The King James Version suggests Paul's Epistle was long, as in lengthy; however, a more accurate meaning is likely that the letters he is forming as he writes are large in size. The Rheims Bible says, "What manner of letters I have." Paul's dwindling eyesight may have caused him to write using large letters.

Text	KJV	Tyndale	Geneva	Bishops'	NET
James 5:16	The effectual fervent prayer of a righteous man availeth much.	The prayer of a ryghteous man avayleth moche, yf it be fervent.	For the fervent prayer of a righteous man avayleth moch.	*For* the fervent prayer of a righteous man availeth much.	The prayer of a righteous person has great effectiveness. Note: *Grk* is very powerful in its working

John Eadie, a well-recognized biblical scholar, comments: "[The KJV reading] is so far tautological [needlessly repetitious], since to be effectual and to be of much avail are not very different. . . . The more literal rendering is 'the prayer of a righteous man availed much, as it worketh.'"[11] The NET translation captures the meaning quite closely.

Perhaps the greatest triumph of the King James Version is that it stands as a testament to God's commitment to accomplish his eternal purposes by partnering with finite, imperfect men and women. Although no two identical copies of the 1611 King James Bible were ever produced, God's authoritative Word has passed on for centuries to new generations.

10

Branches on the Family Tree

The Four Siblings of the 1611 King James Version

Francis Fry (1803–86) invested his life in business and community service. He served as director and chairman of the Bristol waterworks and sat on the board of the Bristol and Gloucester Railway. But Fry's aspirations did not lie in business or public service; more than anything, he wanted to contribute to the scholarly study of sixteenth-century Bibles and the King James Version. His devotion launched his page-by-page investigation of at least 190 copies of the five folio editions of the King James. Fry was considered one of the greatest bibliographers of

The original 1611 King James Version was reprinted in four similar folio editions (1611–13, 1617, 1634, and 1639–40). Photo: A. May.

the nineteenth century, and he compared editions to see if he could trace textual differences between the five folios of the King James Version. His investigations led to the publication in 1865 of *A Description of the Great Bible—1539, Cranmer's Bible 1540–41, King James's Bible 1611–40*.

Fry's work became the standard for all succeeding studies of the King James, but his method of removing leaves from the various King James editions and rearranging them to determine which leaves were original and which were reprints led to confusion. Scholars who later conducted research using the Bibles Fry had used found it difficult to identify and classify the leaves as originals or reprints. Nevertheless, his work is indispensable to a study of the five folios. Today, many 1611 copies have Fry's collation verifying that they are correct copies. This has led to false assumptions about the "purity" of their copies. It is impossible to determine a "pure" 1611 copy.

The various editions of the King James Version are textually similar. The printer's goal was to reproduce the same text and format used in the 1611 edition in each of the subsequent five folio

The Tyndale 1525 showing that the doxology has been omitted in Matthew 6:13, as noted in the table below. The 1525 is an incomplete translation due to Tyndale's forced flight from Cologne.

editions while incorporating corrections and spelling updates. With exceptions for minor corrections, each subsequent edition attempted a page-for-page replication of the previous edition.

The 1611 Folio Edition

The 1611 folio is the first edition of the King James Version. Its most distinctive features are the Cornelius Boel copper-engraved general title page (a woodcut title was used in the New Testament) and the unique reading in Ruth 3:15, "He went into the citie." The title page reads, "Appointed to be read in Churches"—the wording that provided impetus for the King James Version's popular identity as the Authorized Version. As stated earlier, although King James I never officially pronounced the version "the authorized Bible," it was given unofficial authorized status since it was controlled from beginning to end by the king and printed by royal printer Robert Barker.

The 1611–13 Folio Second Edition

The second edition of the King James Version was printed between 1611 and 1613 and included a woodcut title page for both the general title and the New Testament title. Because this edition included the reading, "She

Readings Identifying the King James Version

The following chart records selected examples of the most common King James Version readings contrasted with readings from other versions.

Text	King James Version– modern editions	Rheims NT 1582 (basic Latin text)	*Textus Receptus* Greek Text	Modern Greek Text	Tyndale 1526–34	ESV 2001 (and most other modern versions)
Matthew 6:13; the doxology in Lord's Prayer	For thine is the kingdom, and the power, and the glory, for ever.	omitted	included	omitted	omitted 1525 and 1526; included in 1534[1]	omitted, but placed in a footnote recognizing it is in later manuscripts
Matthew 17:21	Howbeit this kind goeth not out but by prayer and fasting.	included	included	omitted	included	omitted, but included in a footnote
Matthew 18:11	For the Son of man is come to save that which was lost.	included	included	omitted	included	omitted, but included in a footnote
Mark 15:28	And the scripture was fulfilled, which saith, And he was numbered with the transgressors.	included	included	omitted	included	omitted, but included in a footnote
Mark 16:9–20 Ending of Mark	Now when Jesus was risen early . . . confirming the word with signs following.	included	included	omitted	included	omitted, but in brackets

Passage	Text					
	of the water.... whosoever then first ... stepped in was made whole of whatsoever disease he had.					included in a footnote
John 7:53–8:11 Woman taken in adultery	And every man went unto his own house.... Go, and sin no more.	included with variations	included	omitted	included	omitted, but in brackets
Acts 8:37	And Philip said, If thou believest with all thine heart, thou mayest. And he answered and said, I believe that Jesus Christ is the Son of God.	included	included	omitted	included	omitted, footnoted
Acts 24:6b–8a	And would have judged according to our law ... Commanding his accusers to come unto thee.	included	included	omitted	included	omitted, but included in a footnote
Romans 16:24	The grace of our Lord Jesus Christ be with you all. Amen.	included	included	omitted	included	omitted, but included in a footnote
1 John 5:7b–8a Comma Johanneum	[Bear record] in heaven, the Father, the Word, and the Holy Ghost: and these three are one. And there are three that bear witness in earth.	included	included	omitted	included	omitted, no reference to missing text

went into the citie," in Ruth 3:15, it was dubbed the "She Bible." The second edition also includes other errors:

- Matthew 26:36 substitutes the word *Judas* for *Jesus*.
- The first page of the dedication reads, "The Translators OE the Bible" rather than "of."
- The eighth line of the dedication reads "Chkist" instead of "Christ."
- In "The Names and order of all the Books," 1 and 2 Corinthians are substituted for 1 and 2 Chronicles.

Additional differences can be found between the two editions, including different woodcut initials.

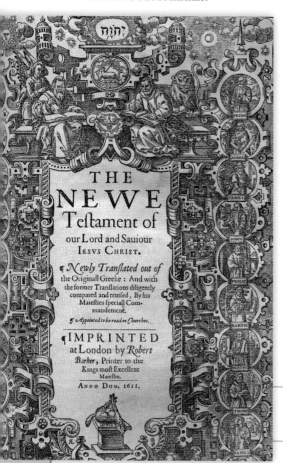

A 1613 smaller-sized folio features type with 72 lines per leaf instead of the standard 59 lines of the other five folios. This edition also differs on nearly every page from the larger folios. The first two editions along with the three additional folio editions were typeset so that each leaf ends with the same word. This typesetting choice made it easy to confuse pages, and therefore many copies were produced with mixed printings. This 1613 version is known for its numerous errors, several of which are notable:

- Genesis 27:44 substitutes "passé" for "turn."

New Testament title leaf of the second edition 1611–13 King James Version "She" edition includes "appointed to be read in churches."

- Ezekiel 23:7 substitutes "delighted" for "defiled."
- Psalm 11:1 substitutes "flie" for "flee."
- 1 Corinthians 11:17 substitutes "I praise you" for "I praise you not."
- 1 Peter 1:22 substitutes "selves" for "souls."

The knotted story of the printing and collation of the first two editions of the King James Version is difficult to untangle. Biblical scholar David Norton observes, "It [the mixture of readings] suggests a degree of collation between the first and second editions that produced quite a few deliberately chosen readings."[2] If certain readings were chosen by the translators for textual reasons or corrected by the original manuscript, those readings would carry authority. The frustration for readers today is that it is impossible to know the precise criteria by which certain readings were selected by the translators.

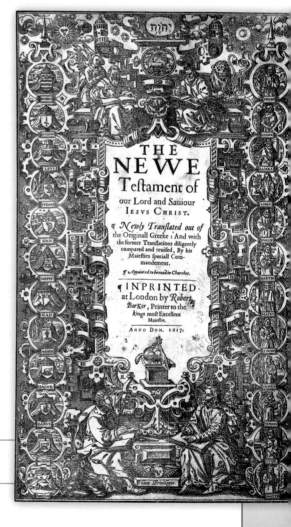

The 1617 Folio Third Edition

This third major edition closely duplicates the second edition. It was the first to correct the reading in Psalm 69:32 from "and your heart shall liue that seeke good" (1611 and 1613 editions), to "and your heart shall liue that seeke God" (1617, 1634, and 1640 editions). The modern spelling of *seek* and *live*

Title leaf to the third folio edition of the King James Version (1617).

was first used in the 1640 edition.[3] The 1617 edition also includes a unique spelling in Jeremiah 18:3, *whelles*, while *wheels* is used in all other editions. The 1617 edition is important because it demonstrates the great amount of mixture that entered the first two editions. Nonetheless, it seems likely that the editors of the 1617 King James used the 1613 edition as they compared readings to correct errors from the 1613 against the 1611 edition.

Another interesting feature of the 1617 edition is that the initial *I* at the beginning of Psalm 122 bears the image of the New Testament writer John. In the 1611, 1613, and 1640 editions, the initial displays only a simple, decorative *I*. The 1634 edition replicates the 1617, and John's image (spelled *Iohn*) is again used to illustrate the initial *I*.

The 1634 Folio Fourth Edition

The 1634 folio is textually similar to the preceding editions. The general title page adds to printer Robert Barker's name (which had appeared as printer in former editions) the words "and by the assigns of John Bill," and his name appears again in the 1640 edition. The 1634 text agrees with the 1617 edition in nearly every reading. A few minor differences exist: In the introductory material of the 1634 text the phrase,

Title leaf to the fourth folio edition of the King James Version (1634).

"To finde Easter for euer," is printed on different pages and only one displays a large woodcut at the bottom of the page. Hebrews 12:1 reads, "Let us runne with patience the race that is set before us" (1634 and 1640 editions), instead of, "Let us runne with patience *unto* the race that is set before us" (1611, 1613, and 1617 editions; emphasis added).

The 1639–40 Folio Fifth Edition

Most consider the fifth folio the finest of the five folio editions of the King James Version. It improved upon previous editions by adding alternate readings, which were placed in the margins in roman type. The fifth edition also reflects the changes in spelling that had occurred in the intervening years since the printing of the 1611 first edition. In 1611 the letter *u* was used instead of *v* in the middle of words, but a *v* was used for the *u* when it was the first letter. For example, in the 1611 edition (Ps. 43:3 and Ps. 44:1), the words *unto* and *have* appear as *vnto* and *haue*; however, in the 1640

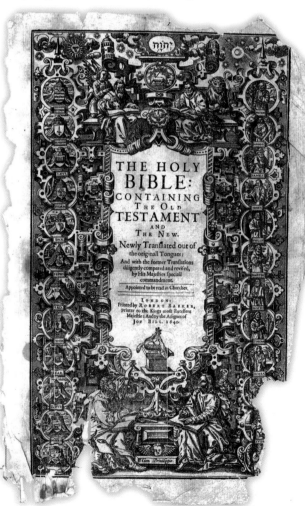

New Testament title/general title leaf of the fifth folio edition of the King James Version (1639–40).

edition the words are spelled *unto* and *have*, reflecting modern spelling that disregards letter placement. The modern letter *J* also appears as *I* in the first four folios (The Booke of Iudges) and only as *J* in the 1640.

The first line of the title page of the dedication in the 1640 edition reads, "TO THE MOST HIGH," while the first line in the other four editions reads, "TO THE MOST," with "HIGH" on the second line. Another distinguishing feature of the 1640 edition is the worn and sometimes incomplete border that appears around each individual page. Gaps at the corners confirm whether a Bible is a 1640 edition.

Editors of the King James Version did not intend for the five folio editions to be revisions of preceding editions; each page was supposed to be an exact reprint, with only minor changes introduced by the editors. But after Francis Fry examined and rearranged individual pages from the five folios, historians found it difficult to identify pure, unmixed copies of any of the five editions. (Copies untouched by Fry can be found in libraries and collections that predate his life in the nineteenth century and are, therefore, good starting places for reexamining his findings.) But in spite of human error, minor omissions, deletions, and transpositions, the message of God's Word was not diminished, and the truth of Scripture was carried into the world with power. For the next four hundred years the Bible that English-speaking people turned to was the King James Version.

11

The Growing Family

Direct Descendants of the King James Version

B etween the years of 1640 and 1769, errors caused by the increased number of poorly edited Bibles and the constant need for revision by Oxford and Cambridge printers—two other printers with royal sanction to print Scripture during this time—led scholars to question the final authority of the 1611 King James Version. As a result, the purity and purpose of the Bible became a subject of debate. In response, two well-known biblical scholars from Cambridge and Oxford attempted to end the controversy.

In 1769 Benjamin Blayney, a biblical scholar from Hertford College, Oxford University, addressed the controversy when he reported the results after completing his 1769 Oxford revision of Cambridge biblical scholar Dr. F. S. Paris's 1762 Cambridge edition of the Bible. Controversy had arisen between Oxford Press and Cambridge Press regarding which publisher was producing the most accurate Bible. Blayney wrote in *Gentleman's Magazine*,

> I have carefully collated the 1611 folio, the 1701 Bishop Lloyd's fine edition, and two Cambridge editions of late date and corrected many former errors. These corrections made the new edition [1769] of such a standard of purity as, it is presumed, are not to be met within any other edition hitherto extant. . . . And though

Dr. Paris made large corrections in this particular edition published at Cambridge [1762 edition], there still remained many necessary alterations which escaped the doctor's notice.[1]

Blayney's words fanned the smoldering coals of controversy regarding the accuracy of biblical versions into a firestorm.

The Oxford–Cambridge debate centered around the accuracy of the first edition King James Version and its use of spelling, punctuation, and italics as well as its inclusion of printers' errors. Dr. Paris had attempted to produce a standardized edition of the King James for Cambridge Press, and competitor Oxford Press had employed Blayney to continue the revision work. But the exploration of deeper questions spurred Blayney and Paris in their efforts:

- Could a perfect Bible translation be produced?
- Was the task insurmountable?
- Was it necessary or even possible for a line of *perfect* revisions to flow in succession from the original text?

The questions still fascinate many today. Some modern-day KJV enthusiasts believe that

Open in front is the 1616 King James revision, lying on top of it is the 1629 revision, lying in the back is the 1638 revision, and upright in the back is the 1762 Paris revision.   Photo: A. Sanchez.

inerrancy and preservation are inseparable issues and argue that Blayney's completed edition was perfect and, therefore, possessed the characteristics of theological inerrancy.[2]

Most people believe the King James Version sitting on their shelves today reflects precisely the same text as the 1611 edition. While the wordings are similar, however, a careful comparison of the modern King James Version and the 1611 edition demonstrates numerous variations. Although these variations are not theologically significant, they do reveal details about the history of the 1611 version. Some of these differences reflect deliberate changes to correct printers' or translators' errors in previous editions, which inadvertently introduced new ones. The financial windfall that flowed from the popular version led to printing shortcuts, hurried production, and inferior proofing, resulting in errors. Then a few printers, aware of the misprints, attempted to revise and correct the readings, thereby creating minor discrepancies between various textual readings.

Two distinct issues of the King James Version bore the date 1611, and the readings in each issue differed in a number of places. Even casual comparison reveals that not all differences between the two can be attributed to printers' errors. Where did these variations originate, and who made the changes? These questions have no easy answers, but scholars have speculated about possible answers, one of which is that multiple print shops with multiple editors may have been used, and separate printers and editors may have taken liberties with the translators' manuscript. The mystery may never be solved, but the textual and historical data surrounding the questions deserve investigation.

Minor Revisions Prior to the 1616 Edition

In the seventeenth century, certain sizes and styles of Bibles were used privately while others were reserved for public use. The five large folio, black-letter editions of the King James published from 1611 to 1640 were designed for readings from the pulpit. The various editions issued from 1613 to 1769 were also large folio revisions. A number of less important editions were also

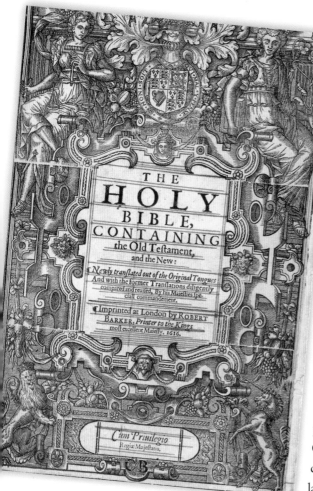

published that popularized the KJV by adding improved marginal notes, italics, and roman-letter font.

In 1612 the first quarto (midsized) roman-letter edition was published by Robert Barker, the king's printer. This smaller-size edition was intended for private use. The title page omits the phrase, "Appointed to be read in Churches"—wording that was commonly included in the early, larger folio editions. While this edition closely follows the 1611 "He" text, it corrects some of the 1611 edition's mistakes. The 1612 reading in Ruth 3:15 uses the spelling *hee*. In yet another example, shown in the illustration on page 190, in Exodus 14:10 the 1611 repeats the phrase, "The children of Israel lift up their eyes, and behold, the Egyptians marched after them, and they were sore afraid," however, the 1612 corrects the verse by printing the phrase only once.

Another 1612 quarto edition in roman type reads *she* in Ruth 3:15 and differs in other ways as well. The marginal notes at Mark 7:4 differ in the 1611 folio and 1612 quarto editions.[3] Like the 1612 quarto, two editions of the 1612 octavo (smaller size) also include both readings of the 1611 in Ruth 3:15. These editions correct the duplication of the lines in Exodus 14:10 and correct the margins of Mark 7:4. Other than this, these octavos closely follow the 1611 edition. They also omit the statement, "Appointed to be read in Churches." My copy of the 1613 octavo includes the common printing error that substitutes the word *Printers* for *Princes* in Psalm 119:161.

The Need for a Revision Recognized (1616)

Printer's errors, findings of textual critics, and market demand drove the need for revision. The 1616 small folio edition blazed new trails in the printing of the King James Version. It was the first small folio to use roman letters instead of the black letters of the larger folio editions. The general title and New Testament title pages feature a common woodcut title used by the Barkers with the initials of Christopher Barker (CB) displayed at the bottom, even though the Bible was printed by Robert Barker. The page facing the first chapter of Genesis shows an elaborate woodcut of the tree of knowledge in the Garden of Eden. The 1616 features a beautiful format with unusual headpieces (graphic designs at the top of the page) at the beginning of each book of the Bible that do not appear in any other King James edition.

The 1616 edition was the first serious attempt to edit the complete Bible, revising the text in a number of places. Although it accurately edited the original 1611 printing, it did not gain popularity and is considered a rare find among collectors. The 1616 exerted almost no influence on the subsequent folio editions of 1617, 1634, and 1640. Typesetting large black-letter editions was so difficult and costly that even when printers found errors, they often ignored them. Select corrections from the various editions appear in the following chart, along with the text of a modern printing of the Cambridge University's 1999 King James Version.

Text	1611 "He Bible"	1616 "She Bible"	Cambridge KJV 1999
Leviticus 26:40	the iniquity	their iniquity and the iniquity	their iniquity
Deuteronomy 16:5	the gates	thy gates	thy gates
2 Chronicles 32:5	prepared Millo	repaired Millo	repaired Millo
Job 39:30	there is he	there is she	there *is* she
Jeremiah 49:1	inherit God	inherit Gad	inherit Gad

Original Translators Insist on New Revisions (1629)

Credit for the first thorough revision of the King James Version belongs to two original 1611 translators: Samuel Ward and John Bois. Whether Ward and Bois initiated the revision themselves or responded to a request issued by Cambridge University is not known. They may have recognized the problems associated with the KJV's dependence on the Bishops' Bible and its antiquated English, but since they were part of the Cambridge Company of translators, the decision was most likely jointly agreed upon by the men and the university.

Based on charters granted by British royals, both Oxford and Cambridge universities claimed the right to print King James Version Bibles. In 1629 Cambridge chose to exercise the right, and Thomas and John Buck, printers to the University of Cambridge, printed the first Cambridge edition of the King James Version. (Oxford did not exercise its printing rights until 1675.) The 1629 edition was a small folio format in roman lettering with a distinguished copperplate title page and was the product of major revisions. No evidence exists that official authority was ever granted for the project;

nevertheless the edition was still referred to as the Authorized Version, and the title page reads, "Appointed to be read in Churches."

In addition to using the beautiful roman type in the 1629 edition, editors paid careful attention to words printed in italics, spelling, punctuation, and marginal references. Despite a bias against notes among Anglican bishops, the 1629 revision expanded upon marginal notes. These notes, however, did not carry the theological weight of the notes in the Geneva Bible. Most referenced the meanings of particular Hebrew or Greek words. For instance, 2 Kings 23:33 reads, "That he might not reigne in Jerusalem." The marginal note says, "Or, because he reigned." Romans 6:13 reads, "As instruments of unrighteousness," and the accompanying note states, "Gr [Greek], arms or weapons." The 1629 edition was the first to record the misprint in 1 Timothy 4:6 that reads "unto thy doctrine" instead of "unto the doctrine." The following chart reveals selected revisions included in the 1629 King James Version:

Text	1611	1629	Cambridge KJV 1999
Exodus 26:8	and the eleuen	and the eleven curtains	and the eleven curtains
Deuteronomy 5:29	My commandements	all My commandments	all my commandments
Deuteronomy 10:10 (margin)	fortie dayes	former days	forty days
1 Samuel 1:20 (marginal note)	Heb. reuelation of dayes	Heb in revolution of days	Heb. in revolution of days
Mark 15:41	Galile	Galilee	Galilee
1 Corinthians 12:28	helpes in gouernmēts	helps, governments	helps, governments

The Revision Process Succeeds (1638)

The Bible revisions of the seventeenth century brought an economic windfall to printers, and Cambridge entered the market to capture a share of those profits. The 1638 edition, produced in a readable roman type, was published to help Cambridge gain a foothold in the market share.

In 1638 Ward and Bois, joined by Thomas Goad and Joseph Mead, translation scholars who joined the work of the revision, continued the efforts they began with the 1629 edition. Under their direction, printers Thomas

Buck and Roger Daniel printed what proved to be an accurate revision in a large folio similar to the original 1611 folio. Most of the errors in the original 1611 were corrected. Special attention was paid to uniform rendering of the italics. In addition to improvements in the margins and the rendering of italics, new readings were also introduced into the text itself.

The 1638 revision became the standard edition until 1762 and was quite possibly the finest King James Version ever printed. Unfortunately, some of the 1629 corrections were not carried into the 1638. From the period of 1638 to 1762 the text of the King James Version remained stable in the form it was published in the 1638 revision.

Text	1611 and 1629	1638 Revision	Cambridge KJV 1999
Matthew 12:23	Is this the sonne of Dauid?	Is not this the sonne of David?	Is not this the son of David?
1 John 5:12	hath not the Sonne	hath not the Sonne of God	hath not the Son of God
Acts 6:3[4]	whom we may appoint	whom ye may appoint	whom we may appoint
John 14:6	the Trueth	and the truth	the truth

Profits at the Expense of Accuracy

In the years following the first printings of the King James Version, the Geneva Bible still exerted significant influence. After 1616, however, Archbishop William Laud successfully suppressed the printing of Geneva Bibles in England, making it illegal to print them. Recognizing that the Geneva notes were still popular among Puritans, foreign printers entered the English Bible printing market. In 1642 Amsterdam printer Joost Broerz began printing the King James Version. His version included Geneva notes and Junius's annotations on Revelation. (Junius was a sixteenth-century Huguenot and joint author of a Latin version of the Old Testament.)

Printing the Bible was good for the economy, but the economic climate produced overzealous printers who often lacked good editing skills. Not all editors followed the *standard* 1638 King James edition, a fact which can be seen in the many variations in editions between these two major revisions.

During the period from 1630 to 1762, the public demand for Bibles caused printers to shortcut proofreading procedures, which often resulted in gross errors that disgraced some Bible publishers. For instance, the seventh commandment in Exodus 20:14 reads, "Thou shalt not commit adultery." One edition that omitted the letters *n-o-t* became known as the "Wicked Bible." The absence of those three letters has made this edition the most notorious Bible ever produced. In the Brake-Hellstern rare Bible display at the Dunham Bible Museum in Houston, Texas, the "Wicked Bible" receives more attention than any other Bible in the museum collection. Another 1638 King James edition provides an erroneous reading based on word substitution in Luke 7:47. "Her sins which are many are *forgotten*."

Other error-ridden King James Bibles have become Bible collectors' favorites. A 1653 KJV became known as the "Unrighteous Bible" because of its reading in 1 Corinthians 6:9, "Know ye not that the unrighteous shall inherit the kingdom of God?" Another of the infamous *error Bibles* is the "Vinegar Bible" of 1716–17. The top of the page heading in Luke 20 reads, "Parable of the Vinegar," instead of, "Parable of the Vineyard." The

The "Wicked Bible" offered a distinctive reading of Exodus 20:14, "Thou shalt commit adultery."

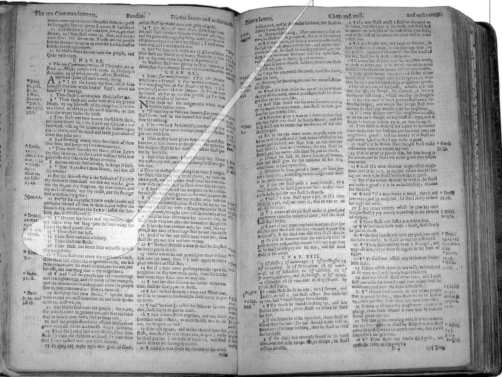

Mischief at the Press

The silence of the night was broken by muffled steps. Two dark-clad figures crept forward through the darkness, their shoes padded in burlap secured with twine. Guided by moonlight, they approached the side door of the London printing house as they strained for the sounds of approaching footsteps. The two figures pried at the side door with crowbars, and the wooden structure yielded with little effort. Within moments they were inside the print shop where they headed straight for the press that lay prepared with the next day's job typeset in an open tray.

One man lit a candle and scanned the type while a second man blocked the dim light from the view of the window. Then slowly and deliberately the first man leaned forward and removed three metal letters of type from the page setup: *n-o-t*. He pocketed the letters he had removed from the seventh commandment, Exodus 20:14, "Thou shalt not commit adultery." The verse now read, "Thou shalt commit adultery." Three letters became the focus of an investigation, imprisonment, and controversy that stirred debate for the next four centuries.

The following morning the door of the print shop was discovered open, but nothing seemed disturbed. No one was apprehended, and the burglary went undetected.

The crime, however, soon became public. While he was not to blame for the crime, printer Robert Barker soon bore the burden of responsibility. When the missing word was discovered after copies of the completed Bible were already in circulation, Barker, printer of the 1631 King James octavo, was fined 300 British pounds (approximately $500 by modern standards). The scandal and the financial penalty were the beginning of the end for Barker. He was forced into bankruptcy and died, literally in the poor house—a tragic end for a man who contributed so much to the early printing of the most influential book in the English-speaking world.

Barker's partners, John Bill and Bonham Norton, were known for their litigious entanglements with Barker and growing frustrations with a string of court decisions against them. For years a conspiracy theory has circulated that Norton and Bill were responsible for the printing omission, based on their reputation for burglary and related illegal misdeeds. Although some experts explain the exclusion of the word as a simple seventeenth-century printing error, the elements of coincidence in the "Wicked Bible" provide tantalizing reasons to speculate about Bill's and Norton's possible complicity.

printer, John Baskett, overlooked so many mistakes in printing this Bible that it was dubbed a "Baskett-full-of-errors."

The First Standard Edition (1762)

More than one hundred years passed before another serious attempt was made at a revision. During this time increased literacy and higher education led to increased intolerance for misprints, errors, and inferior printing, which resulted in a cry for Bibles faithful to the original text. Several editions had revised elements of the text of the King James Version, but no version had successfully eliminated all the errors. F. S. (Thomas) Paris was determined to improve upon previous attempts at revision and edited the then-current King James Version for Joseph Bentham at Cambridge in 1762.

Paris made a serious attempt to correct spelling, punctuation, italics, and printers' errors. His edition, more than any since 1611, formed the basis for the King James Version still used in the twenty-first century. Unfortunately, the 1762 version attained very little circulation and was criticized by some.

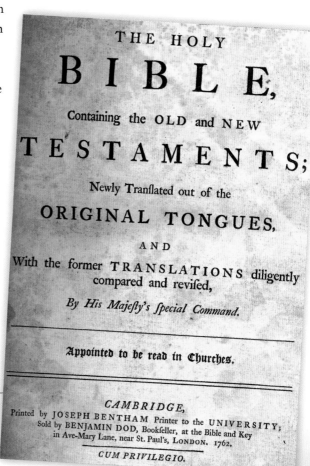

THE HOLY
BIBLE,
Containing the OLD and NEW
TESTAMENTS;
Newly Translated out of the
ORIGINAL TONGUES,
AND
With the former TRANSLATIONS diligently
compared and revised,
By His Majesty's special Command.

Appointed to be read in Churches.

CAMBRIDGE,
Printed by JOSEPH BENTHAM Printer to the UNIVERSITY;
Sold by BENJAMIN DOD, Bookseller, at the Bible and Key
in Ave-Mary Lane, near St. Paul's, LONDON. 1762.
CUM PRIVILEGIO.

Title leaf of the King James Version revised by F. S. (Thomas) Paris in 1762.

Nevertheless, it satisfied scholars' desire for an accurate English translation, and it also paved the way for Benjamin Blayney's *magnum opus* in 1769.

Even the least important features fell under the scalpel of editing in Paris's edition. Several noticeable errors occurred in the revision of italics, which were used to indicate English words that were necessary to accurately express the concept from the original language. For example, in 2 Kings 25:4 the 1611 version correctly reads, "of warre *fled* by night," whereas the 1762 reads, "of *war* fled by night." And in Psalm 13:3 Paris mistakenly altered "the *sleep* of death" to the 1611 reading "the sleep of *deat*."

The new version also introduced a significant marginal note in Acts 7:45. The text reads, "Which also our fathers that came after, brought in with Jesus. . . ." Paris's note says, "Or having received." The 1881–85 Revised Version and the 1901 American Standard Version make no mention of the alternate rendering of the Greek phrase. But the 1982 New King James Bible published by Thomas Nelson uses the same rendering and places it in the text itself, not just in the margin: "Which our fathers, having received it in succession. . . ." The following chart reveals the influence of the 1762. It mirrors the text used in modern KJVs.

Text	1611 KJV	1762 Cambridge KJV	1999 Cambridge KJV
Matthew 16:16	Thou are Christ	Thou are the Christ	Thou art the Christ
Luke 19:9	the son of Abraham	a son of Abraham	a son of Abraham
John 15:20	than the Lord	than his Lord	than his Lord
Romans 4:12	but also walk	but who also walk	but who also walk

The Revision that Stands the Test of Time (1769)

Building on Thomas Paris's 1762 Cambridge edition, Benjamin Blayney edited the King James Version in 1769, and Thomas Wright and W. Gill of Oxford printed it. Incorporating and expanding Paris's work, Blayney's text became the standard King James Version for the next one hundred years. Blayney's central contributions included revised spelling, italics, and marginal notes. He also revised chapter summaries and, in some cases, expanded them by as much as one-third. Blayney's edition continued the use

THE

HOLY BIBLE,

CONTAINING

The Old and New Testaments :

TRANSLATED OUT OF

The ORIGINAL TONGUES:

AND WITH THE

FORMER TRANSLATIONS

Diligently Compared and Revised,

By His MAJESTY's Special Command.

Appointed to be read in Churches.

O X F O R D,

Printed by *T. Wright* and *W. Gill*, Printers to the U N I V E R S I T Y:
And sold by *R. Baldwin*, and *S. Crowder*, in Paternoster Row, London;
and by *W. Jackson*, in Oxford. 1769.

CUM PRIVILEGIO.

of Bishop William Lloyd's chronology, which was first introduced in Paris's 1762 edition.

Despite Blayney's careful attempt to eliminate errors, mistakes were carried into the 1769 version. Although he depended heavily on Paris's edition, in some instances he corrected Paris's work and in other instances he repeated 1611 KJV readings.

Text	1611 KJV	1762 Paris	1769 Blayney	1999 Cambridge KJV
Genesis 10:7	Sabtecha	Sabtecah	Sabtechah	Sabtecha
Deuteronomy 10:2	brakest	brakedst	brakedst	brakest
Psalm 135:5	our LORD[5]	our Lord	our Lord	our Lord
Jeremiah 40:1	the word that	the word which	the word which	the word that
Nahum 3:16	flieth	fleeth	fleeth	flieth
Acts 7:28	diddest	killedst	diddest	diddest
James 2:16	be you warmed & filled	be *ye* warmed and be ye filled	be *ye* warmed and filled	be *ye* warmed and filled

The battle for literary superiority in Bible publishing continued between Oxford and Cambridge. While it might be expected that Oxford Press consulted the Oxford-Blayney edition and Cambridge Press consulted the

Cambridge-Paris edition as they printed Bibles, both publishers consulted both the Blayney and Paris editions. Generally speaking, modern editions today follow Blayney's edition, but this is not true in all cases. The following chart shows a sampling of differences and similarities between the various editions, demonstrating that Oxford and Cambridge showed no particular loyalty to their own editions, which demonstrates the publishers' priority for accuracy of the text over promoting their own publications.

Text	1611 KJV	1762 Cambridge (Paris) KJV	1999 Cambridge KJV	1769 Oxford (Blayney) KJV	2002 Oxford KJV
Deuteronomy 10:2	brakest	brakedst	brakest	brakedst	brakest
Jeremiah 40:1	the word that	the word which	the word that	the word which	the word that
Nahum 3:16	flieth	fleeth	flieth	fleeth	fleeth

These two eighteenth-century editions modernized the English Bible and prepared the way for work in the nineteenth century. With only a few exceptions the notes and especially the italics remained the same in subsequent editions. Unfortunately, a fire occurred soon after the printing and destroyed the impression of Blayney's folio edition.[6]

Text	1611 KJV	1769 Revision	1999 Cambridge KJV
2 Corinthians 5:2	earnestly, desiring	earnestly desiring	earnestly desiring
Revelation 13:15	to give	to give them	to give
Proverbs 6:19	and him that soweth	and he that soweth	and he that soweth

By the mid-nineteenth century, the lucrative Bible market had caught the attention of Americans. Between 1847 and 1851 the American Bible Society attempted a revision under the leadership of American scholar Edward Robinson. Using recently published Bibles in London, Oxford, Cambridge, and Edinburgh, a committee of seven men compared and collated the four British versions to a standard American edition. This process shaped basic translation principles for the new revision. James W. McLane, a Presbyterian minister from New York, drew up other rules to guide the committee in its work. The work continued for three and a half years before the results were presented to the committee, who rejected the effort based on common dissatisfaction with a number of changes represented in the revisions.[7]

Revision Revised after One Hundred Years:
Cambridge Paragraph Bible (1873)

The failure of the American Bible Society influenced subsequent translation work and prolonged the life of the Blayney edition, which continued to be printed by Oxford University Press. In 1831 a controversy emerged when Thomas Curtis challenged the accuracy of contemporary editions of Scripture in reflecting the readings of the original 1611 King James Version. Curtis published his findings in 1833 in *The Existing Monopoly; an Inadequate Protection of the Authorized Version of the Scripture*. Thomas Turton, professor at Cambridge, and Edward Cardwell, professor at Oxford, took up the cause to defend the accuracy of modern translations. In response to the controversy, Oxford published an exact reprint of the 1611 King James Version. In the introduction, the publisher said,

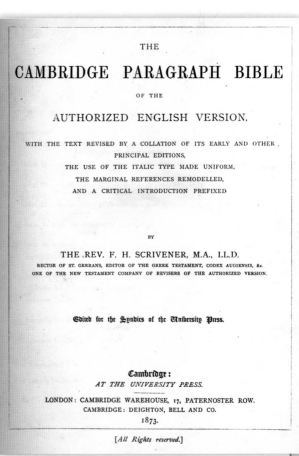

THE

CAMBRIDGE PARAGRAPH BIBLE

OF THE

AUTHORIZED ENGLISH VERSION,

WITH THE TEXT REVISED BY A COLLATION OF ITS EARLY AND OTHER
PRINCIPAL EDITIONS,
THE USE OF THE ITALIC TYPE MADE UNIFORM,
THE MARGINAL REFERENCES REMODELLED,
AND A CRITICAL INTRODUCTION PREFIXED

BY

THE REV. F. H. SCRIVENER, M.A., LL.D.

RECTOR OF ST. GERRANS, EDITOR OF THE GREEK TESTAMENT, CODEX AUGIENSIS, &c.
ONE OF THE NEW TESTAMENT COMPANY OF REVISERS OF THE AUTHORIZED VERSION.

Edited for the Syndics of the University Press.

Cambridge :

AT THE UNIVERSITY PRESS.

LONDON: CAMBRIDGE WAREHOUSE, 17, PATERNOSTER ROW.
CAMBRIDGE: DEIGHTON, BELL AND CO.
1873.

[*All Rights reserved.*]

Title leaf to the Cambridge Paragraph Bible 1873.

[It is] so exact as to agree with the original Edition page for page, and letter for letter; retaining throughout the ancient mode of spelling and punctuation, and even the most manifest errors of the Press. Without this extreme degree of accuracy the Reader would not have been able to judge by its means, whether the original Standard can still be exactly followed, and how far the deviations introduced at different periods, and which have now had possession of our Bibles for many years, can reasonably be abandoned.[8]

The resurrection of the 1611 edition of the King James Version at first seemed possible. But the publication of the 1833 facsimile of the 1611 translation demonstrated the impossibility of going back to the 1611 version. In the intervening two hundred years between editions, great strides had been made in printing, diction, and spelling. A return to the misprints of the 1611 was not an option.

Even though the 1769 edition was considered the finest text of its day, collation work for an Eyre and Spottiswoode KJV (the king's printer) identified 116 errors. The resulting controversy fueled a desire to produce an accurate text and reinforced the need for a new translation; that controversy culminated in the publication of the Cambridge Paragraph Bible in 1873.

Could the controversy between Oxford and Cambridge universities be brought to an acceptable conclusion? F. H. A. Scrivener attempted to bring the two schools together to support one accurate, critical revision of the 1611 with the 1873 Cambridge Paragraph Bible. For many years scholars praised his success in creating the most accurate of all the revisions of the Authorized Bible. He carefully and laboriously compared word for word the 1611 edition, improved the marginal notes, and modernized spelling. The text, arranged in paragraph form, afforded the reader the luxury of complete thoughts grouped together and read in context rather than in fragmented segments, as in the separate verse divisions in the 1611 and its revisions.

The plethora of revisions and translations weakened the hold of the King James Version dominance. When Scrivener completed the Cambridge Paragraph Bible in 1873, he was aware that work on the Revised Version had been underway for approximately three years (it was not completed until 1885). He felt a critical edition of the 1611 was necessary—even if it served only as an accurate textual tool for the Revised Version. So Scrivener accepted an appointment to the revision committee for the English Revised Version, which indicates that members undoubtedly consulted the Cambridge Paragraph Bible.

Scrivener's work included an appendix that compared all of the major and minor editorial revisions of and departures from the 1611 King James Version. In addition to the hundreds of editorial corrections between 1611 and 1769, the Paragraph Bible restored about 125 previously abandoned readings in those editions. Examples of some of these words that had departed from the 1611 KJV are provided in this table.

Text	1611 KJV	1762 Cambridge, 1769 Oxford	1873 Cambridge Paragraph Bible	1999 Cambridge KJV
Matthew 23:24	straine at a gnat	strain at a gnat	strain out a gnat	strain at a gnat
Mark 6:53	Genesareth	Gennesaret	Genesaret	Gennesaret
Mark 10:18	there is no man good, but one	*there is* none good, but one	*there is* none good but one	*there is* none good but one
Mark 14:32	Gethsemani	Gethsemane	Gethsemane	Gethsemane

The table below shows short texts restored from 1611 and omitted in revisions between 1611 and 1873:

Text	1611 KJV	1762 Cambridge, 1769 Oxford	1873 Cambridge	1999 Cambridge KJV
Genesis 37:36	Medanites	Midianites	Medanites	Midianites
Romans 11:23	bide	abide	bide	abide
1 Timothy 2:9	shamefastness	shamefacedness	shamefastness	shamefacedness

The Oxford-Cambridge controversy over the style of the King James Version significantly diminished respect for the version. While scholars acknowledged the accuracy and smooth expression of the KJV, most believed its diction, spelling, and scholarship pointed to the obvious conclusion that the time had come for a new translation.

The battle for Bible translation supremacy had begun. After 250 years of literary dominance, the King James Version's reign was in question, and a new translation was about to threaten the throne. In February 1870, both houses of the Convocation of Canterbury unanimously passed a resolution to appoint a committee of scholars to begin the work of a new translation. The convocations were, and still are, provincial assemblies of the clergy that hold great power; however, they often disagree. In a significant act of solidarity, the 1870 Convocation planned the details for the new revision of the Authorized Version, but over the course of time, the project grew beyond the scope of the original proposal.

The Revised Version was completed in 1885 and later included the American edition's 1901 revisions. It became the first genuine text revision since the 1611 King James Version, reflecting work that extended beyond editorial changes. The new revision was not initially accepted, nor did it gain universal approval in the intervening years. Scholars embraced the Revised Version, but the general public clung to the established and familiar King James Version.

Today's proliferation of modern translations began in the mid-nineteenth century. Since 1831, individuals, denominations, committees, and religious sects have birthed Bible versions. Some are classified as revisions of the King James Version while others are categorized as translations from the Greek and Hebrew. Those who support the superiority of the 1611 King James Version often refuse to accept revisions other than the 1611 or the final revision of 1769. In spite of one's opinion about the superiority of the King James Version over other versions, the translation's continued popularity bears witness to its enduring legacy as England's most famous literary achievement.

> In spite of one's opinion about the superiority of the King James Version over other versions, the translation's continued popularity bears witness to its enduring legacy as England's most famous literary achievement.

The Scofield Reference Bible (1909)

One King James study Bible has quite possibly influenced more conservative Christians in the twentieth century than any other. The Scofield Reference Bible, a widely circulated King James study Bible, was edited and annotated by Cyrus I. Scofield in 1909. Oxford University used the traditional King James Version text of 1769 for the text of the Scofield Bible, which first appeared in 1909 and was revised by the author in 1917 and again in 1967 by E. Schuyler English. The most recent Scofield edition revised archaic expressions and brought them into twentieth-century vernacular. In the introduction to the 1967 edition, the editor describes his selected departures from the standard King James Version:

> For example, "bakemeats" is obsolete, as is "botch" in its meaning of a *boil*; "minish" is archaic, as is "ouch" meaning *setting*; today we use "restrain" instead of "let,"

The Bible and the Baptist

I entered a small Christian bookstore in the town of Shelbyville, Illinois, with a sense of excitement. Several days previously a local jeweler had presented a lengthy explanation of an eschatological chart to my wife and me and encouraged us to think about whether we would one day meet Christ as Savior or Judge. That night Carol and I decided we wanted to meet him as Savior, and we both accepted Jesus Christ into our lives. We had been advised by our spiritual mentor to purchase a Bible and read it through.

That day as I scanned the bookstore shelves, my eyes fell on a Scofield Reference Bible. The language of the King James Bible somehow felt like *holy language* to me. I liked the feel and especially enjoyed the explanatory information available in the notes. "This Bible can explain the things I don't understand," I reasoned to myself.

As I handed my Bible to the clerk, he scrutinized my selection and then glanced up at me. "This is a Baptist Bible!" he warned.

I wasn't sure what he meant, but our friend the jeweler, who had so carefully explained the Bible chart and encouraged us to receive Christ, had recommended the Scofield Bible. I thanked the clerk for his admonition but assured him that the Scofield was the Bible I wanted.

My Scofield Bible guided me through the early years of growth in my Christian life. I soon discovered that the truth of God's Word was not based upon notes written in the margins, but upon the words in the text.

which is archaic in the sense of *hindering*. Word changes have been made when clarification is necessary. It is not a new translation but it is the language of the King James Version that has been modified for modern readers.

The King's Version Still under Revision (1982)

Many Christians today still prefer the King James Version over newer translations.[9] But there also have been attempts to provide a King James Version for the modern reader, such as the one led by Thomas Nelson Publishers in 1982.

The New King James Version translation project began with the vision of Arthur Farstad (d. 1998) in 1975. More than sixty people met in Chicago and Nashville and produced guidelines for the revision. From these meetings Thomas Nelson Publishers commissioned 130 Bible scholars, church leaders, and lay Christian workers to create a modern revision that would retain the accuracy, purity, and stylistic beauty of the 1611 King James Version. James Price (Temple Baptist Theological Seminary) edited the Old Testament, Arthur Farstad (Dallas Theological Seminary) edited the New Testament, and William McDowell (Florida Southern College) edited the English language usage.[10]

The New Testament revision was completed in 1979 and the complete Bible in 1982.

A selection of modern King James Versions: 21st Century King James Version (1994), New King James Version (1982), New Cambridge Paragraph Bible (2005), Scofield Reference Bible (1909), and Revised Version (1881–85). Photo: A. May.

The translators attempted to remain faithful to the original language while adhering to linguistic principles and textual studies, incorporating the most recent archaeological finds, and updating the language to conform to current usage. The translators consulted the original language texts used in the long line of King James translations and revisions. The 1967–77 Stuttgart edition of the *Biblia Hebraica* for the Old Testament, with comparisons made to the Jacob ben Chayyim edition published by Daniel Bomberg in 1524–25, formed the base for the Old Testament. The Septuagint and Latin Vulgate were also consulted. The New Testament followed the *Textus Receptus*, in spite of the fact that Farstad served as an editor of the Majority Text (a variant text to the Byzantine text-type). The revisers employed the dynamic equivalent linguistic theory.[11]

Once again the translators relied upon processes quite similar to those used in earlier revisions. Changes in word order, syntax, vocabulary, and spelling dominated the work. The major noticeable differences occurred in the change of the pronouns *ye, thou, thee, thy,* and *thine* to *you* and *your*. Verb forms such as *leadeth* and *speaketh* were modernized to *leads* and *speaks*.

Public acceptance of the New King James Version was mixed. Modern scholars criticized the version's minor revisions, asserting that the language of the version was neither seventeenth century nor twentieth century. Other criticisms were leveled: The version was not easy to read, nor did it follow modern textual-critical scholarship. It was based on the long-abandoned Byzantine textform. But many Christians who had embraced the King James Version for many years found the New King James refreshing and readable. Today the New King James Version represents a large market share of Bible sales.

To help convince the public of the new Bible's authenticity, Thomas Nelson published a facsimile of the 1611 King James Version in a matching cover with its 1982 New King James Version. Readers were encouraged to compare editions to verify the accuracy of the New King James with the

1611 edition. While the Greek text-type was the same as used by the translators of 1611, the actual Greek New Testament was primarily the text of F. H. A. Scrivener that was published in the nineteenth century.

The New Cambridge Paragraph Bible (2005)

The publication of the New King James Version did not satisfy the desire for revision by publishers and many of its readers. Cambridge University launched a project to modernize the text of the King James Version called the Paragraph Bible, which was published in 2005. David Norton, an English language scholar from New Zealand, superintended this revision of the Cambridge Paragraph Bible of 1873. The publisher planned to modernize the 1611 King James English without producing an actual revision, creating a new text that would reflect the work of the 1611 translators and not subsequent revisions. Any modernization of the text was not to interfere with the original text or translation and should relate only to spelling, punctuation, and vocabulary. Taking the basic text of the original 1611 King James Version, Norton applied three guidelines in the revision of the New Cambridge Paragraph Bible:

1. Modernize, unless the meaning of the text is changed or obscured; be wary of transgressing against etymology.
2. Preserve genuine forms of words but not variant spellings.
3. Where possible, use variant acceptable forms to represent clearly identifiable semantic variations.[12]

The following table compares readings between the 1611 and the New Cambridge Paragraph Bible:

Text	1611 King James Version	1873 Cambridge Paragraph Bible	2005 New Cambridge Paragraph Bible	1999 Cambridge KJV
Matthew 1:5	Boos	Booz	Booz	Booz
Matthew 2:1	Hierusalem	Jerusalem	Jerusalem	Jerusalem
Matthew 9:34	casteth out the deuils	casteth out the devils	casteth out the devils	casteth out devils
Acts 7:35	by the handes	by the hand	by the hands	by the hand

Even though a modern word might be better understood by modern readers, passages in the New Cambridge Paragraph Bible retained archaic word forms from the 1611 KJV:

Text	1611 King James Version	2005 New Cambridge Paragraph Bible	Modern form	Cambridge KJV 1999
1 Samuel 30:13	agone	agone	ago	agon
Matthew 13:21	dureth	dureth	endure	dureth
Exodus 28:36	grave	grave	engrave	grave
2 Kings 9:26	plat	plat	a plot [of ground]	plat

The New Cambridge Paragraph Bible relies upon the traditional *Textus Receptus* as its Greek New Testament instead of the critical Greek New Testament used by most modern translations. It was welcomed by those

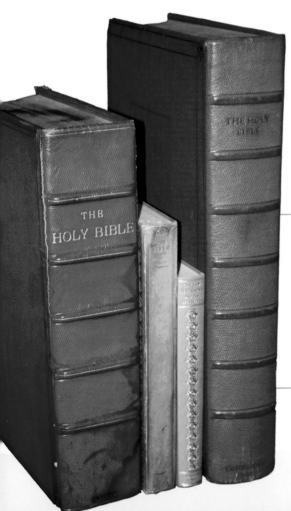

Collector's editions of fine quality printed King James Versions: 1935 Oxford Lectern Bible (considered the finest and most consistent example of composition on the most excellent quality paper); the 1925 Nonesuch Bible (quality printing); the 1963 Nonesuch Bible (known for its well-designed layout and print quality); the 1763 Baskerville Bible (considered Baskerville's *magnum opus* and his most magnificent edition). Photo: A. May.

Curiosities of the King James Bible

A small number of what some people identify as *errors* in the King James Bible can be viewed simply as printing and editing curiosities. Errors generally occurred due to a lack of skill in editing or from fallible printers rushing to meet great demand.[13] For example, printer John Baskett's error-ridden version, called the "Vinegar Bible," was so riddled with inconsistencies it was dubbed a "Baskett-full-of-errors." Additional printing errors include:

"He/She Bible" (1611–13) The original King James Bible appeared in two editions. One has been dubbed the "He Bible" and the other the "Great She Bible" for their distinct translations of Ruth 3:15, "And he/she went into the citie." Scholars generally agree that the *he* reading originally appeared in the first edition. The *she* reading appears in the second and all subsequent editions (except for certain 1612 and 1613 quartos and octavos, which read *he* or *hee*) because *she* was considered the correct reading. But the supporting Hebrew manuscripts (primarily Syriac) allow for either reading. In fact, the 1885 English Revised Version reads *he* and records in the margin that some ancient sources use the word *she*.

"Judas Bible" (1611) The "She Bible" and the New Testament of the 1611–13 folio mistakenly print the word *Judas* for *Jesus* in Matthew 26:36. A similar error occurs in the first issue of the 1610–11 Geneva Bible in John 6:67.

"Revenge Bible" (1613) In a quarto Bible printed by Robert Barker, Romans 12:17 reads, "Recompense to man evil for evil" (instead of "Recompense to no man evil for evil").

"Wicked Bible" (1631) Barker's octavo edition of the King James Version printed a colossal mistake in Exodus 20:14, "Thou shalt commit adultery."

who love the King James Version and wanted a revision that did not abandon the 1611. The Paragraph Bible's strength lies in its reflection and retention of the assets of the popular 1611 version.

In spite of the fact that the language of the new Bible does not reflect modern English usage, after four hundred years the King James Version is still preferred by significant numbers of Bible readers in the English-speaking world. While some people continue to choose the King James

"Forgotten Sins Bible" (1638) A pocket-size (duodecimo) edition of the King James Version features an error in Luke 7:47, "Her sins which are many are forgotten" (where *forgiven* is intended).

"More Sea Bible" (1641) An octavo edition printed by Barker renders the last sentence of Revelation 21:1, "and there was more sea," which should have been, "and there was no more sea."

"Easter Bible" (1648) John Field of London issued a quarto King James Version that read in the title page of Esther, "The Book of Easter."

"Unrighteous Bible" (1653) Printer John Field's small pocket edition of the King James Version renders 1 Corinthians 6:9, "Know ye not that the unrighteous shall [for *shall not*] inherit the kingdom of God?"

"Vinegar Bible" (1716–17) John Baskett's folio edition of the King James Version misprinted the page heading over Luke 20 as the "Parable of the Vinegar" instead of the "Parable of the Vineyard."

"Sting Bible" (1746) In this small Bible printed by Thomas Baskett, Mark 7:35 reads, "the sting of his tongue" (instead of, "the string of his tongue").

"Murderer's Bible" (1801) An Oxford University Press octavo edition of the King James Version misprints "murderers" (for "murmurers") in Jude 16.

"Standing Fishes Bible" (1806) A two-volume London quarto printed by G. Woodfall for George Eyre and Andrew Strahan reads in Ezekiel 47:10, "The fishes shall stand" (where "fishers" was intended).

"Wife-Hater's Bible" (1810) An Oxford University Press octavo of the King James Version rendered Luke 14:26, "If any man hate not his father . . . , and his own wife also, he cannot be my disciple" (the word *wife* should have been *life*).

Version based on style or familiarity, others unequivocally claim the King James to be superior to other versions. Both consumer preferences may guarantee the viability of the King James Version well into the twenty-first century.

12

American Cousins

Entering the New World

The long voyage, sleepless nights, and bouts of seasickness washed away in the swirling surf as the weary Pilgrims left their ships and waded ashore in the New World. Weeks of hunger, cold, and overcrowding had come to an end. Their eyes drank in the sight of shoreline, trees, and solid ground—ground their small band would call home.

The hardship had been worth the wait. Before lying down to sleep their first night in the New World, men, women, and children offered prayers of thanks. Utopia awaited—a land far from the grip of the British throne, the repression of the Anglican Church, and the influence of papal authority. Worship in this new land could take place without discrimination, harassment, or persecution. With their Bibles and the promise of God's Spirit among them, the Pilgrims set their hopes on a bright future. With dedication to God and commitment to forging a new life infusing their souls, failure was not an option.

The Pilgrims landed in Plymouth, Massachusetts, in 1620 with their Bibles in their hands and a vision of a New World governed by God's Word. With the Church of England an ocean away, the Pilgrims saw their new home as a sanctuary from former persecution. The colonists who established the first permanent settlement of Jamestown, Virginia, in 1607 came as refugees from the Church of England. Their first charter assured freedom in religious worship, church establishment, and the right to conduct evangelism among the Native Americans.

The Puritans, who began immigrating to America in 1628, were known first and foremost for their belief in the Bible and their appetite for English translations.[1] They preferred the Geneva Bible with its Calvinistic commentary notes; linking the sacred text with study notes gave added credibility to the Puritan emphasis on piety. Historically, church leaders had viewed laity reading the Bible as a potentially dangerous practice; however, new attitudes and thinking among the Puritans had brought a change, and the laity were now encouraged to read the Bible. They appreciated the guidance of scholarly notes written by professional clergy, and the Puritans' spiritual leaders taught that reading the Bible along with the Geneva commentary notes and listening to their pastor's sermon could lead the pious into true spirituality.

> Taking seriously the doctrine of the authority and infallibility of Scripture, Puritans attempted to apply the Bible to every area of political, religious, and social life.

Taking seriously the doctrine of the authority and infallibility of Scripture, Puritans attempted to apply the Bible to every area of political, religious, and social life. American historian and author Harry Stout writes that with the continued growth of Puritanism, "questions of national polity and social order increasingly received attention from the learned divines."[2] When it came to the clergy, however, many preferred a Bible without commentary.

The King James Version of 1611 provided a translation that was accurate and scholarly without including theologically biased notes. Stout writes, "Where the Geneva Bible and its marginalia served well the purpose of an embattled religious minority with thoughts fixed firmly on martyrdom and the world to come, it was less useful in fashioning binding principles of a social organization and order in this world."[3] The Puritans' application of oversimplified religious principles to social and religious society led to what many consider the darkest era in American religious history. The Salem witch trials became forever identified with Puritanism.

In 1630 John Winthrop brought the first recorded copy of a King James Version to America (a 1614 edition). Henry Dunster (1609–59), the first president of Harvard College (1640–59), owned another early copy of the King James Version, which is now housed in the Harvard University Library.[4] Within just a few years, the King James Version became the Bible of the American colonies.

The Puritans' strict and legalistic use of the Bible eventually gave way to the Great Awakening in the eighteenth century and a more moderate reading of the Bible, resulting in the development of biblical educational principles, the establishment of colleges, and the consolidation of political influence. The King James Version enabled the clergy to forge a more moderate approach to theology and ecclesiastical practice. Churches entered a time of steady growth both numerically and spiritually.

A leaf from the 1663 Eliot Bible, the first edition of the first Bible published in America.

Eliot Indian Bible: The King James Version Meets the Native American

The first New Testament printed in the new world was written in the Algonquin language and was called the Eliot Indian Bible. Published in 1663 in Cambridge, Massachusetts, by Samuel Green and Marmaduke Johnson, the Eliot Indian Bible was dedicated to Charles II of England. The last man to read Algonquin, James Trumbull, died in 1897.

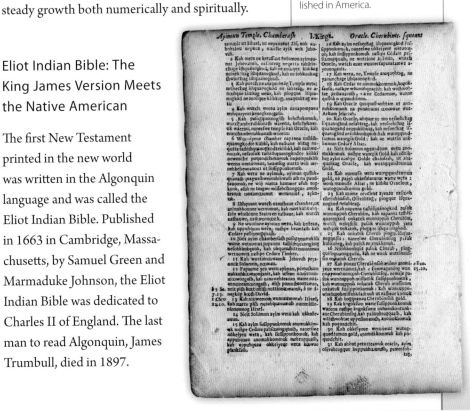

John Eliot arrived in America in 1631 and became a missionary to the Indians in the region of Massachusetts at age forty-two. Over the next twenty-five years he organized twenty-four congregations and trained twenty Native American pastors while he worked on the Algonquin translation. In thirty years Eliot reported 11,000 converts to Christianity. Insightful and perceptive questions raised by the Indians are recorded by American historian Marion Simms: "Whether there might not be something, if only a little, gained by praying to ye devil? Why does not God, who has full power, kill ye devil that makes all men so bad? If all the earth be burned up, where shall hell then be?"[5]

The basis for the Eliot Bible may have been the King James Version. One of Eliot's blunders in translation is seen in 2 Kings 2:23, where the KJV reads, "Goe up, thou baldhead." Eliot made the mistake of translating *bald-head* as *ball-head*: "Go up, thou ball-head."[6] Since the Geneva and Roman Catholic Douay Bibles read, "*Come* up, thou balde head" (emphasis added), Eliot must not have used the Geneva or the Douay Bible. Certainly Eliot's training at Cambridge could have included Hebrew, which also reads in translation, "Go up." If he used an English translation as his guiding text, the most likely version was the KJV. Since editions later than the 1611 large folio edition incorporated the same reading, determining which King James edition is impossible.

The Colonial Bible

England refused to give the American colonies permission to print Scripture on the new continent. They made the colonists import all Bibles from England so they would have to pay taxes and revenues to England. In a response that ultimately failed, the American Continental Congress tried to import 20,000 Bibles from Holland and Scotland.[7]

The American Revolution and independence from England signaled a new era for Bible printing. In 1777 entrepreneur Scotsman Robert Aitken set out to publish the *editio princips* (first edition) of the New Testament in America. The work was a complete King James Version in small octavo size,

A leaf from the Aitken Bible, which was the first English Bible (King James Version) printed in America.

and it appeared on the market in 1782.[8] The printer's address listed on the title page reads, "Three doors above the coffee house, in Market Street." The "Bible of the Revolution," as it is called, received full congressional support; it is the first and only Bible ever to receive such approval. The statement used by Congress and published in the Aitken Bible preliminaries reads:

> *Resolved,* That the United States in Congress assembled highly approve the pious and laudable undertaking of Mr. Aitken, as subservient to the interests of religion, as well an instance of the progress of arts in this country, and . . . they recommend this edition of the Bible to the inhabitants of the United States, and hereby authorize him to publish this recommendation in the manner he shall think proper. Cha. Thomson, Secy.[9]

The 1789 *Massachusetts Spy* newspaper ad by printer Isaiah Thomas.

Bibles printed in the colonies rather than imported from Britain were more affordable. Nevertheless, while American merchants and farmers often enjoyed material comforts, cash in the new nation was regularly in short supply. To entice potential buyers to make purchases, Bible printer Isaiah Thomas advertised the sale of a large family Bible in the local newspaper, the *Massachusetts Spy*, on December 10, 1789. In addition to a lengthy description of the beauty and size of this Bible, the ad included the following:

To make payment easy to those who wish to be encouragers of this laudable undertaking, and to be in possession of so valuable property as a Royal Quarto Bible, and who are not able to pay for one all in Cash—from such the Publisher will receive one half of the sum or 21 shillings, in the following articles, viz. Wheat, Rye, Indian Corn, Butter, or Pork, if delivered at his store in Worcester, or at the store of himself and Company in Boston, by the 20th day of December, 1790: the remaining sum of 21 shillings to be paid in Cash, as soon as the books are ready for delivery. This proposal is made, to accommodate all, notwithstanding the sum of 21 shillings will by no means be the proportion of Cash that each Bible bound, will cost the Publisher.

Near the end of the Revolutionary War, Presbyterian minister Dr. John Rogers suggested that a copy of the Aitken Bible (KJV) be given to each

Phantom American Bibles: A Collector's Dream Search?

Is it still possible for twenty-first-century Bible collectors to discover rare treasures? Perhaps.

One story claims that in spite of British prohibitions, two English Bibles were printed in America prior to the Aitken Bible of 1782. Early American printer Isaiah Thomas claimed that Gamaliel Rogers and Daniel Fowle secretly printed 2,000 copies of the first New Testament in a small duodecimo format. Thomas had completed an internship with Zechariah Fowle, who had served as an apprentice to Gamaliel Rogers and Daniel Fowle. According to Thomas's book, *The History of Printing in America*, Zechariah stated that Daniel had referred to the duodecimo edition of the New Testament on several occasions.[10] Thomas discusses the report in detail to counter arguments of those who dispute his claim; however, if an American printing of the Bible occurred, the printers managed to produce such a perfect imitation of the London edition that no copies have ever been identified.

Thomas related a second story: In the mid-eighteenth century, Massachusetts printers Kneeland and Green supposedly printed seven or eight hundred copies of a quarto for Daniel Henchman. This version would have been the first complete Bible printed in the colonies, appearing shortly after the New Testament of Rogers and Fowle. In order to prevent prosecution, Kneeland and Green printed the Bible in secret and forged the London imprint from a copy printed by Mark Baskett, printer to the King's Most Excellent Majesty.[11] The London and Massachusetts editions differ only in subtleties of typography, making it extremely difficult for scholars to identify the printers as Kneeland and Green. As with the Rogers and Fowle edition, no Bible has ever been found that can be identified as a Kneeland and Green.

Most experts regard Thomas's stories as fiction since the only known early copies of an American Bible were printed by Robert Aitken in 1777 (New Testament) and 1782 (complete Bible). But the lack of evidence for *phantom* Bibles does not necessarily mean they did not exist. Early American printers were creative entrepreneurs who worked in secret and could have printed Bibles as Thomas recounts, and there is no evidence he had any motive to concoct false reports.

So, Bible collectors, keep looking. If you find a Kneeland and Green or a Rogers and Fowle, be sure to let the world of Bible collectors in on your find. I'd love to be the first to know.

member of the Continental army. George Washington favored the proposal, but because his army was disbanding, he thought it financially irresponsible to approve such a measure. A facsimile of the letter communicating his sentiments, a treasured glimpse into the history of the Bible in America, was featured in *The Bible of the Revolution*, published by the Grabhorn Press for John Powell in 1930.[12] In a letter dated June 11, 1783, George Washington writes:

> Your Proposition respecting Mr. Aitkin's [*sic*] Bible would have been particularly noticed by me, had it been suggested in season. But the late Resolution of Congress for discharging Part of the Army, taking off near two thirds of our Numbers, it is now too late to make the Attempt. It would have pleased me well, if Congress had been pleased to make such an important present to the brave fellows, who have done so much for the Security of their country's Rights & Establishment.[13]

The Civil War Bible

The King James Version exerted a powerful influence on the men who fought in the Civil War.[14] In May 1861, with the war just under way, the board of the American Bible Society made it known to all distributors both in the South and North that they intended to supply all soldiers with copies of the Bible.[15] In August 1861 President Abraham Lincoln made a proclamation that forbade trade with the enemy, which made it difficult for the society to provide Bibles and New Testaments to the Confederate Army across enemy lines. During the next year, however, after negotiating with governmental agencies to gain special army permission, the society was able to provide Bibles to the Confederates. In 1863 it was reported that the Maryland Auxiliary placed 86,424 Bibles in Confederate hands.[16]

In spite of genuine efforts to get the Bible into the hands of all soldiers of both the Union and Confederate armies, Bibles became scarce in the South. By 1863 northern prisoners in Richmond were selling copies of Bibles they had bought from the American Bible Society for thirty cents to Confederates at inflated prices of twelve to fifteen dollars. With that money, the prisoners were able to buy food.[17]

Even the *mother country* got into the commercial enterprise of selling Bibles to the former colonies. Sharing Southern sympathies, in 1862 the Confederate States Bible Society in England printed 50,000 New Testaments, 10,000 Bibles, and 250,000 portions of Scripture in order to make them available free of charge to soldiers of the Confederacy.[18] Distribution was dangerous, since it meant ships were forced to run the sea blockade the Northern forces had set up to isolate the Southern armies. In spite of the challenges, several shipments successfully reached the South, although in some cases the Union blockade intercepted the ships, and the Bibles were taken as contraband.

Over the years I have collected copies of all the Bibles printed during the Civil War. One very interesting New Testament bears an inscription on the flyleaf identifying the "Rebel ship *Minna*," which attempted to run the

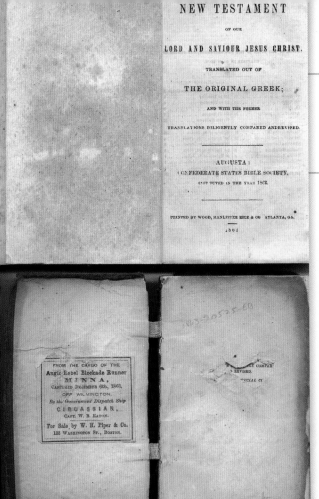

Shown are two rare and important Civil War New Testaments: 1862 Confederate New Testament printed in Atlanta, and 1863 New Testament that the rebel ship *Minna* attempted to smuggle into the South.

Northern blockade. The *Minna* was captured, and her Bibles were confiscated and sold at public auction in the North.

In 1862 the Confederate States Bible Society published a New Testament in Atlanta, Georgia. It was a simple copy, bound with heavy brown paper covers and measuring 2 3/8 x 5 inches. A crude sewing of the leaves and plain cover reveals the society's attempt to print New Testaments very inexpensively. Today these New Testaments are extremely rare.

During the war the American Bible Society supplied more than three million Bibles and New Testaments to soldiers fighting on both sides of the conflict. The 1860 and 1861 editions represent the greatest percentage of the total number, although during each year of the war the American Bible Society printed New Testaments to be distributed to soldiers. In 1866 (the Jubilee year of the founding of the American Bible Society), when the Civil War was over, the society printed a large run of New Testaments to replenish the supply lost during the war.

13

Behold the Legacy

Inspiration and Contribution

T he King James Version was paid the ultimate compliment when the translators of the 1881–85 Revised Version of the New Testament stated in their introduction:

> We have had to study this great Version [the KJV] carefully and minutely, line
> by line; and the longer we have been engaged upon it the more we have learned
> to admire its simplicity, its dignity, its power, its happy turns of expression, its
> general accuracy, and, we must not fail to add, the music of its cadences, and the
> felicities of its rhythm. To render a work that had reached this high standard of ex-
> cellence still more excellent, to increase its fidelity without destroying its charm,
> was the task committed to us.[1]

Although the King James Version competes against hundreds of modern translations, this four-hundred-year-old classic remains a popular translation and retains a large share of the Bible sales market. Some consumers choose the King James based on family preference or historical tradition. Others believe the language of the KJV communicates a sense of dignity and reverence. Still others select this version because they believe the translation is based on a more accurate and authoritative Greek New Testament text. And some who

choose the KJV hold to a theology and doctrine of preservation of Scripture that they believe points to the superiority of the version. These as well as other reasons continue to make the King James Version a popular translation four centuries after its introduction.[2]

Words That Endure

The King James Version's legacy and contribution to the English language can be recognized in phrases that have become well-known idiomatic expressions:[3]

"fall flat on his face" (Num. 22:31)
"a man after his own heart"
     (1 Sam. 13:14)
"the land of the living" (Job 28:13)
"pour out one's heart" (Ps. 62:8)
"pride goes before a fall" (Prov.
     16:18)

King James Bibles were often beautified with fore edge paintings of the exposed leaf edges and elaborate book covers. Shown above is a fore edge scene depicting Oxford University (1640), and to the right is a front-and-back book cover embroidered with a portrait of King David (1634). Photos: C. Brake.

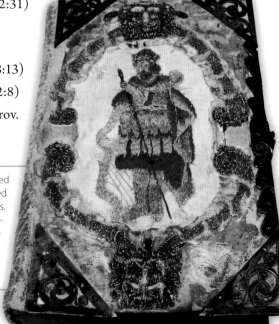

"like a lamb to the slaughter" (Isa. 53:7)

"sour grapes" (Ezek. 18:2)

"the salt of the earth" (Matt. 5:13)

"give up the ghost" (John 19:30)

"the powers that be" (Rom. 13:1)

"a thorn in the flesh" (2 Cor. 12:7)

Modern facsimiles of early English Bibles with original dates and dates of modern publications. Left to right: 1526 Tyndale (2002), 1388 Wycliffe (2000), 1535 Coverdale (1975), 1539 Great Bible (1991), 1611 King James Version (1961), 1560 Geneva (2007), and 1611 King James Version (1833). Photo: M. May.

The King James Version Today

Some people believe the 1611 King James Version is the *only* Bible inspired by God.[4] I am often asked:

"Which Bible is the best?"

"Why don't we decide on one version and have everyone use it?"

"Since the King James Version has stood the test of time, shouldn't we regard it as the best?"

What should our response be to questions like these?

Those who elevate the King James Version to icon status unfortunately force others who love the version to engage in fruitless and sometimes misdirected arguments that diminish the value of this theologically and historically important work. King James enthusiasts sometimes focus on the version's more peripheral elements, such as its beautiful but dated language, instead of engaging in serious investigation of the version's textual merits.

How should the King James Version be viewed in light of its history and legacy? Should it be examined in relation to modern linguistic theory and new manuscript discoveries? How should we view the archaic language of *thees* and *thous* and vastly outdated vocabulary? Should we regard the KJV as the only version inspired by God? Or should we acknowledge it as a *royal monument of English literature,* place it on the shelves with other antiquated books, and move our focus to modern translations?

I will focus on just two questions that I believe are of primary importance in this discussion: (1) Is the KJV inspired? and (2) What is the best translation?

Is the King James Version Inspired?

What do we understand to be the meaning of the term *inspiration*? The Bible addresses this question directly. Second Timothy 3:16 reads, "All Scripture is God-breathed and is useful for teaching, rebuking, correcting and training in righteousness" (NIV). The wording of the King James Version similarly states, "All scripture is given by inspiration of God, and is profitable for

Word and, ultimately, to empower them to change the hearts of their nation and their world.

As I sat under the mango trees, my thoughts moved toward the message I had been assigned to deliver in a few short days, addressing the many needs of these pastors' hearts. As I studied I was surprised to discover that the Murle language version of the New Testament was based on the text of the King James Version that had been translated almost four hundred years earlier; the King James Version was the beloved and familiar text of my African students.

Several years prior to my visit to the Murle pastors, while teaching in the Amharic language in a local Bible school in Ethiopia, I was challenged by a student regarding the wording of a passage of Scripture I was reading. When I compared my Bible to that of my students, I realized they were reading from an earlier Amharic translation of the Bible derived from the text of the King James Version. When I or other missionaries pointed out differences between the texts, students became confused, and our Western, logical explanations caused suspicion. My African students felt strongly that their edition of the Bible was the *true* version.

Their attachment to a beloved version represents an important issue that has engaged translators, clergymen, and Bible lovers across continents and over the span of four hundred years: Which is the best translation?

doctrine, for reproof, for correction, for instruction in righteousness." In this verse the predicate of the words *all Scripture* includes the term *God-breathed*, which is used only in this single instance in Scripture. Paul is claiming that, at least for the documents of the Old Testament that existed at the time, the words of Scripture originated with God himself.

The inspiration of Scripture extends to the New Testament as well. Paul implies the authority of Scripture in 1 Timothy 5:18, "For the Scripture says, 'Do not muzzle the ox while it is treading out the grain,' and, 'The worker deserves his wages'" (NIV). Paul is quoting from Deuteronomy 25:4 in the Old Testament and Luke 10:7 in the New Testament, referring to both passages as Scripture. Peter attributes authority to the writings of Paul by equating his writings with other Scriptures: "He writes the same way in all his letters, speaking in them of these matters. His letters contain some things that are hard to understand, which ignorant and unstable people distort, as they do the other Scriptures, to their own destruction" (2 Peter 3:16 NIV).

The Bible itself witnesses to its inspired status, yet the original manuscripts of Scripture did not survive; they perished within a century of their appearance. Thus is it accurate to say that because we do not have the original manuscripts, our Bibles are not inspired? Perhaps we should go so far as to say that because most people in the West do not have command of the languages in which the original Scriptures were written, they do not have access to the inspired text. While these statements may be accurate in some exaggerated technical sense, Christians and Bible scholars throughout history agree that insofar as our English translations render the meaning of the Word of God as intended by the original authors in a language we can understand, they are inspired. This is true for the King James Version as well as for modern translations.

> Legitimate arguments can be offered for preferring the King James Version, and compelling arguments can be offered for using modern translations.

The more difficult questions are: What is the original text of the Scriptures (a study of textual criticism), and what is the intended meaning of the original author (interpretation as presented in modern commentaries and study tools)? These questions can only be answered by diligent study of the Book of Books.

What Is the Best Translation?

Inspiration, however, is not the central question in debates over translation preferences. Legitimate arguments can be offered for preferring the King James Version, and compelling arguments can be offered for using modern translations.

Which is the best translation? One way to answer is this: It depends on why you're reading. If you want an enjoyable, edifying experience of one of the English language's greatest treasures, the King James Version is likely your best option. If you're reading for a sterling example of early seventeenth-century translation, again, the King James Version is likely the best way to go. And if you want to read a translation of poetry, rhythm, and music that befits the Word of God, look no further than the King James Version. Many argue, however, that if a twenty-first-century reader of English wants as clear an understanding of the original autographs as possible, other translations serve better than the KJV. The few scholars that support a text that closely resembles the Greek text of the KJV believe it is more reliable because of the large number of extant manuscripts it represents against the modern critical text that is based on the earliest manuscripts.[5] Obviously readers themselves will have to decide which translation is best for them.

From Folio to iPhone

The King James Version was translated in an era of history when the English language was revered; a man's words were the measure of his education. Language unlocked doors of power, fulfilled dreams, and created literature of influence. Those who controlled words could shape not only their own world but the future.

Early twentieth-century Bible scholar Robert Dearden comments on the singular role of the King James Bible in history:

> Splendors of the court of St. James furnish the setting for the celebrated First Authorized Version. This is perhaps the most brilliant gem in the diadem of that Monarch. Down through the ages the Bible had held its sway due chiefly to the tireless efforts of noted individual translators. But the year 1611 was to mark a new epoch in Bible history. That year witnessed the creation of the celebrated Authorized King James Version of the English Bible printed by Robert Barker in London.[6]

The year 2011 marks the four-hundredth anniversary of the publication of the King James Version. Today a version of this four-hundred-year-old Bible can be purchased in shopping malls or over the Internet, selected in deluxe leather or recyclable bindings, and read on Kindle, disk, iPhone, or as a conventional book. But what relevance do we twenty-first-century Christians find in a Bible first published in 1611? Most of us need not look far to discover that the King James Version is woven into the fabric of our personal stories and the wider stories of our faith communities. Its cadence and rhythms have drawn the world to its sheer literary beauty. The truth of the KJV has instilled courage in martyrs, brought peace to the dying, graced victims with forgiveness, and guided prodigals to their homes. It has counseled both commoners and kings with an unchanging message through the ages.

The King James Version became a conduit of faith for generations around the globe and the Scripture upon which a new nation was founded. The words of the KJV were read over rough-hewn tables in the early homes of American settlers and carried in the saddlebags of circuit-riding preachers. Its principles shaped the foundation of the American judicial system, and its truth produced a democracy that serves as a beacon of hope to the world.

The translators themselves spurned the worship of the text they produced, for God alone is worthy of our worship. Yet the King James Version stands as a translation of unparalleled influence; it truly is the crown jewel of the Golden Age of English literature. As such, it is certainly worthy of the valued place it holds in the history of Christian faith and the history of the world.

Acknowledgments

Scholars readily accept the truth behind the time-worn saying, "We stand on the shoulders of those who have gone before us." Many of those broad shoulders are acknowledged in the bibliography of this book. However, modern-day book publishing requires more than just the knowledge it takes to research the data and to record it on paper. It takes a plethora of competent writers, editors, photographers, literary agents, and creative designers. I wish to acknowledge with deepest gratitude the men and women who made this book possible.

Photography

Angela Sanchez, Amanda May, Carol Brake, Bob Bahner, and Michael Brake for their photos of my rare Bible collection; John Hellstern for photos of his rare Bibles (Speed's map 1611 and Wicked Bible 1631); Michael Morgan for the photo of his Blayney's 1769 title page; and Rusty Maisel for photos of Bibles.

Thanks to the Lupton family for permission to incorporate the original artwork of their father, Lewis (Luppy) Lupton. A special thanks to daughter Julia Button and Commander Christopher Mather, Royal Navy, retired, for their help in digitizing Lewis's artwork. A reprint of Lewis Lupton's twenty-five-volume *A History of the Geneva Bible*, incorporating his extensive artwork, is available from Tentmaker Publications.

General Office Assistance

Marian O'Connor, Emi Koe, and Kristen Badriaki, Multnomah Biblical Seminary staff, for their encouragement and selfless labor in assisting me in this project.

Daniel Lockwood, president, Multnomah University, for his encouragement and support during the period of research and writing.

Library Assistance

Phil Johnson, librarian, Multnomah University, for the use of interlibrary loan and online research and Pam Middleton, who assisted in obtaining sources and graciously put up with me in my regular pursuit of "just one more source" for verifying my thoughts.

Literary Agents

David Sanford and Tim Beals at Credo Communications for encouragement when things did not go well.

Mike Petersen, Tyndale Publications, a friend who constantly encouraged me in the process.

Editing and Design

Carol Brake, Tim Beals, Stephen J. Grabill, Chad Allen, and Lois G. Stück for their suggestions and editing of the manuscript. Brian Brunsting and Robin Black for their interior design.

A special thanks to Shelly Beech for her gentle temperament and expertise in editing the manuscript.

Appendix 1

The King James Version Compared with Sixteenth-Century Translations and Modern Versions

The King James Version and Sixteenth-Century English Translations of Matthew 6:9–13

King James Version "He" Bible (1611)

[9] Our father which art in heauen, hallowed be thy name. [10] Thy kingdome come. Thy will be done, in earth, as it is in heauen. [11] Giue vs this day our daily bread. [12] And forgiue vs our debts, as we forgiue our debters. [13] And lead vs not into temptation, but deliuer vs from euill: For thine is the kingdome, and the power, and the glory, for euer, Amen.

Bishops' Bible (1602)

[9] Our father, which art in heauen, halowed be thy name. [10] Let thy kyngdome come. Thy will be done, as well in earth, as it is in heauen. [11] Giue vs this day our daily bread. [12] And forgeue vs our debts, as we forgeue our

debters. [13] And lead vs not into temptation, but deliuer vs from euill. For thine is the kyngdome, and the power and the glory, for euer, Amen.

Rheims New Testament (1582)

[9] Our Father who art in heaven, hallowed be thy name. [10] Thy kingdom come. Thy will be done on earth as it is in heaven. [11] Give us this day our supersubstantial bread. [12] And forgive us our debts, as we also forgive our debtors. [13] And lead us not into temptation. But deliver us from evil. Amen.

Geneva Bible (1560)

[9] Our father which art in heauen, halowed be thy Name. [10] Thy kingdome come. Thy will be done euen in earth, as it is in heauen. [11] Giue vs this day our daily bread. [12] And forgiue vs our dettes, as we also forgiue our detters. [13] And leade vs not into tentation, but deliuer vs from euil: for thine is the kingdome, and the power, and the glorie for euer, Amen.

Great Bible (Whitchurch, 1540)

Oure father which art in heaven, hallowed be thy name. Lett thy kyngdome come. Thy will be fulfylled, as well in earth, as it is in heaven. Geve us this daye oure daylye bread. And forgeve us our dettes, as we forgeve oure detters. And leade us not into temptacyon: but delyver us from evyll. For thyne is the kyngdome and the power, and the glorye for ever. Amen.

Coverdale Bible (1535)

[9] O oure father which art in heauen, halowed be thy name. [10] Thy kyngdome come. Thy wyll be fulfilled vpon earth as it is in heauen. [11] Geue vs this daye oure dayly bred. [12] And forgeue vs oure dettes, as we also forgeue oure detters. [13] And lede vs not in to temptacion: but delyuer vs from euell. For thyne is the kyngdome, and the power, and the glorye for euer. Amen.

Tyndale Bible (1534)

[9] Oure father which arte in heuen, halowed be thy name. [10] Let thy kyng-dome come. Thy wyll be fulfilled as well in erth as it ys in heven. [11] Geue vs this daye oure dayly breede. [12] And forgeue vs oure treaspases even as we forgeue oure trespacers. [13] And leade vs not into temptacion: but delyuer vs from euell. For thyne is the kyngdome and the power and the glorye for ever. Amen.

Modern Translations of Matthew 6:9–13

New American Standard Bible (1995)

[9] Pray, then, in this way: "Our Father who is in heaven, hallowed be Your name. [10] Your kingdom come. Your will be done, on earth as it is in heaven. [11] Give us this day our daily bread. [12] And forgive us our debts, as we also have forgiven our debtors. [13] And do not lead us into temptation, but deliver us from evil. [For Yours is the kingdom and the power and the glory forever. Amen.]"

New International Version (1984)

[9] This, then, is how you should pray: "Our Father in heaven, hallowed be your name, [10] your kingdom come, your will be done on earth as it is in heaven. [11] Give us today our daily bread. [12] Forgive us our debts, as we also have forgiven our debtors. [13] And lead us not into temptation, but deliver us from the evil one."

Holman Christian Standard (2003)

[9] Therefore, you should pray like this: Our Father in heaven, Your name be honored as holy. [10] Your kingdom come. Your will be done on earth as it is in heaven. [11] Give us today our daily bread. [12] And forgive us our debts, as we also have forgiven our debtors. [13] And do not bring us into temptation, but deliver us from the evil one. [For Yours is the kingdom and the power and the glory forever. Amen.]

English Standard Version (2001)

⁹ Pray then like this: "Our Father in heaven, hallowed be your name. ¹⁰ Your kingdom come, your will be done, on earth as it is in heaven. ¹¹ Give us this day our daily bread, ¹² and forgive us our debts, as we also have forgiven our debtors. ¹³ And lead us not into temptation, but deliver us from evil."

New Living Translation (2004)

⁹ Pray like this: Our Father in heaven, may your name be kept holy. ¹⁰ May your Kingdom come soon. May your will be done on earth, as it is in heaven. ¹¹ Give us today the food we need, ¹² and forgive us our sins, as we have forgiven those who sin against us. ¹³ And don't let us yield to temptation, but rescue us from the evil one.

New English Translation (2005)

⁹ So pray this way: Our Father in heaven, may your name be honored, ¹⁰ may your kingdom come, may your will be done on earth as it is in heaven. ¹¹ Give us today our daily bread, ¹² and forgive us our debts, as we ourselves have forgiven our debtors. ¹³ And do not lead us into temptation, but deliver us from the evil one.

God's Word Translation (1995)

⁹ This is how you should pray: Our Father in heaven, let your name be kept holy. ¹⁰ Let your kingdom come. Let your will be done on earth as it is done in heaven. ¹¹ Give us our daily bread today. ¹² Forgive us as we forgive others. ¹³ Don't allow us to be tempted. Instead, rescue us from the evil one.

New American Bible (1970)

[9] This is how you are to pray: Our Father in heaven, hallowed be your name, [10] your kingdom come, your will be done, on earth as in heaven. [11] Give us today our daily bread; [12] and forgive us our debts, as we forgive our debtors; [13] and do not subject us to the final test, but deliver us from the evil one.

Appendix 2

Chronology of the King James Version

1619	First complete Bible published by Norton and Bill, successors of the Barkers
1625	King James dies and Charles I becomes king
1629	First Bible printed in Cambridge with revisions included
1631	Infamous "Wicked Bible" error in Exodus 20:14, "Thou shalt commit adultery"
1633	First King James Version published in Scotland
1634	Fourth folio edition
1639–40	Last folio, considered the finest of the five folios
1642	Folio published by Joost Broerz with Geneva notes
1641–51	English Civil War
1649–60	The Commonwealth
1653	Infamous "Unrighteous Bible" error in 1 Corinthians 6:9, "Know ye not that the unrighteous shall inherit the kingdom of God?"
1660	Restoration of Charles II (crowned king in 1649)
1660	Very large two-volume folio of the first Bible of the Restoration
1666	Great London fire may have destroyed original King James Version manuscript
1675	First King James Version published in Oxford (spelling revised)
1714	First King James Version published in Ireland
1717	Famous "Vinegar Bible" published by John Baskett
1722	The most beautiful Bible ever printed, published by James Watson in Edinburgh
1777	First New Testament printed in America by Robert Aitken of Philadelphia
1782	First complete King James Version printed in America
1800	Machlin's large seven-volume folio with engravings and pictures designed by eminent artists
1873	Cambridge Paragraph Bible, revised and in paragraph form
1881–85	English Revised Version published in Oxford and Cambridge
1901	American Standard Version

1903–5	Nonesuch Bible, considered one of the finest printed by Francis Meynell
1909	Scofield Reference Bible
1952	Revised Standard Version
1982	New King James Version
1994	The 21st Century King James Version
2005	New Cambridge Paragraph Bible

Notes

Hear Ye, Hear Ye . . .

1. The Hampton Court Conference lasted three days: January 12, 16, and 18, 1604. The early sessions of the conference focused on a discussion of the issues facing the Anglican Church. On the second day the suggestion was made for a new translation. While the narrative in this chapter has been dramatized, the details of the proceedings of the conference are based on research recorded by William Barlow in *The Summe and Substance* (London: John Windet, for Mathew Law, 1604). It should be noted that Barlow's objectivity has been called into question, but no alternative source has come to light that discredits his account.

Chapter 1 A Nation Finds Her Tongue

1. This Augustine should not be confused with Augustine, the bishop of Hippo.

2. J. A. Giles, ed., *Bede's Ecclesiastical History and the Anglo-Saxon Chronicle* (London: George Bell and Sons, 1887), 67–68.

3. Robert McCrum, William Cran, and Robert MacNeil, *The Story of English* (New York: Elisabeth Sifton Books, 1986), 62.

4. G. Geoffrey Shepherd, "English Versions of the Scripture before Wycliffe," in *The Cambridge History of the Bible: The West from the Fathers to the Reformation*, vol. 2, ed. G. W. H. Lampe (Cambridge: Cambridge University Press, 1969), 375.

5. McCrum, Cran, and MacNeil, *The Story of English*, 67.

6. Ibid., 69.

7. Norman L. Geisler and William E. Nix, *A General Introduction to the Bible* (Chicago: Moody Press, 1986), 545.

8. Shepherd, "English Versions," 365.

9. Ibid., 378.

10. Joseph Bosworth, *The Gothic and Anglo-Saxon Gospels* (London: John Russell Smith, 1865), ii–iii. The Wycliffe and KJV translations were added to Bosworth's *Gothic and Anglo-Saxon Gospels*.

11. Although the French language greatly influenced English, English as a widely spoken vernacular remained resilient. The Hundred Years' War between England and France (1337–1453) motivated the English to speak their own language rather than French. McCrum, Cran, and MacNeil, *The Story of English*, 78.

12. The first Christmas song appeared about 1350. "Hand by hand we shall us take / And joy and bliss shall we make / And for the devil of hell man hath forsaken / And God's Son is made our mate." David C. Fowler, *The Bible in Middle English Literature* (Seattle: University of Washington Press, 1984), 59.

13. Ibid., 3–52. Fowler discusses in great detail the development of drama during the Middle Ages.

14. Alister E. McGrath, *In the Beginning: The Story of the King James Bible and How It Changed a Nation, a Language, and a Culture* (New York: Doubleday, 2001), 36.

15. While most scholars today recognize that Wycliffe did not translate the entire Bible himself,

he was the man most closely associated with its translation.

16. F. F. Bruce, "John Wycliffe and the English Bible," *Churchman* 98, no. 4 (1984): 300. Bruce mentions Robert Gosecteste (thirteenth century) as an exception and notes that Greek was taught in Oxford in 1320–21.

17. Wycliffe preceded Luther in opposing the selling of indulgences. A common rhyme during Luther's time poked fun at indulgences: "As soon as the coin in the coffers ring, the soul from purgatory springs."

18. Quoted in Anne Hudson, *Lollards and Their Books* (London and Ronceverte, WV: Hambledon Press), 153. Oxford Bodleian MS Laud Misc. 200 folio 201. The text was translated from Latin by the fourth-year high school Latin class at Coram Deo Academy, Flower Mound, Texas, under the supervision of Advanced Latin Instructor Daniel R. Fredrick, Ph.D.

19. In 1401 the church issued the *De heretic comburendo*, which promised death to heretics for reading a Bible in the vernacular. In 1408 the infamous Constitutions were formulated forbidding a Bible in English without church approval in direct response to the overwhelming reception of the English Wycliffe Bible.

20. Baruch is one of the deuterocanonical books included in Roman Catholic, Eastern Orthodox, and Oriental Orthodox Old Testaments but not in the Protestant Old Testament. The deuterocanonical books are books and passages of the Old Testament that are not accepted as part of the Jewish Bible.

21. John Foxe, *Acts and Monuments* (London: Seeley, Burnside, and Seeley, 1844), 3:245.

22. The Constitutions of 1408 forbade the translation of the Bible into English without the express permission and oversight of the Roman Catholic Church.

Chapter 2 Fanning the Flames

1. Lewis Lupton, *Tyndale, Translator* (London: Olive Tree, 1986), 27. Lupton believes the clothes portrayed in this portrait are not consistent with Tyndale's period.

2. Some say no evidence exists that Tyndale spent this time in Cambridge, but most of Tyndale's travels cannot be verified with certainty.

3. While the story is widely circulated, it may not be based in actual fact.

4. While the popular story is often told, scholars doubt its authenticity. The full title of Foxe's book is *Actes and Monuments of these Latter and Perillous Days, Touching Matters of the Church*, although most people know it as *Foxe's Book of Martyrs*.

5. W. J. Heaton, *The Bible of the Reformation* (London: Francis Griffiths, 1910), 166.

6. Miles Coverdale, "Introduction to Apocrypha," Coverdale Bible (1537) quarto.

7. After 1800 the books of the Apocrypha were included only in select editions.

8. Thomas Matthew was the pseudonym for John Rogers. Rogers feared his association with Tyndale would prejudice the acceptance of his translation; use of a pseudonym veiled his association.

Chapter 3 The Theological Tug-of-War

1. Also known as the "Breeches Bible" for its reading in Genesis 3:7, "They sewed fig leaves together and made themselves breeches."

2. Mark Galli, "Courage When It Counted," *Christian History* 16, no. 4 (1995): 9. I am indebted to Galli, who provides a full account of Cranmer's life and execution.

3. An imperial edict prohibited *suspect* Bibles in Latin, French, and Dutch. At the Council of Trent the theological faculty of Louvain was commanded to prepare an authorized edition. A. S. Herbert, *A Historical Catalog of the Printed Editions of the English Bible 1525–1961*, vol. 2 (New York: American Bible Society, 1961), 936.

4. Erasmus's Paraphrases were English translations of the New Testament from the Latin. Interestingly, Queen Mary Tudor translated the Gospel of John while she was still a princess.

5. J. Isaacs and H. W. Robinson, eds., *The Bible in Its Ancient and English Version* (Oxford: Oxford University Press, 1940), 193.

6. In 1547 Edward VI, by authority of Parliament, ordered the repeal of the Lollard heresy laws, which had required enforcement of a variety of religious ceremonies, abolished all images, banned clerical marriages, and so on.

7. It is suggested that Bishop Cox first proposed a new translation. See Alfred W. Pollard,

Records of the English Bible (London: Oxford University Press, 1911), 290.

8. Prior to 1800 the number of folds in the printer's sheet determined the size used to describe a Bible. A large page folded once was a folio; it had two leaves printed on front and back, making four printed pages. When the sheet was folded twice it was a quarto (4to), four leaves front and back (eight pages); when folded to eight leaves (sixteen pages), an octavo (8vo); when folded to twelve leaves (twenty-four pages), a duodecimo (12mo); and when folded to sixteen leaves (thirty-two pages), a sextodecimo.

9. One of the Bishops' Bible's most fascinating inclusions is a note citing a current event that appears alongside Psalm 45:9, "Ophir is thought to be the Island in the west coast, of late found by Christopher Columbus: from whence at this day is brought most fine gold."

10. Listed in Herbert, *Historical Catalog*, 71.

11. The title page, however, reads "Authorized and appointed to be read in Churches."

12. F. F. Bruce, *The English Bible: A History of Translations from the Earliest English Versions to the New English Bible* (Oxford: Oxford University Press, 1970), 94.

13. The 1606 edition marked the end of the Bishops' Bible, but the New Testament was printed as late as 1618.

Chapter 4 Puritans, Petitions, and Plots

1. Benson Bobrick, *Wide as the Waters: The Story of the English Bible and the Revolution It Inspired* (New York: Simon and Schuster, 2001), 199.

2. James I, king of England, *The Workes of the Most High and Mightie Prince, James* (London: Robert Barker, 1616). These works were all bound in one volume.

3. Schmidtchen argues that the insertion of the genealogies in English might have prevented it from being identified as a *papist* Bible, which was condemned in the kingdom. Paul W. Schmidtchen, "Bibles Once Owned by King James I," *Hobbies—The Magazine for Collectors* (April 1964): 106–7.

4. The lack of sound evidence makes the story doubtful.

5. James, as a Scotsman, embraced the Reformed principles of the Geneva Bible but did not approve of its view on kingship and authority. His decision to support a new translation was based as much on politics and efforts to secure his power base as king as it was on a desire to abandon the Geneva Bible. Puritans had expected his support for the Geneva Bible rather than a new translation.

6. In Scotland James had answered to a council, but in England he was monarch. His desire for sole power over the kingdom was stronger than his theological convictions. In fact, James hated the Presbyterian Church in Scotland for its failure to give proper authority to bishops. Andrew Melville had openly declared his public support of James but privately proclaimed Christ the true King of Scotland. His accusation that James was "God's silly vassal" did not endear him to James. James did not have the slightest intention of supporting the Presbyterian agenda. McGrath, *In the Beginning*, 140.

7. In the seventeenth century two crude firearms were available. One was called the *matchlock*, which held a slow-burning match that sparked the gunpowder and exploded, sending the projectile down the barrel. The other was called a *wheel lock*, a device in which a wheel spun rapidly, striking a metal bar to explode the powder.

8. The Puritans wanted to purify the Church of England from the practices of Elizabeth that they associated with the pope. They hoped James would help them rid the church of many questionable practices.

9. McGrath, *In the Beginning*, 156. The four Puritans were John Rainolds, president of Corpus Christi College; Laurence Chadderton, master of Emmanuel College; John Knewstubs, fellow at St. John's College; and Thomas Sparke, minister of Bletchley in Buckinghamshire.

10. Geneva Bible notes in the 1599 edition speak harshly about the rights of kings; these were objectionable to James I: Exod. 1:22; 2 Chron. 15:15–18; Dan. 6:22; 11:36.

11. An interesting development, since the 1579 Bassadyne Bible was dedicated to James of Scotland.

12. Geddes Macgregor, *The Bible in the Making* (London: John Murray, 1961), 111.

13. Olga S. Opfell, *The King James Bible Translators* (Jefferson, NC: McFarland, 1982), 30.

14. Plantagenet Somerset Fry, *Kings and Queens: A Royal History of England and Scotland,*

2d ed. (London: Dorling Kinderseley, 1997), 130–31.

Chapter 5 The Men and Their Mission

1. The major source naming the translators is a list printed by Bishop Gilbert Burnet (1643–1715), who suggests the number of translators was forty-seven, not fifty-four as the King James mentions. The differences may be accounted for by the fact that some translators died and others could be appointed or added when needed as suggested in principle fifteen of Bancroft's rules: "Three or four of the most Ancient and Grave Divines . . . not employed in translating . . . to be overseers of the translations." Burnet's list does not include Bancroft or Bilson, who certainly influenced the translation.

2. A *prebend* is a stipend given to a member of the clergy by a cathedral or college for service rendered. The term *living* refers to the general principle of awarding positions that had stipends attached such as prebends, deanships, and bishoprics. *Prebendary* is a cleric receiving a prebend; it can refer to an honorary canon with no stipend. These prebends may come from tithes of farm produce or lands owned by a parsonage; the higher the prebend, the higher the standard of living.

3. The story is in keeping with Lancelot's reputation for giving to the poor, generally anonymously. Right Reverend Father John, *A Sermon Preached at the Funeral of the Right Honorable and Reverend Father in God Lancelot the late Lord Bishop of Winchester* (London: G. Miller for Richard Badger, 1629), 20. This event is recorded by Opfell, *King James Bible Translators*, 30–31.

4. No one doubts the translators' qualifications, but there was a certain disparity as to abilities and contributions. Some were very fine translators and others only average.

5. Price and Ryrie mention that the Jerusalem Chamber was used years later for the Revised Version in 1870, the New English Bible in 1961, and the Revised English Bible in 1989. David Price and Charles C. Ryrie, *Let It Go among Our People: An Illustrated History of the English Bible from John Wyclif to the King James Version* (Cambridge: Lutterworth Press, 2004), 121.

6. Herbert, *Historical Catalog*, 70.

7. The date of death, when known, will follow the name so one can see the translator's relation to the translation and publication of the King James Version (1604–11).

8. Andrews attended the coronation of James and Anne and had the honor of opening the royal robes for the anointing. At this ceremony, William Shakespeare was granted groomsman status.

9. Father John, *Sermon Preached at the Funeral*, 18.

10. Lewis Lupton, *A History of the Geneva Bible: England's Word* (London: Olive Tree Press, 1992), 32.

11. Opfell, *King James Bible Translators*, 32.

12. Queen Elizabeth I often employed buccaneers—sailors who raided Spanish ships in particular; the most famous was Sir Francis Drake.

13. Opfell, *King James Bible Translators*, 35.

14. The Millenary Petition, a Puritan document said to be signed by one thousand ministers, voiced their opposition to church practices and expressed their desire for reform in the church.

15. Opfell, *King James Bible Translators*, 60.

16. Alexander W. McClure, *The Translators Revived* (Worthington, PA: Maranatha, n.d.), 168.

17. No one really knows how the hunting accident happened.

18. Ward Allen published the notes John Bois penned on the pages of the Bishops' Bible of 1602. These notes have helped historians sort out the process of translation. Ward S. Allen, *Translating for King James* (Nashville: Vanderbilt University Press, 1969). This is clear from Bois's note quoting Harmer's reading at 1 Peter 2:24, "*Caried up our sins to the tree. D. Harmer*," 91. Interestingly, Harmer's suggestion was not included in the KJV, which reads: "Bare our sinnes in his owne body on the tree." The marginal reading says, "or, to," a partial concession to Harmer.

19. Opfell, *King James Bible Translators*, 87.

20. Ibid., 94.

21. Thomas Fowler, *The History of Corpus Christi College* (Oxford: Horace Hart, Clarendon Press, 1893), 127–29.

22. Price and Ryrie, *Let It Go*, 122.

23. Allen, *Translating for King James*, 17–19.

24. Some Roman Catholic scholars point out the use of the phrase "Sow'd cockle, reap'd no corn" in Shakespeare's *Love's Labour's Lost*, act 4, as a reference to the Rheims New Testament,

which in Matthew 13:25–30 uses the term *cockle* where all other versions use *tares*. See Hugh Pope, *English Versions of the Bible* (Westport, CT: Greenwood Press, 1972), 275.

25. Joseph Pearce, *The Quest for Shakespeare* (San Francisco: Ignatius Press, 2008). Roman Catholic scholar Pearce argues persuasively that Shakespeare was a Roman Catholic, but that does not clarify what his actual daily practice was nor how openly he may have held this viewpoint. Pearce promises in a future book to show from Shakespeare's plays that he was devoted to Catholicism.

26. Pollard, *Records of the English Bible*, 61.

27. Records differ in number, perhaps due to untimely deaths of certain translators and names of men that appear on different lists who probably had minor input on the translation.

28. Richard Bancroft sent a letter with instructions to the translators to follow specific rules in translating. Bancroft suggests these principles were those of the king himself. Pollard, *Records of the English Bible*, 331. The translation's rules appear on pages 53–54.

29. Adam Nicolson, *God's Secretaries* (New York: HarperCollins, 2003), 74.

30. "The Translators to the Reader," *The Holy Bible*, King James Version (London: Robert Barker, 1611), n.p.

31. The KJV translators inconsistently used *you* and *your* instead of *ye, thy*, and *thine* in the preface and dedication. This era was a period of transition in the use of the second person plural. Even the 1560 Geneva introduction used *you* instead of *ye* and *your* instead of *thine*.

32. Quoted in Ward Allen, *Translating the New Testament Epistles 1604–1611* (Ann Arbor, MI: University Microfilms for Vanderbilt University Press, 1977), xix.

33. There is no question that the king himself had tremendous influence on the outcome of the translation of the KJV. He appointed Anglican Bishop Bancroft to establish the principles, and as this principle clearly states, he gave input into the guiding principles themselves. So to call this translation the King James Version is not far from accurate.

34. This principle had a lofty purpose, but in reality it prevented the possibility of an overbal- ance of Puritan influence amid a majority of Anglican translators.

35. Robert H. Stein, "Is Our Reading the Bible the Same as the Original Audience Hearing It?" *Journal of the Evangelical Theological Society* 46, no. 1 (March 2003): 68. Stein discusses in some detail the evidence for ancients reading aloud and listening to messages from Scripture and other literature.

36. Ibid., 71. See also William Harris, *Ancient Literacy* (Cambridge: Harvard University Press, 1991), 272, 328–30; and Harry Y. Gamble, *Books and Readers in the Early Church: A History of Early Christian Texts* (New Haven: Yale University Press, 1997), 339–41.

37. Allen, *Translating the New Testament Epistles*, xxv.

38. Paul J. Achtemeier, "Omne Verbum Sonat: The New Testament and the Oral Environment of Late Western Antiquity," *Journal of Biblical Literature* 109, no. 1 (1990): 5.

39. McGrath refers to an account in Hebrew scholar John Selden's (1584–1654) *Table Talk*. A KJV translator read the text aloud to other delegates and sought suggestions for improvements. McGrath, *In the Beginning*, 187.

40. Nicolson, *God's Secretaries*, 221. Nicolson also suggests that only about 8 percent of the phraseology in the Bishops' Bible found its way into the King James translation (*God's Secretaries*, 73). This also suggests that the text for the KJV submitted to the printer, Robert Barker, was not a completely annotated Bishops' Bible but more likely a handwritten manuscript.

41. In at least one verse, Jeremiah 38:16, the translators followed the Septuagint in reading "the king" where the Hebrew names the king, "Zedekiah the king."

Chapter 6 Tracing the Path

1. Kurt Aland and Barbara Aland, *The Text of the New Testament* (Grand Rapids: Eerdmans, 1987), 53.

2. The church in Rome was a significant force during the first three centuries as the developing authority of the bishop in Rome gave power to the church there.

3. Aland and Aland, *Text of the New Testament*, 66. The Alands write: "The widely acclaimed Caesarean text of the New Testament, we must

insist, is thus far purely hypothetical. . . . All claims for the Caesarean text, however confidently expressed, rest on dubious foundations."

4. Scholars generally accept the Alexandrian text-type as the oldest; certainly our oldest existing manuscripts are of the Alexandrian text-type. Whether they reach back to the original is the question scholars continue to argue.

5. Dr. Daniel Wallace, executive director of the Center for the Study of New Testament manuscripts and recognized New Testament scholar, points out that in actuality there are a number of differences. The Hodges-Farstad Majority Text differs from the *Textus Receptus* in 1,838 places. The critical text differs from the TR in about 5,000 places, but it differs from the Majority Text in 6,577 places. This means that the TR has some readings that are not Byzantine (the first manuscript that Erasmus used is the head of a Caesarean family of manuscripts, codex 1) but are more authentic than the Majority Text.

6. Darlow and Moule identify *Codex Vaticanus* gr.330 and 346 as two of the manuscripts borrowed from the Vatican and a Venice manuscript MS.S. Marc. 5. T. H. Darlow and H. F. Moule, *Historical Catalogue of the Printed Editions of Holy Scripture in the Library of the British and Foreign Bible Society*, vol. 2 (New York: British and Foreign Bible Society, 1903–11), 576.

7. Samuel Prideaux Tregelles, *An Account of the Printed Text of the Greek New Testament* (London: Samuel Bagster and Sons, 1854), 9–15.

8. This portion is a lacuna (a portion missing from the text).

9. The story reveals what I was thinking at the time. I had heard that the addition of the *comma* was inserted above the line by a later scribe (not the one who transcribed the text itself). The original scribe included the comma *Johanneum* as part of his Greek text most certainly from a Latin manuscript. Wallace points out that Erasmus corrected the Greek text due to the scribe's lack of Greek knowledge. Erasmus actually had omitted the comma because there was no Greek manuscript evidence for it. While any promise to include it in his Greek NT (if a manuscript were found) may be fictitious, when Codex Montfortianus came to his attention, he inserted it in his text.

10. Desiderius Erasmus, *In Annotationes Novi Testamenti Prefatio* (Basel, Switzerland: Johann Froben, 1516), 385.

11. The manuscript dates around 1520, and scholars believe the Franciscan Friar Roy translated the reading back into Greek from the Latin Vulgate. It may have been prepared at Stunica's request. The reading appears in the Complutensian Polyglot in a slightly different form (the work of Stunica) and in all Greek New Testaments. Luther's edition of the German included it in a Frankfurt edition in 1576 and in some Wittenberg editions until 1596. Eberhard Nestle, *Introduction to the Textual Criticism of the Greek New Testament* (Oxford: Williams and Norgate, 1901), 5. Nestle says it was included in all Greek manuscripts after 1534. He must be referring to a text that included it in 1534 (perhaps Colinaeus's 1534 New Testament). Certainly all the major Greek texts such as Erasmus (1516–35) and the Complutensian included it, but no other Greek manuscript has come to light that included the reading. Metzger points out that three later manuscripts added the reading in the margins. Bruce M. Metzger, *A Textual Commentary on the Greek New Testament*, 2nd rev. ed. (New York: United Bible Societies, 2005), 102–3. No actual evidence exists that the story has any validity, but the story and controversy live on. Dr. Daniel Wallace notes, "There are eight Greek manuscripts known to have the *comma Johanneum*—four in the text and four in the margin. He recently discovered a ninth manuscript that has the reading earlier than 1520, a 14th century manuscript. (See http://www.csntm.org/tcnotes/archive/TheCommaJohanneumInAnOverlookedManuscript where Dr. Wallace describes the new find.)

12. Tregelles, *An Account of the Printed Text*, 26.

13. There were two dates attached to the same edition.

14. Darlow and Moule, *Historical Catalogue of the Printed Editions*, vol. 2, 599.

15. Although this was the first printed Greek New Testament to have verse divisions—the same divisions used by the Geneva New Testament and the King James Version—it was Pagninus in 1528 who was the first to use verse divisions in the whole Bible. Pagninus's divisions, however, had no impact nor were they the same as Stephanus's.

16. Bruce M. Metzger, *The Text of the New Testament: Its Transmission, Corruption, and Restoration*, 2nd ed. (New York: Oxford University Press, 1968), 105.

17. Dr. Wallace points out, "Codex 76 (14th century) is the lone Greek MS that has *her*; there are a few Old Latin MSS that have it, as well as Vulgate MSS (though these Latin MSS could be read as *his* since the Latin form is ambiguous). In addition, Pseudo-Athanasius (whose date is unknown) has *her* as does the *Catenae in euangelia Lucae et Joannis* (a patristic source with various authorities cited loosely)."

18. The Rheims New Testament and the Bishops' Bible also read "her."

19. This would probably be the 1602 reprint edition of Stephanus.

20. John Eadie, *The English Bible* (London: Macmillan, 1876), 211.

21. While Lachmann followed the printed Greek New Testaments for his printed edition, he specifically examined manuscripts directly and included his findings in his edition of the printed New Testament.

22. A number of other important textual critical scholars from 1707 through 1881 such as, John Mill, Jacob Wettstein, John Bengel, Richard Bentley, Samuel Tregelles, and Constantin Tischendorf were instrumental in the development of modern textual criticism. It was Tischendorf's discovery of *Codex Sinaiticus* in 1874 that influenced Westcott and Hort's work.

23. Brooke Foss Westcott and Fenton John Anthony Hort, *The New Testament in the Original Greek*, 2 vols. (Cambridge, MA, and London: Macmillan, 1881).

24. Hermann Freiherr von Soden, *Die Schriften des Neuen Testaments in ihrer altesten erreichbaren Testgestalt* (Berlin, Germany: Alexander Duncker, 1902–13).

25. The Alands list a number of weaknesses in von Soden's theory of textual criticism. Aland and Aland, *Text of the New Testament*, 22–23.

26. F. H. A. Scrivener, *The Authorized Edition of the English Bible (1611)* (Cambridge: Cambridge University Press, 1884), 43.

27. Translator scholar George Abbot was very influential in persuading the group that the Apocrypha should be included.

28. James I, *The Workes*, "Basilikon Doron," 151.

29. Lewis Lupton, *England's Word*, 105.

30. Ibid., 45.

31. Brooke Foss Westcott, *A General View of the English Bible* (London: Macmillan, 1872), 269.

32. It must be kept in mind that the vast majority of modern textual critics do not accept the Greek text that the King James translators used. They prefer the critical text that incorporates the modern discoveries and awareness of older manuscripts and papyri. It is not the purpose of this book to debate the pros and cons of textual criticism, only to discuss how it affects the 1611 King James Version.

33. William David McBrayer, "Preface," in *The New Testament in the Original Greek According to the Byzantine/Majority Textform*, ed. Maurice A. Robinson and William G. Pierpont (Atlanta: Word, 1991), xi.

34. It is interesting to note that a recent master's thesis found more than thirty unique Byzantine readings in the Gospel of Mark in *Codex Sinaiticus*. Matthew Williams, *Uniquely Byzantine Readings in Codex Sinaiticus* (Portland: Multnomah Biblical Seminary, 2009).

Chapter 7 Rejection, Rewriting, and Revision

1. Lupton, *England's Word*, 40. Lupton gives no supporting evidence for his comment.

2. The manuscript from the Bodleian Library has been published in Ward S. Allen and Edward C. Jacobs, *The Coming of the King James Gospels* (Fayetteville, AR: University of Arkansas Press, 1995).

3. Charles Butterworth estimates that 39 percent of the Bible phrases and clauses he surveyed first appeared in the KJV. Sixty-one percent of English phrases and clauses had reached their final literary form in the following translations (Wycliffe, Tyndale, Matthew's, Coverdale, Great Bible, Geneva, and Bishops'). He gives the breakdown as follows: Wycliffe, 4 percent; Tyndale and Matthew's, 18 percent; Coverdale and the Great Bible, 13 percent; Geneva, 19 percent; Bishops', 4 percent; all other versions before 1611, 3 percent; and unique to King James, 39 percent. He also notes how other estimates may conflict with his method. Charles C. Butterworth, *The Literary Lineage of the King James Bible 1340–1611*, 231, n. 97.

4. James G. Carleton has conclusively demonstrated that words from the Rheims (R) ended up in the KJV. The Rheims, published in 1582, was the last translation prior to the KJV that was referred to frequently in the "Translators to the Readers." Carleton observes: "One cannot but be struck by the large number of words which have come into the Authorized Version from the Vulgate through the medium of the Rhemish New Testament." For example, in the Rheims Matthew 8:30 reads, "But your very hairs of the head are all numbered." KJV states, "But the very hairs of your head are all numbered." The other versions used by the KJV translators are clearly different. Carleton, *The Part of Rheims*, 32.

5. This is the text generally referred to as the *Textus Receptus*, although it is more accurately a text of Stephanus 1550.

6. Allen, *Translating for King James*. The original manuscript CCC-312–Fulman belongs to Corpus Christi College.

7. Opfell, *King James Bible Translators*, 102–3.

8. Allen, *Translating the New Testament Epistles*, 76.

9. The Geneva Bible reads, "Let another take his charge," while the Bishops' Bible reads "And his Bishoprick let another take." The term references the imprecatory Ps. 109:8, where the word *office* is in both the King James and the Bishops', and the marginal note cites the word *charge*. The idea of associating the word *Bishoprick* with the curse did not please Smith and Bilson. They complained that Bancroft changed it to "Bishoprick," altering the wording to read, "On that glorious word Bishoprick, even for Judas, as at Acts 1v20."

10. William Fulke wrote his *Counterblast* in *The Text of the New Testament of Jesus Christ, Translated Out of the Vulgar Latin by the Papists of Traiterous Seminarie at Rheims*, against the Rheims New Testament in 1589. He placed the Bishops' Bible side by side with the Rheims and proceeded to point out its errors. It drew attention to the new Roman Catholic version, and many began to read it.

11. A number of important Latin works were being published and made available to scholars. The *Antwerp Polyglot* contained an interlinear Latin translation of Pagninus's Hebrew text, and in 1579 Tremellius published a Latin translation of the Hebrew Old Testament. No doubt many good Latin texts were available, and a case could be made showing some Latin reading in the Bishops' Bible; for example, Isaiah 53:1 in the Bishops' reads, "But who hath given credence unto our preaching"; the Geneva reads, "Who will believe our report"; the KJV reads, "Who hath believed our report?"; the Latin Bible of Tremellius uses the Latin term *credidi*, which means "trust," "believe," or "commit."

Chapter 8 Masterpiece from the Mayhem

1. The first Bible printed in England was the work of Thomas Vautroullier in 1575 by printer Christopher Barker. Richard Jugge had been the queen's printer until his death in 1577. Thomas Wilks became the official printer and sold a portion of the business to Barker.

2. Henry R. Plomer, "The King's Printing House under the Stuarts," *The Library*, new series, 2, no. 11 (1901): 359. Plomer traces the history of the printing relationship of Robert Barker, John Bill, and John and Bonham Norton.

3. Lewis Lupton, *Not unto Us*, vol. 24, *A History of the Geneva Bible* (London: Olive Tree Press, 1992), 87.

4. Opfell, *King James Bible Translators*, 111.

5. David A. Norton, *A Textual History of the King James Bible* (Cambridge: Cambridge University Press, 2005), 63. This would account for Miles Smith's and Thomas Bilson's introduction, chapter headings, and summaries.

6. Price and Ryrie, *Let It Go*, 123.

7. Nicolson, *God's Secretaries*, 227.

8. Donald L. Brake, "2011 Census of KJV 1611 'He' Bibles," in *A Royal Monument of English Literature*, 2011.

9. It is common to refer to the 1611 edition as "first edition, first issue" and the 1613 edition as "first edition, second issue," but we are using "first edition" and "second edition" based on David Norton's convincing argument that the 1613 edition is a genuine second edition. Norton, *A Textual History*, 65–67.

10. Norton suggests the "he" reading may have been a hidden error, even if there is evidence for the Hebrew text "he" reading. If the translators saw a variant reading, they surely would have inserted the alternative reading as a footnote. This does not, however, help explain why some of the quartos of 1612 also have the "he" reading. A

feeling by the translators that "he" was legitimate may have support since even some modern translations use "he."

11. McGrath suggests the pelican was linked with the Lord's Supper or Mass associated with the medieval feast of Corpus Christi (the body of Christ). McGrath, *In the Beginning*, 210.

12. The Duke of Sutherland, D. K. Robjohns, had put it up for sale in 1930.

13. Ibid., 279. Broughton's reputation as a prima donna had preceded him and may explain why he was not invited to be a translator. In addition, he may have previously sought Queen Elizabeth's support for a new translation.

14. I have a copy of the Geneva Bible printed in 1776 with Cranmer's prologue from the Great Bible of 1540. Most books focus on the 1644 date as the last edition without knowing of the 1776 and another 1778 edition.

15. McGrath, *In the Beginning*, 284.

16. Lancelot Andrews, *Sermons* (London: George Miller for Richard Badger, 1629), 238.

17. McGrath, *In the Beginning*, 219.

18. Pollard, *Records of the English Bible*, 60. Pollard states that there is no evidence that it was *authorized* in the sense of royal approval. The word *appointed* that appears on the title page is much weaker than the term *authorized*. Had it been authorized by the king, the title page certainly would have used the stronger term.

19. Herbert, *Historical Catalog*. Herbert catalogs multiple editions of the King James Version.

20. Fredric Kenyon, *Our Bible and the Ancient Manuscripts* (New York: Harper and Brothers, 1958), 205.

21. McGrath, *In the Beginning*, 287–89. Complaints about the misprints and inaccuracies in the KJV around 1645 led to demands for a revision. The influence of the Puritans grew during the end of the reign of Charles I; however, the Geneva Bible still did not gain popular support. It was in the restoration of Charles II's reign (1660) that the KJV became the "pillar of the Restoration society" and all demands for a revision of the KJV ceased.

Chapter 9 Maps, Margins, and Mythology

1. The precision of the lines forming corners of the page are often used to distinguish editions and prints. For instance, the lines not meeting at the corners indicate editions such as 1617, 1634, or 1639–40.

2. Apparently the creature in the initial appears in some 1611 editions, but not in my copies. The two facsimile copies that have it also include the King James coat of arms. The creature appears in later folio editions, suggesting that the 1611 versions with the creature were printed later and perhaps mixed when assembled.

3. While similar initials appear in the 1602 Bishops' Bible, they are generally different.

4. Barker may have had more than five presses and more than one office. If Barker had used five printing presses, each press would have required about seventy-three plates to produce the 1,464 pages (each plate front and back had four pages). Each folio page was run through the printing press twice, once on the front and once on the back.

5. The genealogies were an exception to the numbering system. They were numbered in Arabic numerals at the head of the page.

6. Quires signed Aa–Zzz; Norton, *A Textual History*, 66.

7. Alfred W. Pollard, *The Holy Bible: A Facsimile in a Reduced Size of the Authorized Version Published in the Year 1611* (London: Oxford University Press, 1911), 33.

8. *The 21st Century King James Version* (Gary, SD: Deuel Enterprises, 1994).

9. Francis Fry, *A Description of the Great Bible—1539, Cranmer's Bible 1540–41, King James's Bible 1611–40* (London: Willes and Sotheran, 1865), 32.

10. I chose the 2001 New English Translation (NET) because I feel it is one of the most literal of the modern translations.

11. Eadie, *The English Bible*, 225.

Chapter 10 Branches on the Family Tree

1. David Price points out that it is absent in this reading in Tyndale 1525 (I would also add the 1526 edition) but included in the 1534 edition and in all other sixteenth-century versions which would differentiate between the Catholic and Protestant Bibles. Price suggests this is evidence that the Vulgate is the earlier reading, since modern textual criticism views the reading as an interpolation. Why Tyndale excluded the reading in his earlier edition and included it in later editions

(included in all Erasmus's editions) is a mystery. Price and Ryrie, *Let It Go*, 47.

2. Norton, *A Textual History*, 80.

3. Norton gives a detailed collation of the 1617 folio with the first and second editions. Ibid., 188–91.

Chapter 11 The Growing Family

1. Benjamin Blayney, "Account of the Collation and Revision of the Bible," *Gentleman's Magazine* 39 (October 1769): 518.

2. *Theological inerrancy*: the Bible as written by God is without error.

3. The text of Mark 7:4 reads, "As the washing of cups and / pots, brazen vessels, and of / tables." The marginal note reads, "*Sextaius is about a pinte and an halfe* and also *or beds,*" while the 1611 marginal note reads, "or beds. Sextaius is about a pinte and an halfe." The notes read in the opposite order.

4. This change in the text is claimed by some to have been inserted for theological reasons by the Puritans; however, here it is inserted under the "Royal License." Other renderings can be found in Scrivener, *Authorized Edition*, appendix A.

5. *LORD* is the KJV spelling of the Hebrew term *Yahweh,* and *Lord* renders *Adonai*. The Hebrew text reads *Adonai,* making the translation *Lord* the correct one.

6. Confusion exists whether Paris's or Blayney's editions were lost in a fire. J. R. Dore mentions the 1762 edition burned and only six copies were saved. J. R. Dore, *Old Bibles: An Account of the Early Versions of the English Bible* (London: Eyre and Spottiswoode, 1888), 348. A. S. Herbert refers to a fire that destroyed the 1769 edition. Herbert, *Historical Catalog*, 283. Scrivener mentions fires that destroyed a good portion of both editions. Scrivener, *Authorized Edition*, 30.

7. Scrivener, *Authorized Edition*, 36–37.

8. *The Holy Bible, an Exact Reprint Page for Page of the Authorized Version* (Oxford: Oxford University Press, 1833), 1.

9. One of the latest attempts to provide a King James Version for the modern reader, *The 21st Century King James Version*, published in 1994 by 21st Century King James Publishers, a division of Deuel Enterprises, Gary, South Dakota, has made a unique contribution to the modern debate. They have seriously attempted to update the language of the 1611 KJV and avoided the common criticisms of various detractors. The result is an easy-to-read KJV without the loss of any potential doctrinal content. They maintained the use of *thee, thou, hath, art, cometh,* and *hast* since the editors believe these are still understood today and have some advantages over modern usage because of their parallels with the Greek text of the New Testament. It remains to be seen whether this new edition will affect the common KJV sales and popularity or just be passed over as another KJV imitator.

10. Sakae Kubo and Walter F. Specht, *So Many Versions?* (Grand Rapids: Zondervan, 1983), 275.

11. *The New King James Version* (Nashville: Thomas Nelson Publishers, 1982), vi.

12. Norton, *A Textual History*, 136–41.

13. Printers' errors in Bibles still happen today. In the first edition of the 1995 *Ryrie Study Bible: New American Standard*, in Philippians 3:17 the endings of four lines are missing. An earlier *Ryrie Study Bible New Testament* published by Harcourt Brace Jovanovich in 1976 had to be withdrawn because it included old and wrong authorship notes at the end of the Epistles. Of course this Bible is now a collector's item.

Chapter 12 American Cousins

1. Literacy in all social classes had been increasing from the mid-sixteenth century. The growing literacy among all populations was the seedbed in which Puritanism flourished. They were thirsty for reading God's Word. The Bible provided the head of every home "direction for his apparel, his speech, his diet, his company, his disports, his labour, his buying and selling, yea and for his very sleep." Nicolson, *God's Secretaries*, 122–23.

2. Harry S. Stout, "Word and Order in Colonial New England," in *The Bible in America*, ed. Nathan O. Hatch and Mark A. Noll (New York: Oxford University Press, 1982), 25.

3. Ibid., 26.

4. P. Marion Simms, *The Bible in America* (New York: Wilson-Erickson, 1936), 93.

5. Ibid., 189.

6. Ibid., 190.

7. Harold R. Willoughby, *Soldiers' Bibles through Three Centuries* (Chicago: University of Chicago Press, 1944), 17.

8. The first English New Testament printed in America was printed by Isaiah Thomas in 1777.

An error in 1 Timothy 4:16, "thy doctrine" (first found in the 1629 Cambridge revision) for "the doctrine" suggests Thomas used the revised edition of the King James Version.

9. Quoted in Willoughby, *Soldiers' Bibles*, 18.

10. Isaiah Thomas, *The History of Printing in America, with a Biography of Printers, and an Account of Newspapers, in Two Volumes* (Albany, NY: Joel Munsell, 1874), 123.

11. Ibid., 107–9.

12. Willoughby, *Soldiers' Bibles*, 20–21.

13. Robert R. Dearden Jr. and Douglas S. Watson, *An Original Leaf from the Bible of the Revolution* (San Francisco: John Howell, 1930), 27–28.

14. The Bible in America during the Revolutionary War and the Civil War was almost exclusively the King James Version.

15. The American Bible Society was founded in 1816 as a nonprofit, nondenominational organization established for the purpose of distributing Bibles to every individual either free or at a very reasonable price. They were particularly known for their distribution of Bibles during the Civil War.

16. Dearden and Watson, *An Original Leaf*, 27.

17. Paul C. Gutjahr, *An American Bible: A History of the Good Book in the United States, 1777–1880* (Stanford, CA: Stanford University Press, 1999), appendix 3. Gutjahr charts the sale of Bibles during the nineteenth century. He notes that the prices of the ABS Bibles were carefully recorded in the minutes of the American Bible Society.

18. Dearden, *An Original Leaf*, 29.

Chapter 13 Behold the Legacy

1. The New Testament of Our Lord and Saviour Jesus Christ (English Revised Version) (Cambridge: University Press, 1881), ix.

2. For a complete comparison of modern versions with the King James Version, see Donald L. Brake Sr., "Versions, English," in *The New Interpreter's Dictionary of the Bible*, ed. Katharine Doob Sakenfeld (Nashville: Abingdon Press, 2009).

3. McGrath lists many other expressions that have had an influence on the English language. *In the Beginning*, 263–64.

4. Some men such as Al Lacy, *King James only* defender, hold that the revision of Blayney in 1769 is perfect. KJV only advocates have come to grips with the realization that the 1611 edition of the KJV has errors and claim the 1769 edition as their inspired version. One reason is that it is the seventh edition, which is the number of perfection. To them, all other corrections in later editions are not true KJV editions. Al Lacy, *Can I Trust My Bible?* (Littleton, CO: Al Lacy Publications, 1991), 144.

5. Most modern scholars of textual criticism do not support the text used by the King James translators; however, a small number of scholars are able defenders of the text known as the Majority Text or Byzantine textform. See Zane Hodges and Arthur Farstad, *The Greek New Testament According to the Majority Text* (Nashville: Thomas Nelson, 1985); Harry A. Sturz, *The Byzantine Text-Type and New Testament Textual Criticism* (Nashville: Thomas Nelson, 1984); and Robinson and Pierpont, *New Testament in the Original Greek*. It is not the purpose of this book to evaluate the merits of these views but to state that a legitimate argument exists to support the text from which the King James Version was prepared.

6. Robert R. Dearden Jr., *The Guiding Light on the Great Highway* (Philadelphia: John C. Winston, 1929), 231.

Selected Bibliography

Achtemeier, Paul J. "Omne Verbum Sonat: The New Testament and the Oral Environment of Late Western Antiquity." *Journal of Biblical Literature* 109, no. 1 (1990): 3–27.

Ackroyd, P. R., and C. F. Evans, eds. *The Cambridge History of the Bible.* 3 vols. Cambridge: Cambridge University Press, 1980.

Aland, Kurt, and Barbara D. Aland. *The Text of the New Testament.* Grand Rapids: Eerdmans, 1987.

Allen, Ward S. *Translating for King James.* Nashville: Vanderbilt University Press, 1969.

———. *Translating the New Testament Epistles 1604–1611.* Ann Arbor, MI: University Microfilms for Vanderbilt University Press, 1977.

Allen, Ward S., and Edward C. Jacobs. *The Coming of the King James Gospels.* Fayetteville, AR: University of Arkansas Press, 1995.

Andrews, Sir Lancelot. *Lancelot Andrews, Sermons.* London: George Miller for Richard Badger, 1629.

Baber, Henry. *An Historical Account of the Saxon and English Versions of the Scriptures, Previously to the Opening of the XVth Century.* London: Paternoster Row, 1810.

Barlow, William. *The Summe and Substance.* London: John Windet for Mathew Law, 1604.

———. *The Summe and Substance.* Gainesville, FL: Facsimiles and Reprints, 1965.

Blayney, Benjamin. "Account of the Collation and Revision of the Bible." *Gentleman's Magazine* 39 (October 1769): 148–51.

Bobrick, Benson. *Wide as the Waters: The Story of the English Bible and the Revolution It Inspired.* New York: Simon and Schuster, 2001.

Bosworth, Joseph. *The Gothic and Anglo-Saxon Gospels.* London: John Russell Smith, 1865.

Brake, Donald L., Sr. *The New Testament in English Translated by John Wycliffe.* Portland, OR: International Bible Publications, 1986.

———. "Versions, English." In *The New Interpreter's Dictionary of the Bible.* General editor, Katharine Doob Sakenfeld. Nashville: Abingdon Press, 2009.

———. *A Visual History of the English Bible: The Tumultuous Tale of the World's Best-selling Book.* Grand Rapids: Baker Books, 2008.

Brake, Donald L., and John Hellstern, eds. *A Royal Monument of English Literature: The King James Version 1611–2011.* Vancouver, WA: Hellstern and Brake, 2011.

Bruce, F. F. *The English Bible: A History of Translations from the Earliest English Versions to the New English Bible.* New York: Oxford University Press, 1970.

———. "John Wycliffe and the English Bible." *Churchman* 98, no. 4 (1984): 294–306.

Butterworth, Charles C. *The Literary Lineage of the King James Bible 1340–1611.* Philadelphia: University of Pennsylvania Press, 1941.

Carleton, James G. *The Part of Rheims in the Making of the English Bible.* Oxford: Clarendon Press, 1902.

Carruthers, S. W. *The Westminster Confession of Faith.* 7th ed. Manchester, England: R. Aikman and Son, n.d.

Cotton, Henry. *Editions of the Bible and Parts thereof in English, from the Year MDV to MDCCL.* Oxford: University Press, 1852.

Daniell, David. *The Bible in English.* New Haven and London: Yale University Press, 2003.

Darlow, T. H., and H. F. Moule. *Historical Catalogue of the Printed Editions of Holy Scripture in the Library of the British and Foreign Bible Society.* 4 vols. London: British and Foreign Bible Society, 1903–11.

Dearden, Robert R., Jr. *The Guiding Light on the Great Highway.* Philadelphia: John C. Winston, 1929.

Dearden, Robert R., Jr., and Douglas S. Watson. *An Original Leaf from the Bible of the Revolution.* San Francisco: John Howell, 1930.

de Hamel, Christopher. *The Book: A History of the Bible.* London: Phaidon Press, 2001.

Dore, J. R. *Old Bibles: An Account of the Early Versions of the English Bible.* London: Eyre and Spottiswoode, 1888.

Eadie, John. *The English Bible.* Vols. 1–2. London: Macmillan, 1876.

Erasmus, Desiderius. *In Annotationes Novi Testamenti Prefatio.* Basel, Switzerland: Johann Froben, 1516.

Fowler, David C. *The Bible in Middle English Literature.* Seattle: University of Washington Press, 1984.

Fowler, Thomas. *The History of Corpus Christi College.* Oxford: Horace Hart, Clarendon Press, 1893.

Foxe, John. *Acts and Monuments.* London: Seeley, Burnside, and Seeley, 1844.

Fry, Francis. *A Description of the Great Bible—1539, Cranmer's Bible 1540–41, King James's Bible 1611–40.* London: Willes and Sotheran, 1865.

Fry, Plantagenet Somerset. *Kings and Queens: A Royal History of England and Scotland.* 2nd ed. London: Dorling Kinderseley, 1997.

Fulke, William. *A Defense of the Sincere and True Translations of the Holy Scriptures in the English Tongue.* London: Henrie Bynneman, 1583. Reprinted by the Parker Society. Cambridge: Cambridge University Press, 1843.

Galli, Mark. "Courage When It Counted." *Christian History* 16, no. 4 (1995): 9–15.

Geisler, Norman L., and William E. Nix. *A General Introduction to the Bible.* Chicago: Moody Press, 1986.

Giles, J. A., ed. *Bede's Ecclesiastical History and the Anglo-Saxon Chronicle.* London: George Bell and Sons, 1887.

Gutjahr, Paul C. *An American Bible: A History of the Good Book in the United States, 1777–1880.* Stanford, CA: Stanford University Press, 1999.

Heaton, W. J. *The Bible of the Reformation.* London: Francis Griffiths, 1910.

Herbert, A. S. *A Historical Catalog of the Printed Editions of the English Bible 1525–1961.* Vol. 2. New York: American Bible Society, 1961.

Hodges, Zane, and Arthur Farstad. *The Greek New Testament According to the Majority Text.* Nashville: Thomas Nelson, 1985.

Isaacs, J., and H. W. Robinson, eds. *The Bible in Its Ancient and English Version.* Oxford: Oxford University Press, 1940.

James I. *The Workes of the Most High and Mightie Prince, James.* London: Robert Barker, 1616.

John, Right Reverend Father. *A Sermon Preached at the Funeral of the Right Honorable and Reverend Father in God Lancelot the Late Lord Bishop of Winchester.* London: G. Miller for Richard Badger, 1629. Reprinted in *XCVI Sermons by the Right Honorable and Reverend Father in God, Lancelot Andrews.* London: George Miller for Richard Badger, 1929.

Kubo, Sakae, and Walter F. Sprecht. *So Many Versions?* Grand Rapids: Zondervan, 1983.

Lacy, Al. *Can I Trust My Bible?* Littleton, CO: Al Lacy Publications, 1991.

Lupton, Lewis. *A History of the Geneva Bible.* 24 vols. London: Olive Tree, 1992.

MacGregor, Geddes. *The Bible in the Making.* London: John Murray, 1961.

Maier, John, and Vincent Tollers, eds. *The Bible in Its Literary Milieu.* Grand Rapids: Eerdmans, 1979.

McBrayer, William David. "Preface." *The New Testament in the Original Greek According to the Byzantine/Majority Textform.* Edited by Maurice A. Robinson and William G. Pierpont. Atlanta: Word, 1991.

McClure, Alexander W. *The Translators Revived.* Worthington, PA: Maranatha, n.d.

McCrum, Robert, William Cran, and Robert MacNeil. *The Story of English.* New York: Elisabeth Sifton Books, 1986.

McGrath, Alister E. *In the Beginning: The Story of the King James Bible and How It Changed a Nation, a Language, and a Culture.* New York: Doubleday, 2001.

Metzger, Bruce M. *The Text of the New Testament: Its Transmission, Corruption, and Restoration.* 2nd ed. New York: Oxford University Press, 1968.

———. *A Textual Commentary on the Greek New Testament,* 2nd rev. ed. New York: United Bible Societies, 2005.

Murray, Iain H. "Lewis Lupton, Mr. Standfast, 1909–1995." *The Banner of Truth.* London: Banner of Truth Trust, 1996.

Nicolson, Adam. *God's Secretaries.* New York: HarperCollins, 2003.

Niemeyer, H. A., ed. "Formula Consensus Ecclesiarum Helveticarum Reformatarum." *Collectio Confessionum in Ecclesiis Reformatis Publicatarum.* Lipsiae: Sumptibus Iulii Klinkhardt, 1840.

Norton, David A. *A History of the English Bible as Literature.* Cambridge: Cambridge University Press, 2000.

———. *A Textual History of the King James Bible.* Cambridge: Cambridge University Press, 2005.

Opfell, Olga S. *The King James Bible Translators.* Jefferson, NC, and London: McFarland, 1982.

Paine, Gustavus. *The Men behind the King James Version.* Grand Rapids: Baker Books, 1977.

Pearce, Joseph. *The Quest for Shakespeare.* San Francisco: Ignatius Press, 2008.

Plomer, Henry R. "The King's Printing House Under the Stuarts." *The Library,* new series, 2, no. 11 (1901): 353–75.

Pollard, Alfred W. *The Holy Bible: A Facsimile in a Reduced Size of the Authorized Version Published in the Year 1611.* London: Oxford University Press, 1911.

———. *Last Words on the History of the Title-Page.* New York: Burt Franklin, 1971.

———. *Records of the English Bible.* London: Oxford University Press, 1911.

Pollard, A. W., and G. R. Redgrave. *A Short-Title Catalog of Books Printed in England, Scotland, and Ireland: 1475–1640.* New York: Bernard Quaritch, 1926.

Pope, Hugh. *English Versions of the Bible.* London: B. Herder, 1952.

Price, David, and Charles C. Ryrie. *Let It Go among Our People: An Illustrated History of the English Bible from John Wycliff to the King James Version.* Cambridge: Lutterworth Press, 2004.

Robinson, Maurice A., and William G. Pierpont. *The New Testament in the Original Greek: Byzantine Textform.* Southborough, MA: Chilton Book Publishing, 2005.

Schmidtchen, Paul W. "Bibles Once Owned by King James I." *Hobbies—The Magazine for Collectors* (April 1964): 106–7.

Scrivener, F. H. A. *The Authorized Edition of the English Bible (1611).* Cambridge: Cambridge University Press, 1884.

Shaheen, Naseeb. *Biblical References in Shakespeare's Plays.* Newark and London: University of Delaware Press, 1999.

Shepherd, G. Geoffrey. "English Versions of the Scripture before Wycliffe." In *The Cambridge History of the Bible: The West from the Fathers to the Reformation.* Edited by G. W. H. Lampe. Cambridge: Cambridge University Press, 1969.

Simms, P. Marion. *The Bible in America.* New York: Wilson-Erickson, 1936.

Stein, Robert H. "Is Our Reading the Bible the Same as the Original Audience Hearing It?" *Journal of the Evangelical Theological Society* 46, no. 1 (March 2003): 63–78.

Stout, Harry S. "Word and Order in Colonial New England." In *The Bible in America.* Edited by Nathan O. Hatch and Mark A. Noll. New York: Oxford University Press, 1982.

Sturz, Harry A. *The Byzantine Text-Type and New Testament Textual Criticism.* Nashville: Thomas Nelson, 1984.

Thomas, Isaiah. *The History of Printing in America, with a Biography of Printers, and an Account of Newspapers, in Two Volumes.* Albany, NY: Joel Munsell, 1874.

"The Translators to the Reader." In *The Holy Bible.* London: Robert Barker, 1611.

Tregelles, Samuel Prideaux. *An Account of the Printed Text of the Greek New Testament.* London: Samuel Bagster and Sons, 1854.

Von Soden, Hermann Freiherr. *Die Schriften des Neuen Testaments in ihrer altesten erreichbaren Testgestalt.* Berlin: Alexander Duncker, 1902–13.

Westcott, Brooke Foss. *A General View of the History of the English Bible.* London: Macmillan, 1872.

Westcott, Brooke Foss, and Fenton John Anthony Hort. *The New Testament in the Original Greek.* 2 vols. Cambridge, MA, and London: Macmillan, 1881.

Williams, Matthew. *Uniquely Byzantine Readings in Codex Sinaiticus.* Portland: Multnomah Biblical Seminary, 2009.

Willoughby, Harold R. *Soldiers' Bibles through Three Centuries.* Chicago: University of Chicago Press, 1944.

Youngblood, Ronald. "Translation Versus Transliteration: The Triumph of Clarity over Opacity." Unpublished paper presented at the Society of Biblical Literature annual meeting, November 2003.

Scripture Index

General Index

Middle English period, 26–35
Modern English period, 35–38
Old English period, 22–26
Erasmus, Desiderius, 42, 126, 132, 133, 135–39,
    264nn5, 9, 11
error Bibles, 211–13, 226–27
excommunication, 30, 38, 82
Existing Monopoly, The (Curtis), 217
external evidence (manuscripts), 132

Fairclough, Richard, 101
faith leading to political action, 29–30
families (text). *See* text-types
Farstad, Arthur, 149, 222
faulty doctrine and worship, 28
Fenton, Roger, 109
First Cambridge Company, 97–99
First Oxford Company, 99–101
First Westminster Company, 93–96
folio, 181, 205–6, 261n8(1)
"Forgotten Sins Bible," 227
format features of KJV, 178–81
    church resources, 181
    size, 181
    variants between editions, 182–83
Fox, Richard, 108
Foxe, John, 34–35, 52
Froben, Johann, 132, 135–36
Fry, Francis, 193–94

genealogies in KJV, 186–87
Geneva, 140
    migration of English Protestants to, 64, 97
Geneva Bible, 15, 66, 67, 73, 74, 84, 210, 230,
    261n5
    as reference tool for KJV, 153
    continuing popularity of, 172–73
    format of, 65
    influence on the KJV, 158, 159
    language of, 116, 117
    marginal notes in, 67, 74, 83, 119, 209, 261n10
    translators of, 64–65
geographic roots of KJV, 129–33
geographical distribution of original New Testa-
    ment books, 128
glosses, interlinear, 24
Golden Legend, The (de Voragine), 40–41
grammatical structures of the KJV, 183–84
Great Awakening, 231

Great Bible, 59, 60, 61, 73–74
    as reference tool for KJV, 111, 153
Greece, 129, 130
Greek New Testament
    of Erasmus, 42, 126, 135–39
    Polyglot, 133–35
Gregory, pope, 22, 23
Gunpowder Plot, 84–85, 87, 123–24
Gutenberg, Johann, 35, 39–40
Gutenberg Bible, 35

Hampton Court Conference, 15, 82–84, 89, 97,
    108
Harding, John, 91, 99
Harmer, John, 106, 154
Harrison, Thomas, 98
"He Bible" (first edition of KJV), 169–70, 226
Hebrew, studies in, 111
Henry VIII, 38, 47, 54, 104
    break with Roman Catholic Church, 57
    licensing of Bibles, 57, 61, 162
Hesychius text-type, 146
Hodges, Zane, 149
Holland, Thomas, 100
Hort, F. J. A., 144–45
humanism, 42
Hutchinson, Ralph, 110
Hutton, Lenard, 107

inerrancy, theological, 205, 241
infallibility of Scripture, 230
influences of other translations on the KJV, 122–
    24, 148, 157, 158–59
inspiration of Scripture, 148, 242–44
internal evidence (manuscripts), 132
interpretation of Scripture, 118, 121, 130, 244
    standard of, 28
    principles for, 34
invasions, 22, 24

James I, 78–80
    as scholar, 79
    defining achievement of his reign, 17
    disapproval of Apocrypha, 147
    influence on translation, 263n33
    state and church, 78, 82, 261n6
    view of kingship and authority, 261n5. *See also*
        divine rule of monarchs; kingship, views of
Jerusalem text-type, 146
"Judas Bible," 226

Kilby, Richard, 100
King, Geoffrey, 96
King James Bible (KJV)
  acceptance of, 174, 176
  as conduit of faith, 246
  as moderating theological influence in America, 231
  attempt at standard American edition, 216–17
  Bancroft's rules for translation of, 116–24, 263nn28, 33
  Cambridge Paragraph Bible (1873), 218–19
  doctrinal and exegetical issues in 188, 190–91
  early editions of
    1611 folio edition (first edition), 195
    1611–13 folio second edition, 195, 198–99
    1617 folio third edition, 199–200
    1634 folio fourth edition, 200–201
    1639–40 folio fifth edition, 201–2
  ensuring accuracy in translation, 111–12
  format features of, 178–81
    church resources, 181
    map by John Speed, 184–86
    size, 181
    variants between editions, 181–82
  genealogies in, 186–87
  geographic roots of, 129–33
  grammatical structures of, 183–84
  Greek texts used by translators, 141–42
  "he" and "she" Bibles (first and second editions), 169–70
  Hebrew texts used by translators, 147
  influences of other translations, 122–24, 148
    of the Geneva Bible, 158, 159
    of the Rheims Bible, 158–59
    of the Vulgate, 157
  literary quality of, 113–14, 115–16, 118, 174, 176, 240–41
  marginal notes in, 119
  minor revisions of, 205–6
  New Cambridge Paragraph Bible (2005), 224–25, 226–27
  opposition to, 171–74
  organization of translation work, 90–93, 115, 120–21
  process used in translation, 110–11, 120–21, 153–55
  Revised Version (1885), 220, 239
  revisions of
    in 1616, 207
    in 1629, 208–9

  in 1638, 209–10
  in 1762, 213–14
  in 1769, 214–16
kingship, views of, 95–96, 119, 120, 172, 261nn5, 6, 10(2). *See also* divine rule by monarchs; James I
Knox, John, 64, 67
Koine
  Greek, 107
  text-type, 146

language, 244
  acquisition of, 155
  significance and development of, 21
Laud, William, 172, 210
Layfield, John, 95–96
Lindisfarne manuscript, 24
literacy, 35, 122–23, 213, 268n1(2)
literary quality of KJV, 113–14, 118, 174, 176, 239, 240–41
Lively, Edward, 91, 97
Lollards, 33, 260n6(2)
Lupton, Lewis, 69

Majority Text, 132–33, 149, 223, 264n5, 269n5. *See also* Byzantine text-type; *Textus Receptus*
manuscript(s)
  copying by scribes, 31, 33, 126–27
  of Bible, 131–33, 244
manuscript formats, seventeenth-century, 165–66
map in KJV (John Speed), 184–86
marginal notes in Bibles
  considered controversial, 17, 45, 55, 59, 74, 119
  in 1629 edition of KJV, 209
married clergy, 109, 110
Mary I, 56, 64, 72–73, 97
Mary Queen of Scots, 78, 79
Matthew, Thomas, 56–57, 64, 260n8
Matthew's Bible, 57, 59, 74, 111, 153
McDowell, William, 222
McLane, James W., 216
Middle English period (development of language), 26–35
Millenary Petition, 81–82, 97, 262n14
missionary endeavors, 22
Modern English period (development of language), 35–38
Montague, James, 107
"More Sea Bible," 227
"Murderer's Bible," 227

New Cambridge Paragraph Bible (2005), 224–26
New King James Version, 222–24
Nicholas of Hereford, 33
Norman Conquest, 22, 25, 26
Norton, Bonham, 163, 212
Norton, David, 224

Oath of Allegiance, 85–86
octavo, 45, 212, 261n8(1)
Old English period (development of language),
   22–26
opposition to KJV, 171–74
oral reading of Scripture, 122–23
Overall, John, 94–95
Oxford, 97, 99, 104–5, 208
   Oxford Press editions of KJV, 203–4, 214–16,
      217–18
Oxford Council, 34

Packington, Augustine, 45
paragraph markers in the KJV, 156
Paris, F. S. (Thomas), 203–4, 213, 214
Parker, Matthew, 73, 74, 75
Perne, John, 106
Pierpont, William, 149
piety, Puritan emphasis on, 230
Pilgrims, 229–30
phantom Bibles, 235
Polyglot Bible (Complutensian Polyglot), 133–35,
   138, 139
Poyntz, Thomas, 47, 48
prebends, 90, 92, 102, 262n2
preservation of Scripture, 148, 205, 240
Price, James, 222
printing
   as a business, 135–36, 164
   significance of, 35–36, 39
   process, 39–40, 166–68
prohibition of Scripture in the vernacular, 28, 33,
   34–35, 36, 38, 260nn19, 22
   results of, 28, 36
Psalter, translations of, 27
Puritans, 97, 105, 116, 172, 210, 261nn5, 8(2)
   and social order, 230–31
   disagreement with official report about Hamp-
      ton Court Conference, 108
   emigration to the New World, 230
   principles of Bible translation, contrasted with
      Anglicans, 116–24
   sympathy with Scottish Reformation, 82
Purvey, John, 33–34

quarto, 44, 65, 206, 261n8(1)
Quentel, Peter, 44

Rabbett, Michael, 109
Radcliffe, Jeremiah, 102
Rainolds, John, 15–16, 84, 89, 99–100, 109, 120
Ravens, Ralph, 107
Ravis, Thomas, 104
Reformation, Reformers, 39, 44, 97, 105, 127, 139
religious instruction, means of, 26, 28
"Revenge Bible," 226
Revised Version (1885), 220
revisions of KJV
   in 1616, 207
   in 1629, 208–9
   in 1638, 209–10
   in 1762, 213–14
   in 1769, 214–16
Richardson, John, 97–98
Robinson, Edward, 216
Robinson, Maurice, 149
Rogers, John. See Matthew, Thomas
Rogers, John (Presbyterian minister), 234
Rolle, Richard, 27

Salem witch trials, 231
Sanderson, Thomas, 109
à Saravia, Hadrian, 95
Savile, Sir Henry, 104–5
Schoeffer, Peter, 44
Scofield, Cyrus I., 221
Scofield Reference Bible (1909), 220–21
Scripture
   authority of, 30, 99, 230, 245
   infallibility of, 230
   inspiration of, 242–44
   interpretation of, 118, 121, 130, 244
   oral reading of, 122–23
   preservation of, 148, 205, 240
   principles for, 34
   standard of, 28
   See also translation of the Bible
Scrivener, F. H. A., 218–19, 224
Second Cambridge Company, 101–3
Second Oxford Company, 103–7
Second Westminster Company, 107–12
Shakespeare, William, 112–13, 263n25
"She Bible" (second edition of KJV), 169–70,
   198, 226
simony, 90

Donald L. Brake's early academic life was better served by his love for sports. High school in a small Illinois town focused more on athletic achievement than developing love for study and research. Academic success was just a necessary step to be eligible for team sports. Lettering in track, baseball, and basketball seemed a far more important occupation than academia.

Thinking no more of academic achievement, his life took a 180-degree turn when he married his high school sweetheart, Carol. Within a year he was anticipating his first son and commuting to Moody Bible Institute to study for the ministry.

Don's new direction in life gave him a ravenous appetite for books, which was reinforced by Dr. Mercer, theology professor at Moody, who cajoled his students to "sell their shoes" to buy a classic text or a freshly penned theology book. His new love for study was honored when he graduated with his ThM from Dallas Theological Seminary (DTS), receiving the Loraine Chafer Theology Award. Don and Carol, with their children Donnie, Debbie, and Michael, left for Ethiopia to serve as missionaries where Don experienced riots and revolution, as well as assisting in translating biblical and theological subjects into Amharic.

After earning a doctoral degree from DTS, Dr. Brake founded Multnomah Biblical Seminary (at Multnomah Bible College); watched the Gulf War as president of Jerusalem University College in Israel; pastored a fabulous flock in Texas; and, of course, collected rare Bibles.

Dr. Brake's academic and professional peers consider him an authority on the history of the Bible and the various translations and versions in both Greek and English from the sixteenth to the twenty-first centuries.

Dr. Brake has taught and led conferences on the subjects of the biblical canon, history of the English Bible, and New Testament textual criticism. He leads tours and study groups to the Holy Land, Greece and Turkey, and Reformation Europe.

He is dean emeritus of Multnomah Biblical Seminary in Portland, Oregon, where he teaches New Testament and theology. Don dreams of the Senior Tour and plays contact sports vicariously through four grandsons, one granddaughter, and the NFL package.

Contact Information

Multnomah Bible College and Biblical Seminary is committed to biblically based higher education, as well as regionally accredited academic excellence. For more information about the college and seminary, please visit Multnomah's website at www.multnomah.edu.

To correspond with Dr. Don Brake, please send your letter via email to dbrake@multnomah.edu or via mail c/o MBS, 8435 N.E. Glisan Street, Portland, OR 97220.

A BEAUTIFUL GUIDE TO THE BIBLICAL LANDS

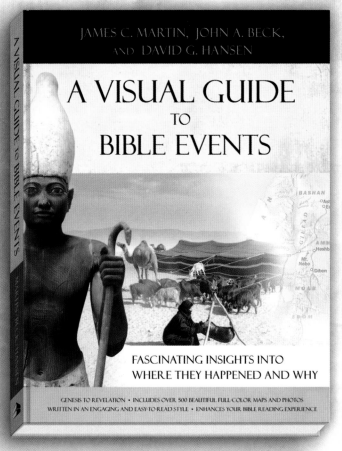

9780801012853   272 pp.

"I have known Jim Martin for many years and have had the privilege of traveling with him as he described many of the biblical sites featured in this book. The subtitle of this visually stunning work lives up to its claim: the authors offer fascinating insights into where and why certain Gospel events took place. This is a meticulously researched and invaluable resource that I know will bring the Scriptures to life for its readers."

—**Ravi Zacharias,** author and speaker

BakerBooks
a division of Baker Publishing Group
www.BakerBooks.com